Meetings with Mary

by Janice T. Connell

Angel Power
Queen of the Cosmos
The Triumph of the Immaculate Heart
Visions of the Children: The Apparitions of the
Blessed Mother at Medjugorje

Meetings
with
Mary

VISIONS
OF THE
BLESSED
MOTHER

Janice T. Connell

WITH A FOREWORD BY ROBERT FARICY, S.J.

BALLANTINE BOOKS
NEW YORK

DECLARATION

The decree of the Congregation for the Propagation of the Faith, A.A.S. 58, 1186 (approved by Pope Paul VI on 14 October 1966) states that the *Nihil Obstat* and *Imprimatur* are no longer required on publications that deal with private revelations, provided that they contain nothing contrary to faith or morals. The author wishes to manifest her unconditional submission to the final and official judgment of the Magisterium of the Church in matters of faith and morals.

http://www.randomhouse.com

Library of Congress Catalog Card Number: 96-96587

ISBN 0-345-39705-5

Cover design by Carlos Beltrán
Cover illustration by Danilo Ducak

Photo research by Omni Photo Communications

Manufactured in the United States of America

First Trade Paperback Edition: November 1996

10 9 8 7 6 5 4 3 2 1

This book was consecrated to God in thanksgiving for the gift of the Incarnation through the Blessed Virgin Mary, at the actual site of the Archangel Gabriel's visit to Mary at Nazareth, in the Grotto of the Annunciation in the Holy Land, during a Mass offered by the Reverends Thomas Stahl, S.J., Thomas King, S.J., Brendan Hurley, S.J., Josef Kadlec, S.J., Daniel O'Connell, S.J., and Harold Bradley, S.J., on March 7, 1995. Father Thomas King, S.J., invoked a special blessing at the holy site upon all those who read this book, all who prepare it, all who handle it. He placed each under the special protection of the Lord Jesus Christ and His entire Nine Choirs of Angels.

Meetings with Mary *is dedicated to the children of Mary, Mother of God, with great love and gratitude through the inspiration of the Holy Spirit.*

CONTENTS

Contents

Contents

ACKNOWLEDGMENTS

The visionaries and locutionists, their families, spiritual directors, interpreters, translators, assistants, and facilitators, for the graciousness with which they shared their experiences.

The countless dedicated children of Mary throughout the world who personally helped on this project for the glory of God and, in their humility, are known to Him alone.

My revered brothers and sisters throughout the world who toil lovingly and tirelessly in the Marian Centers on behalf of the Blessed Mother and her Divine Son. Their commitment and generosity bring the beautiful apparitions of the Blessed Mother to the four corners of the earth.

The Marian prayer groups throughout the world who prayed this book into being.

My family, especially my husband Ed, whose love for the Blessed Mother has provided inspiration and encouragement, our daughter Betsy, our sons, Ted, Will and Derek, and our grandchildren, Mary Christian and Ricky. Their love has given life to this joyous book.

My professional colleagues whose graciousness facilitated this book, especially Thomas V. Fritz, Margaret M. Heckler, Gino Marchetti, Joy Flowers Conti, Carol Los Mannsman, J. Jerome Mannsman, Harold Cassidy, Robert Sensale, Robert R. Redfield, Brian J. Tiboni.

My Marian colleagues who heroically supported the vision contained in this book, especially Claire and Bob Schaefer, the late Frances Reck and Bill Reck, Marjorie and Stanley J. Karminski, Rita Klaus, Larry Galloway, John Haffert, Rosalie Turton, Courtney Bartholomew, Mother Angelica, Sister Isabel Bettwy, Sister Margaret Catherine Sims, Sister Agnes McCormick, Sister Emmanuel, Dennis Nolan, David Manuel, Emily and Tom Petrisko, Thomas Rutkowski, John Hill, Wayne Wieble, Eleanor Wetzel, Tom Collins, Inga McNeil, Susan A. Muto, Terry Colofrancisco, Maureen and Ted Flynn, John and Isabel McGilviry McGregor, the Anthony Azorres family, Joan and John Mitchel, Sue and Bernard Ellis, Debbie and Don Ralph.

Robert Faricy, S.J.; Thomas King, S.J.; Edward O'Connor, C.S.C.; Thomas Thompson, S.M.; Luke Zimmer, S.S.C.C.; Adrian Van Kaam, C.S.Sp.; Michael Scanlan, T.O.R.; and Tomislav Pervan, O.F.M., for their committed devotion to the Mother of God, and for their discernment, scholarship, and encouragement, all of which find expression in this book.

Joëlle Delbourgo, whose wisdom and courage guided its pages.

Leigh Ann Sackrider for her expertise and graciousness.

The generous staff at Ballantine Books for their dedication and commitment to this project.

Marcy Posner and Matthew Bialer for their assistance.

AUTHOR'S NOTE

This book represents the contributions of Father Thomas King, S.J. of Georgetown University, who edited and guided this text. May the Blessed Mother of his Order reward his graciousness abundantly.

The sisters of Our Lady of Mount Carmel mobilized Herculean prayer support on behalf of this book. May the Queen of Heaven smile tenderly on her dear daughters of Loretta, Pennsylvania; San Diego, California; La Plata, Maryland; and Lafayette, Louisiana; especially Mother Teresa Margaret.

Mariologist Father René Laurentin deserves immense gratitude for much of the information that is available concerning the contemporary apparitions of the Blessed Mother. May his gifts reap a bountiful harvest for the Holy Trinity.

Father Michael Scanlan, T.O.R., and Mark Miravalle,

S.T.D., pastored the beginnings of this book. May their efforts bear sweet fruit for the Kingdom of Mary's Son.

Any mistakes or errors are totally due to my inadequacies.

The Spirit of God descended upon Jesus on Mount Tabor
and proclaimed: "This is my beloved Son, with whom I am
well pleased; listen to him" (Matthew 17:5). God has revealed all things in His Word, His Son. There are no answers or revelations that surpass the Gospel of Jesus Christ.
The entire vision, locution and response, and revelation—
which God has already spoken, answered, manifested, and
revealed to us—is Jesus. He is given to us as our brother,
saviour, companion, and reward.[1] Saint Paul told us that in
the Son of God are hidden all the treasures of the wisdom
and knowledge of God (Colossians 2:3). One of His gifts to
us is His Blessed Mother Mary.

Books, movies, newspapers, newsletters, television
documentaries, audio and video tapes abound that report
current apparitions of the Blessed Mother of Jesus. Many
such apparitions contain alleged messages from the Blessed
Mother for these times.

A note of caution regarding reported visionaries and
locutionists comes from the great spiritual master Saint John
of the Cross. He teaches us not to interpret messages reported
by human visionaries literally. Words sourced in humans are
susceptible to change and failure.[2] Saint Paul warned the
followers of Jesus: "But even if we or an angel from heaven
should preach a gospel other than the one that we preached
to you, let that one be accursed!" (Galatians 1:8).

Authentic apparitions of the Blessed Mother shed light

on the Gospel. You will see in this book that her authentic messages throughout the centuries are precisely the same message the Mother of Jesus gave at the wedding feast of Cana: "Do whatever he [Jesus] tells you" (John 2:5).

The truths of the Gospel that are contained in the authentic messages of the Blessed Mother illumine God's Word. The Blessed Mother of Jesus knows the Son of God as no other human being. She, too, quotes the Gospel message of Mount Tabor: "This is my beloved Son, with whom I am well pleased; listen to him."

FOREWORD

Christian tradition has always held that Jesus, at the point of death, gave His Mother Mary to each one of us, and that He gave each of us to His Mother as her son or daughter. The apostle John, present with Mary at the crucifixion, was standing in for each one of us as Jesus said: "Behold your Mother" (John 19:27).

The Blessed Virgin Mary, of course, has nothing divine about her; she is not God. Mary is a human being. She has the status of a creature. However, she is the Mother of Jesus Christ, who does have divine as well as human status. Thus she is the Mother of God. She has no power of her own, but she is, and always will be, the Mother of the most powerful person who ever walked on earth. And she is the Mother of each of us.

She is in Heaven now with her Son Jesus. Sometimes she comes to earth—sent, of course, by Jesus—and appears to people. In her appearances to people, she sometimes speaks, but she brings no new messages, nothing beyond the teaching of Jesus in the Bible. She represents her Son, and she comes to call us to conversion: to sorrow for our sins and to turn to God.

Sometimes her purpose in coming is not confined to just one person or a few; it can be for a whole locality or even for the world. In these cases, the Church investigates to see whether or not there is serious evidence that the Mother of Jesus has really appeared. In most cases of alleged appearances by Jesus' Mother, from early Christian times up until the present, the Church has found no real basis for thinking that it really was Mary; it could have been a mistake, or hallucinations, or psychological problems on the part of the persons who thought they saw her, or even a hoax. But the Church has approved some cases, a small percentage of those claimed, but nevertheless several appearances of the Mother of God.

The Church has approved all of the events in this book except for those that are identified as still under investigation. Does that mean we have to believe that all the approved apparitions throughout the centuries really happened? Do at least Catholics have to believe in the truth of these meetings of people on earth with Mary, the Mother of Jesus? No! No one has to believe it. Church approval, after thorough and stringent investigation, means that official experts have examined the event carefully, and that they have found nothing false. We can therefore accept these events as true.

In each of her comings, Mary appears in such a way that the people to whom she comes can relate to her. To black people she is black. To Koreans she looks Korean.

To Italian people she looks Italian. When the Indian Juan Diego saw her near Mexico City, she appeared as a young Indian girl. And she not only speaks the language of the people she appears to, but she even speaks in the same way, or in the same dialect, or with the same accent they have.

She comes as their Mother because that is what she is. Ours, too.

Jan Connell knows the Lord Jesus and His Mother. She is a woman of deep prayer, prudent, fully orthodox in her Christian beliefs and in her talks and her books. I have known her for a long time. She is a person of total integrity. In this book, she tells us about approved apparitions of the Mother of Jesus to earth, appearances that have meaning for each of us.

Some recent apparitions of the Blessed Virgin Mary have created widespread international interest. Several of the more significant events, carefully chosen, are chronicled in this book, though some may or may not be presently under investigation.

This book provides a timely opportunity for all people to realize what is going on in the world. Those who read it will know the Lord Jesus and His Blessed Mother better.

Robert Faricy, S.J.
Chair, Mystical Theology
Pontifical Gregorian University
Rome, Italy
March 25, 1995

PROLOGUE

The Canticle of Mary

"My soul proclaims the greatness of the Lord;
    my spirit rejoices in God my savior,
For He has looked upon His handmaid's lowliness;
    behold, from now on will all ages call me blessed.
The Mighty One has done great things for me,
    and holy is His name.
His mercy is from age to age
    to those who fear Him.
He has shown might with His arm,
    dispersed the arrogant of mind and heart.
He has thrown down the rulers from their thrones
    but lifted up the lowly.
The hungry He has filled with good things;
    the rich He has sent away empty.
He has helped Israel His servant,
    remembering His mercy,
according to His promise to our fathers,
    to Abraham and to His descendants forever."

LUKE 1:46–55

PART ONE

Holy Mary,

MOTHER OF GOD

It is not by coincidence that you have found this book. Deep in our hearts we all desire to learn of the mysterious world of God's Kingdom; it is not surprising that all of the Western religions have long traditions of human encounters with the Lord, His Blessed Mother Mary, certain saints, prophets, or angels of the celestial court. All the sacred texts speak of those who claim to hear or even see the Lord or His angels and saints. Perhaps you are one of them.

Visions and apparitions of the Blessed Virgin Mary are supernatural favors. They invite everyone into God's heart, and those who find God find all the treasures of creation. As you will see from the stories of pre-twentieth-century apparitions that will unfold in Part I of this book, meetings with the Blessed Mother help awaken us to truth.

From the apostles to Saint Ignatius of Loyola to a group of children in Pontmain, France, many have learned the Mother of God is the Mother of all who invite her into their lives. When the Blessed Mother appears, great things happen on earth and in heaven.

CHAPTER ONE

Queen of Heaven and Earth

Blessed are you who believed that what was spoken to you
by the Lord would be fulfilled.

LUKE 1:45

Rescued Air Force pilot Scott O'Grady looked calm and
healthy on *Dateline NBC* as he reflected on his edge-
of-death experiences behind enemy lines after his F-16 was
shot down over Bosnia on June 2, 1995, by a Serb SAM-6
missile. Captain O'Grady parachuted safely after his F-16
was shot down, evaded capture by the Serbs for six days,
and was rescued by a special team of U.S. Marines in heli-
copters on June 8. He was honored in ceremonies at the
White House and the Pentagon on June 12.

"When they say your whole life flashes before your
eyes, it doesn't just flash before your eyes, but there's photos that click through your mind throughout the entire
time that you just can't—you thought you'd never remember," he told *Dateline NBC*.

"It's just unbelievable that I didn't die," he said emphatically, "whether it would have been from the missile impact, whether it would have been from the seat being able to leave the airplane, to the point where I was on the ground and survived six days." He attributes his survival to all the prayers that were offered for him, and maybe even a miracle.

Captain O'Grady knew of the apparitions of the Blessed Virgin Mary in Medjugorje, a tiny hamlet hidden in the hills of Bosnia, before his plane was shot down over Bosnia. The Blessed Mother of Jesus has told six visionaries in Medjugorje, four of whom have been seeing her daily since June 24, 1981, that her apparitions in Bosnia are her final apparitions on earth: she is calling from the mountains of Bosnia to all people on earth, of every religion, to turn back to God now. The visionaries announce messages she brings from God for everyone.

During his NBC interview, O'Grady acknowledged that he experienced the presence, or spirit, of the Blessed Virgin Mary while he was trapped behind enemy lines in Bosnia. Though he did not say that he actually had an apparition of the Blessed Mother, he said, "I consider[ed] myself religious before but not to where I believe[d] any of that [apparitions]."

Captain O'Grady had learned of the extraordinary daily apparitions of the Blessed Mother in Medjugorje from a family friend. He said of that friend, "She was right [about the Blessed Mother in Bosnia] because I don't know what I saw, but I saw something."[1]

The experiences of Captain Scott O'Grady in Bosnia invite us all to ponder the ongoing presence of the Lord, and His holy ones from the beyond, in the lives of ordinary people engaged in everyday life. Not only the Lord, but

also the Blessed Mother, the angels, the saints, the patriarchs and prophets, the souls in purgatory, and even the
lious spirits from the kingdom of illusion have made
do make themselves known to people on the earth.
y family has its personal stories about loved ones
e lives have been "miraculously saved," or whose pres-
is not severed by death.

/eneration of the Blessed Mother of Jesus is deeply
rooted in many family traditions. The virtues of Mary, her
love and faithfulness to God, have been a guiding light for
two thousand years.

My grandparents, and their grandparents before them,
taught our family that the Lord Jesus began His miracles
by means of His Mother Mary: His Incarnation was the
first. Then He sanctified Saint John the Baptist at the Visitation, when His Mother Mary spoke to John's mother,
Elizabeth. The Blessed Mother's humble words, "They have
no wine," led Jesus to create the finest of wines for wedding
guests at Cana in Galilee. For generations, we have learned
that the Lord Jesus continues to honor His Blessed Mother
by granting miracles through her intercession. After all,
through her, with her, and in her, God became man.

My grandmother frequently reminded us that it is impossible to comprehend the mystery of Jesus Christ, who is
God made man. "Pray for strong faith and never doubt the
Word of God!" was her admonition to all her grandchildren. At Christmastime, Grandmother would look at the
manger scene in our living room with great love and sigh,
"The Infant Jesus is the ultimate expression of God's
mercy upon His people."

As little children, we learned to ask the Blessed

Mother to speak to her Divine Infant about all our needs. We were aware that since Jesus is God, He Himself created the Fourth Commandment and He would always honor His Blessed Mother in the highest possible ways.

Billions of others throughout the history of Christianity have recognized that prayers offered to Jesus, through His Blessed Mother's intercession, are quite powerful. Pope John Paul II has entrusted his papacy to the Blessed Mother's care. It is widely reported that he carries the Consecration of Saint Louis de Montfort in his pocket at all times. *Totus Tuus* ("I am completely yours [O Mary]") is the motto he chose for his papacy.[2]

Who is the Blessed Virgin Mary? Why is she called the Mother of God, the Mother of the Church, and so many other glorious names? The Mother of Jesus Christ is unlike any other creature God has ever created. She alone is the Eternal Mother of the God-man, Jesus Christ. Who can comprehend with a mere human mind what such an honor means?

The Blessed Virgin Mary always cooperates perfectly with God's will. Her will is a perfect mirror of the will of God.

God desires that we choose, through Jesus, to become His own children and heirs of His Kingdom forever. Jesus won the grace for us to occupy the thrones in heaven that were abandoned by rebellious angels who vacated them.[3]

Debased spirits of violence, destruction, degradation, and despair reign in their kingdom of eternal death. They prowl about the earth seeking witless human souls as their prey.[4] It is God's will that we escape their deceptions and live in His Kingdom of peace, joy, and abiding love forever.[5]

Those who choose to become children of God have God the Father for their Father as Jesus taught, the Blessed Mother for their Mother as Jesus announced, and Jesus Christ for their brother.[6]

Since the time of the apostles, people all over the world have come to realize that the surest, the easiest, and the shortest way to Jesus Christ is through the Immaculate Heart of His Blessed Mother.[7] Our Lord Jesus is the same today, yesterday, and tomorrow. He remains forever the perfect Son of the Eternal Father and His Blessed Mother, Mary. A vast army of people has existed throughout the centuries whose hearts belong to Jesus Christ, and because of Him, to His Blessed Mother.

The Lord promised that those who seek Him find Him. The ones who draw near the Blessed Mother receive her Divine Son Jesus from her as first Saint Joseph and the shepherds learned from angels and the Magi learned by following a star.

Those who approach Jesus through His Blessed Mother are often insignificant in the world's esteem, just as the shepherds were. Yet great world leaders, too, approach Jesus through His Blessed Mother just as the Magi once did (Matthew 2:1–11).

The Blessed Mother lived and prayed with the apostles and disciples of Jesus after His death and Resurrection. They regarded her as Mother of the Church. The followers of Jesus, as numerous as the sands of the seashore, have continued that tradition throughout the centuries.

Those who have seen the Blessed Mother include the least as well as the most favored members of society. She has appeared to poor children and to founders of great religious orders, to the farmer in the field and the archduchess in her castle, to old people and busy adults in remote regions of the world and the cities of the great nations.

The Mother of Jesus is the Eternal Mother who brings light, strength, hope, and guidance from God to His precious children of the earth. She alone brings Jesus Christ through the divine power of the Holy Spirit, as she did at the Incarnation (Luke 1:34–36). By her cooperation with the will of God, Mary is the spouse of the Holy Spirit. Those who draw near her draw near the Holy Spirit of eternal love.

Never divine herself, the Blessed Mother in her splendor is a clear mirror of God's splendor. Her bounty is a token of His generosity. Her apparitions, as you shall soon see, are a sign of God's omnipresence and His divine, unconditional love for each person He has created.

Apparitions of the Blessed Mother of Jesus to ordinary, sinful people of all races, nations, and stations in life are reported all over the world as the twentieth century draws to a close. Many of these Marian apparitions of the twentieth century are fraught with urgency and contain apocalyptic warnings. Three hundred years ago, the prophetic voice of Saint Louis de Montfort explained the times in which we now live:

> In the second coming of Jesus Christ, Mary has to be made known and revealed by the Holy Spirit in order that, through her, Jesus Christ may be known, loved and served.[8]

The Blessed Mother is presenting messages in these times as never before in history to believers and nonbelievers alike. As at the wedding feast of Cana, her call is filled with love and confidence: *"Do whatever he tells you"* (John 2:5). She announces to these times, to these generations:

"To know Jesus is to love Him. To love Him is to emulate Him. To emulate Him is to find the Kingdom of God forever."

Messages from the Blessed Mother from the beginning call all people on earth to strong faith in God. She asks for obedience to His commandments, heartfelt prayer, fasting, and daily reading of sacred texts.

The Blessed Mother is filled with love. Visionaries refer to her as pure love. But she is firm. She is decisive and unrelenting as she explains to all people everywhere on earth:

"Each child of God must seek reconciliation with every other person immediately for the love of God."

Ominous portents of global destruction induced by humans lend an urgency to the current Marian apparitions reported all over the world.

Between 1981 and 1988, the Blessed Mother and her Divine Son Jesus appeared to seven children in Rwanda warning of the end of the world and the imminent return of Jesus Christ. The apparitions spoke of "rivers of human blood" that would flow in Rwanda. The local Roman Catholic bishop, Jean Baptiste Gahamanyi, approved the site of the apparitions in his diocese of Rwanda as a place of pilgrimage and devotion. By 1994, however, the homeland of the six girl visionaries and one boy visionary was ravaged by savage civil war. Two of the visionaries were slaughtered during the summer of 1994. As one newsweekly put it, "Hell is on earth in Rwanda."[9]

The extensively investigated apparitions of the Blessed Mother at Medjugorje in Bosnia, which began on a daily basis in 1981, have attracted nearly twenty million pilgrims to the site, though a brutal civil war has raged in that region since 1992. In 1995, the major Western powers and the United Nations remain unable to bring peace to the warring factions in Bosnia, yet the daily apparitions bring this continued message of hope from the Blessed Mother that she first announced in July 1982 at Medjugorje:

> *"Prayer and fasting will stop war. It will change the natural law."*

Captain Scott O'Grady, who survived behind enemy lines against all odds, understands that message well.

The quiet voice of Saint Louis de Montfort speaks chillingly to us in these times: "The devil, knowing that he has but little time, and now less than ever, to destroy souls, will every day redouble his efforts and his combats. He will presently raise up cruel persecutions and will put terrible snares before the true children. . . ."[10]

Statues of the Blessed Mother have been seen by secular people of no religious persuasion to weep blood and tears. In the spring of 1995, a weeping statue of the Blessed Mother that was purchased in Medjugorje and transported to a shrine in Civitavecchia, Italy, was reported to be oozing human blood from the eyes. Economic duress, fear of political corruption, and general uncertainty in Italy have combined to send thousands of people to the site of the weeping statue. Claims of fraud, or miracles, or healings and apocalypse are associated with it. *The Washington Post* reported on June 5, 1995, that Italian police, resurrecting an ancient statute, had become involved in the investigation. Church officials are analyzing the blood flow from the eyes and the circumstances surrounding the appearances of the blood on the face of the statue of the Blessed Virgin Mary.[11]

On March 9, 1992, *The Washington Post* ran a story about Reverend Jim Bruse, associate pastor of Saint Elizabeth Ann Seton Catholic Church in Lake Ridge, Virginia. On November 28, 1991, Thanksgiving Day, Father Bruse had noticed a small statue of the Blessed Mother, Our Lady of Grace, which he'd given to his mother, begin to ooze tears.[12] The fluid was salty to the taste, according to Father Bruse. The statue continued to ooze water from the eyes, and by December 21 the table upon which the statue was placed was covered with water and so was the floor. On Christmas Day, the statue began to ooze blood from the eyes while Father Bruse celebrated Mass. Many eyewitnesses saw this phenomenon. (*U.S. News & World Report*'s March 29, 1992, cover story, "The Case of the Weeping Madonna," described some of the strange "oozing" phenomena.)

On December 27, 1991, a statue of the Sacred Heart that belongs to Father Bruse's family began to ooze blood from the heart area. The blood was so copious that it flowed to the floor in front of eyewitnesses. That afternoon,

Father Bruse's feet began to ache. He removed his shoes only to discover that his socks were wet with blood. When he painfully removed his socks, he was shocked to find wounds on the tops of both his feet. At that moment he experienced a piercing, excruciating pain in his right side, just above his belt. As he grasped his side in agony, he realized that his hand was covered with blood flowing from the wound in his side. "What's going on?" he shouted. Father Bruse, a young, simple priest from rural Virginia, had not heard of the stigmata wounds. He had no idea what was happening to him. His wrists began to exhibit small red spots, about the diameter of a pencil.[13]

On January, 2, 1992, the local bishop, the Most Reverend John R. Keating of the diocese of Arlington, met with Reverend Bruse and his pastor, Reverend Daniel Hamilton. By early March, the bishop's office issued a statement that the Church would not make any claims about the phenomena associated with the statues weeping tears and/or blood, or the appearance of the apparent stigmata of Reverend Bruse. Since there was no determined message with the phenomena, no ecclesiastic judgment would be forthcoming at that time.[14] An effect of the phenomena in Virginia, however, was increased participation in the prayer groups that have formed throughout the vast metropolitan Washington, D.C., area.[15]

What significance might these bleeding statues hold for us? According to experts who have studied the Ebola Zaire virus, it kills its victims so quickly and grotesquely that even medical personnel are confounded.[16] From contact until violent death, the virus destroys the human body within approximately ten days. A person first becomes dizzy, weak, and limp and loses all sense of balance. As he goes into shock, blood begins to ooze from all his bodily orifices. Even his eyes and ears weep blood. The virus is so violent that the internal systems of a human being explode out of his dying body as the deadly virus searches for a new living host.[17] Ninety percent of those who come in contact with the virus die, for there is no cure.

In 1989, an outbreak of the Ebola Zaire virus among imported laboratory monkeys was being investigated by a team of scientists at an Army research facility located within easy commuting distance of Reverend Bruse's parish, where the statues would bleed. Few humans were aware of the presence of the Ebola virus in Reston, Virginia, until a headline in *The Washington Post* on December 1, 1989, announced: DEADLY EBOLA VIRUS FOUND IN VA. LABORATORY MONKEY.

By January 1990, a second outbreak of the Ebola virus occurred at the Virginia center. Physicians and scientists worked tirelessly, under extraordinary stress, to isolate and manage the potentially deadly virus. Two team associates, however, became infected with the virus.

At first, the event contained a potential for great tragedy. The virus looked like the deadly Ebola Zaire. Through unforeseen human infection with the virus, it was learned that Ebola Reston does not kill humans. In fact, though it is deadly to monkeys, it does not even make human beings sick. Scientists have theories, as yet unconfirmed, about why the Reston Ebola virus differs from its deadly African counterpart, Ebola Zaire.[18]

The New York Times reported on June 13, 1995, that six Italian nurses in Zaire who were members of the Little

Sisters of the Poor of the Palazzolo Institute were recent victims of the Ebola Zaire virus. The nuns were buried in Kikwit, Zaire, where they had contracted the deadly virus as they cared for the dying. The Little Sisters of the Poor are renowned for their devotion to the Blessed Mother. One hundred sixty members of the Order continue to work in Zaire, where their entire lives are offered as a poured-out prayer of hope for the people of Africa. A spokesperson at the Order's headquarters in Bergamo, Italy, said of the messages that had come from the deceased sisters' fellow nuns in Zaire: "Their messages gave us an example of hope, of simplicity, of love among sisters. It was a kind of love that seemed to exaggerate, in its lucidity, in the face of such a situation. . . . You cannot care for the poor in astronaut suits. . . . [I]f it draws attention, their deaths won't have been in vain."[19]

To us, as well as those who have witnessed the phenomena in Civitavecchia and in Father Bruse's home and church, bleeding statues may not at first seem to make much sense. But perhaps they are signs of God's love and compassion for us in the face of gruesome death from viruses like Ebola Zaire. Perhaps they are telling us to practice our own humble brand of human compassion, as the nuns in Kikwit did, and as the prayer groups arising in the Washington, D.C., area (and all over the world) are striving to do even now.

The Blessed Mother began to advise people from the hills of Medjugorje in 1982 that prayer and fasting will stop war and change the natural law. She asked all people on earth to immediately form prayer groups, to pray, and to fast.

Thinking people are rightly hesitant about ascribing supernatural causes or remedies to natural disasters, including outbreaks of infectious disease or even war. Yet few have problems recognizing that God, however one defines that indefinable word, speaks through the ordinary circumstance of day-to-day life. In the face of massive outbreaks of certain infectious diseases, or unexpected natural disaster, or war, mere human power sometimes proves inadequate.

We, as a sacrificial, committed community, bring dignity to ourselves and to one another. The U.S. Marines who rescued Captain O'Grady remind everyone of the joy of sacrificial, dedicated preservation of human life. The scientists who endured Biosafety Level 4 hazards to investigate the Ebola virus in order to protect the health of the entire community expressed sacrificial dedication to the preservation of human life. The nurses in Zaire who died because they cared for those dying of the Ebola virus live on in their shining example of sacrificial love that gives hope to the world as long as humanity endures.

Any disaster is an opportunity for great virtue to flourish if people retain the faith that there is a supernatural realm from which they can draw strength in difficult times. The marine rescue team was filled with courage and competence. The scientists who worked to isolate the Ebola Reston virus were filled with courage and competence if one is to believe the saga chronicled in Richard Preston's *The Hot Zone*. The Little Sisters of the Poor who died in Zaire live on as examples of courage and competence because love is stronger than death. Love lives forever.

No one knows exactly why or how prayer and fasting change the natural law, or why they stop war. There are many theories that theologians and philosophers have espoused throughout the centuries. Yet normal people do pray, each in his or her own way. And millions fast. Some do so voluntarily and others do so involuntarily.

Reports continue that the Blessed Mother is appearing throughout the world now to people of all faiths, all races, all nationalities. Her messages have a profound urgency for everyone. She requests all people to form prayer groups, to pray much, and to fast with love on Wednesdays and Fridays. She asks all people on earth to begin immediately to read the sacred texts to discover truth. She reminds people that those who seek God find Him. The Blessed Mother of Jesus promises that those who find God dwell with Him forever in His Kingdom of peace, joy, and abiding love.

Apparitions are not random events. Apparitions are about love. Visionaries throughout time, from Abraham and Moses to those of modern days, share their firsthand experiences with visions, apparitions, and locutions (interior voices) of the Lord Jesus, His Blessed Mother, angels, prophets, and saints. Such information rightfully belongs to everyone, for we human beings make up the human family. As a sacrificial, committed community, we bring dignity to ourselves and to one another.

Divine manifestations change people. People change the world.

Wisdom, understanding, knowledge, counsel, fortitude, piety, and fear of the Lord bring solutions to all human problems. Such gifts are the theme of all authentic Marian apparitions. For that reason authentic apparitions are of profound significance to responsible, thinking people everywhere. Not every apparition is a harbinger of apocalypse. Joyful manifestations of God's gifts, too, are for everyone. They belong to all His people.

Visitations of the Lord, the Blessed Mother, and various holy ones from the beyond that occur all over the world are rooted in the formative spiritual beliefs and traditions of all people. In fact, the very foundation of Christianity rests on the apparitions of the Risen Christ.

Sacred Scripture contains public revelation that concluded in the first century. The Dogmatic Constitution on Divine Revelation from Vatican Council II states that no new public revelations are expected until the "glorious manifestation of our Lord Jesus Christ." The new *Catechism of the Catholic Church* teaches that while public revelation is complete, it has not been made completely explicit. It remains for the faithful to gradually grasp the full significance of public revelation contained in the Scripture and tradition of the Church.[20]

Messages obtained from apparitions, visions, and locutions are called private revelation and do not belong to the deposit of faith. They do not complete or improve the Revelation of Jesus Christ.[21] Private revelations can come from external visions and apparitions such as those Saint Bernadette experienced at Lourdes, interior locutions such as Saint Joan of Arc heard, and interior visions or images such as Saint Thomas Aquinas saw. Private revelation is not sacred text. It may illumine the scriptures, bring guidance, strength, and grace to God's people. Private revelations often help people live more integrated, Gospel-centered lives.

Authentic private revelation never contains anything that is not already disclosed in sacred Scripture. It is imperative, therefore, that those who turn to private revelation know the Scriptures well in order to avoid being deceived.

The responsibility to discern the authenticity of private revelations usually rests with ecclesiastical authority. Vatican Council II, however, urged the faithful to be open and attentive to the ways the Holy Spirit continues to guide the church, including private revelations: "Such gifts of grace, whether they be of special enlightenment or whether they are spread more simply and generally, must be accepted with gratefulness and consolation as they are suited to and useful for the needs of the Church."[22]

There are many famous saints who have had private revelations. Saint Francis of Assisi, founder of the Franciscan Order, Saint Margaret Mary Alacoque, who received the manifestations of the Sacred Heart of Jesus, Saint Ignatius of Loyola, who founded the Society of Jesus, and Saint Catherine Labouré, who was given the Miraculous Medal that proved effective to ward off the plague that devastated the towns and cities of Europe, are only a few among the vast numbers throughout thousands of years who have been so blessed.

Extraordinary apparitions are now reported all over the world. The Vatican is unable to process the unprecedented number of reports of private revelations that it receives daily.[23]

Such are the signs of the times. Normal, quite ordinary people do have encounters that radically alter their lives and the lives of those around them. Often, only in retrospect do people recognize that they have been helped by a celestial being or a celestial message sent at a particularly difficult or significant point in their lives.

There are many visions, apparitions, and locutions, perhaps as many as all the people who have ever lived. Authentic ones convey immense joy and confidence in God's love.

Our Sunday Visitor's Catholic Encyclopedia defines apparitions as:

> The sense-perceptible vision or appearance of Christ, the Blessed Virgin, angels or saints. Many apparitions are recorded in the Scriptures (e.g., Tobit 3:16–17; Genesis 26:24; Luke 1:11, 26). The authenticity of apparitions is a matter for investigation and evaluation by the Church or an experienced spiritual director. Church approval is always required when a popular cultus arises in response to alleged apparitions.
>
> Some of the most important approved apparitions center on visions of Our Lady: the Virgin of Guadalupe (1531); the Miraculous Medal (Paris, 1830); Our Lady of La Salette (1846); Immaculate Conception (Lourdes, 1858); Our Lady of Knock 1879); Our Lady of Fatima (1917). Since 1981 a group of teenagers in Medjugorje, Yugoslavia, have claimed to experience regular apparitions of Our Lady. The authenticity of these apparitions is still under evaluation by the Holy See. . . . The interpretation of private revelations must take into

account their expression in the thought-forms of doctrinally and theologically unlearned persons.[24]

For this book I have selected accounts of apparitions of the Blessed Mother and, in some cases, of the Lord Jesus, recorded from oral histories at shrines and places of pilgrimage, and gathered from universities, libraries, government bureaus, museums, churches, synagogues, mosques, temples, parsonages, convents, offices, homes, and families. Some are based upon unpublished interviews and recollections of eyewitnesses. Many of the apparitions are well known and revered by people all over the world. Details of these famous apparitions are readily available, so I have chosen to present here only their significance as manifested in these times.

The words attributed to the Blessed Mother and her visionaries in this book are the actual spoken words whenever they are available as chronicled by the visionaries. A slight variation in language is unavoidable in translations from non-English-speaking visionaries. In very early apparitions, or where no exact words have been recorded or made available, I have composed passages to convey the meaning of the apparitions as faith has remembered them.

How do we know what happens during an apparition? Alleged surface "facts" surrounding reported apparitions are sometimes obscure: obviously, modern techniques of verification did not always exist. Some of the apparitions of the twentieth century, however, have been investigated with the most up-to-date methods available to modern technology. Dr. Henri Joyeux, of the faculty of medicine at Montpellier University, France, with the assistance of his scientific team, performed in-depth laboratory studies of certain famous contemporary visionaries, most notably the children of Medjugorje during their ecstasies. His findings lend credence to the possibility of the nonhuman origins of the visions of the children of Medjugorje. They are available for the scrutiny of those who seek scientific verification and data concerning such apparitions.[25]

Some visionaries, such as those at Lourdes, Fatima, and again at Medjugorje, were subjected to examinations by the police and other government officials, who accused them of everything from political subversion to seeking personal financial gain. Psychiatrists, neuropsychiatrists and parapsychologists, news media, heads of state, church officials, the curious, the sick, and the devout from everywhere scrutinize visionaries. Because of suspected fraud, people are often quite cynical and demand proof of divine intervention in the affairs of the world. Visionaries therefore must bear much intrusion into their private lives humbly and in silence.

Scripture tells us that the Blessed Virgin Mary bore the Son of God. She named Him Jesus, raised Him, followed Him in His public ministry, and stood beside Him at His crucifixion and death. She was present with the apostles and disciples when the Holy Spirit descended upon them.

Sometime later, Church dogma teaches, she was assumed into Heaven. According to Pope John Paul II, her Assumption is "nothing else but the expression of faith of the Christian people that the Mother of God shares in a unique way in the Resurrection and in the Glory of her own Son."[26] The Pope describes the Blessed Virgin

Mary as "the new Eve, placed by God in close relation to Christ, the new Adam, beginning with the Annunciation, through the night of His birth in Bethlehem, through the wedding feast at Cana of Galilee, through the Cross at Calvary, and up to the gift of the Holy Spirit at Pentecost. The Mother of Christ the Redeemer is the Mother of the Church."[27]

Billions of people today, all over the earth, have gone beyond the surface of history to the depths of the mystery. They believe in the gentle presence of the Blessed Mother in their lives as the Mother of God and Queen of Heaven and Earth. Countless believers have given or would gladly give their lives to honor her. For them, she ever remains queen of their hearts.

Others, too, all over the earth, know of her in the deepest yet still unexplored longings of their hearts. They may not know her name as anything other than Blessed Mother. They also have a relationship with her and hope to be with her in Heaven where a place has been prepared for her and all her children. The reality of her presence is a glimmer of light in a dark world that groans and struggles for truth.

The descriptions that visionaries present of the Blessed Mother are filled with wonder and awe at the beauty, dignity, and glory that she conveys in her apparitions. Her skin color matches the visionary's, for she is Mother. Her language is the familiar accent that the visionary knows. Her voice is eternal sweetness. She is gentleness. She is living peace. She is ceaseless tranquillity. She, with her Son, is unconditional love. She and her children are the family of the Holy Trinity. The pursuit of the Blessed Mother is a journey of human faith aided by history and the deepest hope of the human heart.

The Second Coming of Jesus Christ?

Jesus asked His followers: *"But when the Son of Man comes, will he find faith on earth?"* (Luke 18:8). At the dawn of the twenty-first century, people throughout the world look for the Second Coming of Christ foretold in the Gospel as follows:

> "There will be signs in the sun, the moon, and the stars, and on earth nations will be in dismay, perplexed by the roaring of the sea and the waves. People will die of fright in anticipation of what is coming upon the world, for the powers of the heavens will be shaken. And then they will see the Son of Man coming in a cloud with power and great glory."
>
> LUKE 21:25–27

Many view the proliferation of alleged apparitions of the Blessed Mother in these times, on a global scale, as a portent of that prophesied event.[28] The visionaries in Rwanda actually quote the Blessed Mother and the Lord Jesus speaking of the Second Coming of Jesus Christ and the end of the world. All over the world people are actively seeking answers to the fundamental questions of life and death with seriousness, commitment, and intensity.

Global awareness of spiritual experiences exists now on a scale never before possible. Modern international telecommunications bring the apparitions of the Blessed Mother into the homes of the peoples of the earth in every nation. News reporters broadcast information about apparitions all over the world. Newsletters and fax machines spread messages of the Blessed Mother around the globe within moments.

Is the end of the world near? The passage of each day brings the earth one step closer to the end times—the Parousia, or Second Coming of Christ—referred to 318 times in twenty-two of the twenty-seven New Testament books.[29] Fifteen existential "signs of the times" in Scripture herald the Second Coming of Christ:

> As he was sitting on the Mount of Olives, the disciples approached him privately and said, "Tell us when this will happen, and what sign will there be of your coming, and of the end of the age?"
>
> Jesus said to them in reply, "See that no one deceives you. For many will come in my name, saying, 'I am the Messiah,' and they will deceive many. You will hear of wars and reports of wars; see that you are not alarmed, for these things must happen, but it will not yet be the end. Nation will rise against nation, and kingdom against kingdom; there will be famines and earthquakes from place to place. All these are the beginnings of the labor pains. Then they will hand you over to persecution, and they will kill you. You will be hated by all nations because of my name. And then many will be led into sin; they will betray and hate one another. Many false prophets will arise

and deceive many; and because of the increase of evildoing, the love of many will grow cold. But the one who perseveres to the end will be saved. And this gospel of the kingdom will be preached throughout the world as a witness to all nations, and then the end will come.

"When you see the desolating abomination spoken of through Daniel the prophet standing in the holy place (let the reader understand), then those in Judea must flee to the mountains, a person on the housetop must not go down to get things out of his house, a person in the field must not return to get his cloak. Woe to pregnant and nursing mothers in those days. Pray that your flight not be in winter or on the Sabbath, for at that time there will be great tribulation, such as has not been since the beginning of the world until now, nor ever will be. And if those days had not been shortened, no one would be saved; but for the sake of the elect they will be shortened. If anyone says to you then, 'Look, here is the Messiah!' or, 'There he is!' do not believe it. False messiahs and false prophets will arise, and they will perform signs and wonders so great as to deceive, if that were possible, even the elect. Behold, I have told it to you beforehand. So if they say to you, 'He is in the desert,' do not go out there; if they say 'He is in the inner rooms,' do not believe it. For just as lightning comes from the east and is seen as far as the west, so will the coming of the Son of Man be. Wherever the corpse is, there the vultures will gather.

"Immediately after the tribulation of those days,

> "the sun will be darkened,
> and the moon will not give its light,
> and the stars will fall from the sky,
> and the powers of the heaven will be shaken."
>
> MATTHEW 24:3–29

The great cosmic event comes. Jesus promised:

"And then the sign of the Son of Man will appear in heaven, and all the tribes of the earth will mourn, and they will see the Son of Man coming upon the clouds of heaven with power and great glory. And he will send out his angels with a trumpet blast, and they will gather his elect from the four winds, and from one end of the heavens to the other. . . . Heaven and earth will pass away, but my words will not pass away."

> MATTHEW 24:30–31, 35

People all over the world now ask: "Do we live in apocalyptic times? Is the Blessed Mother gathering the flock of her Son?" The "herd" is certainly being repositioned. The world as humanity now knows it continuously changes before our eyes. Many nations are locked in internecine warfare or suffer from political instability and terrorism. Nuclear weapons are hidden in the bowels of the earth. Environmental ignorance, combined with negligence, has left parts of the world a cesspool of filth. Epidemic disease is rampant with no sign yet of abating. At least one person dies of starvation every minute of every day. The Bible, however, speaks more than 350 times of God's unconditional love for humankind.[30] The Bible promises:

> For the sake of his own great name the LORD will not abandon his people, since the LORD himself chose to make you his people.
>
> 1 SAMUEL 12:22

Floods, hurricanes, tidal waves, sudden volcanic eruptions, earthquakes, unstable global weather patterns all are relentless reminders to each generation of the truth about life on the planet earth. Catastrophes force people to let go of established patterns of life, forget what they have treasured and lost, and focus on the depths of their own existence in an ever-unfolding majesty of renewal and reintegration. The Bible reminds us:

> He never withdraws his mercy from us. Although he disciplines us with misfortunes, he does not abandon his own people.
>
> 2 MACCABEES 6:16

The messages conveyed by visionaries and locutionists about apocalyptic events are prophetic announcements. Those who receive the messages are usually not the best source of interpretation of those messages. Saint Paul spoke of the imminent Second Coming of Jesus Christ. In Scriptural language, "soon" can mean thousands of years. Some of the apparitions of the twentieth century, however, especially at Fatima and Pontmain, to name only two, did deal with events that transpired almost immediately. Eschatological urgency yields to wisdom and understanding when the reality of God's unfathomable love is appreciated.

Splendid, unexpected apparitions of the Blessed Mother announce to the world's population that she comes to these times surrounded with the majesty of the divine and accompanied by the beautiful angels of God. She is continuously identified by visionaries as "pure love." Usually she is surrounded by so much celestial light that visionaries, often without realizing the significance, speak of her as the woman of the Apocalypse, for they see her "clothed with the sun" (Revelation 12:1).

Frequently the dress and veil of the Blessed Mother are described as luminescent white, so dazzling that billions of twinkling stars could be the fabric. Her eyes are like deep pools reflecting the clearest sky. Her skin is like satin. Her voice has the sweetness of a lullaby, the mystery of a rippling stream, and the depth of an echo that calls to the caverns of memory deep in each soul that God has ever created. She is Mother. She is home. She is safety. She is abundance. She is tranquillity. She is the gate of Heaven and the hope of all people.

The Blessed Mother speaks of God who is love. She tells us He dwells in all that lives. She reminds us that we are constantly surrounded by loving, caring, and helping spirits of pure love who desire that we too learn to love. Each person ever created has an eternal destiny. No one is born alone, no one walks the earth alone, and no one dies alone.

The apparitions in this book are a joyful exploration of

some of the more famous and highly significant visions of the Blessed Mother, and in some instances, of her Divine Son Jesus, that impact these times. They give us hints of God, weeping and pining for His poor, broken children to return to His waiting arms. The beautiful, eternal messages of love that are contained in these apparitions are for all people on earth. They are the promise that propels the earth to spin on in countless mornings of hope.

CHAPTER TWO

Queen of All Saints

His dominion is vast
and forever peaceful,
From David's throne, and over his kingdom,
which he confirms and sustains
By judgment and justice,
both now and forever.
The zeal of the LORD of hosts will do this!

ISAIAH 9:7

The concept of the Blessed Virgin Mother of God is rooted in human consciousness. It has intrigued people from the beginning. The virtues and dignity of the Blessed Virgin Mother of God are extolled in the world's art, music, literature, and architecture.

One example is the druids, who in 300 B.C. built a prayer sanctuary dedicated to "The Virgin Who Would Bear the Son of God" in the lovely sacred groves that are now Chartres, France. In the Middle Ages, a glorious cathedral was built on the site in honor of the Blessed Virgin Mary. Pilgrims flock there, even today.

The Blessed Mother of Jesus is unlike any creature who has ever existed. A member of the human race and never divine, she is the Mother of all people. Her role has been described thus: "Mary consented in faith to become the Mother of Jesus. The constant tradition of the Church holds that Mary received the Word of God into her heart and her body at the angel's announcement and thereby brought Life to the world. She conceived in her heart, with her whole being, before she conceived in her womb. First came Mary's faith. Then her Motherhood."[1]

The Blessed Virgin Mary was conceived in her mother Anna's womb, by natural means, as the offspring of her father Joachim, and born free from the slightest stain of sin. This dogma is known as the Immaculate Conception.[2] She who is the Mother of God remains perpetually a virgin.

In 431 the Council of Ephesus declared that Holy Mary is truly Theotokos, the Mother of God, the Mother of Jesus, the Second Person of the Holy Trinity made flesh.[3] The Blessed Virgin Mary's perpetual virginity is threefold: she conceived the Lord Jesus Christ of the Holy Spirit, without seed of man; without injury she brought Him forth; after His birth she preserved her virginity inviolate.[4]

Christian tradition, affirmed by the doctors of the church, maintains that Mary conceived the Son of God not only physically, but also spiritually. Pope Pius IX described the spiritual gifts of Holy Mary:

> God loved her above all creatures to such a degree as to find in her, as in no other, His highest complaisance. Wherefore, out of the inexhaustible riches of His Divinity, He lavished upon her, far more than upon all the angels and saints, such an

abundance of every heavenly gift and grace, that being always utterly free of every stain of sin, and all beautiful and perfect, she was adorned with such fullness of innocence and holiness that, aside from God, no greater holiness and innocence is conceivable, and in fact, no mind except that of God can comprehend it.[5]

From time to time throughout the centuries, certain highly privileged souls have been permitted glimpses of the Blessed Virgin Mother of God. Because there is no past or future where God dwells, and because all of us have existed in the mind of God from the beginning, it is not surprising that certain ones, such as Elijah the Prophet, knew of and even saw the Blessed Mother and her Divine Son before they were born on earth. The story of the apparition to Elijah, according to Carmelite tradition, follows.

Elijah the Prophet

The ancient tradition of the religious order of Our Lady of Mount Carmel is rooted in the experiences of the prophet Elijah. A brilliant light hovered over the great mountain where Elijah dwelled as he aspired to live a life of purity and holiness. He chose to live hidden away from human eyes on the heights of Mount Carmel in Palestine on the shores of the Mediterranean Sea. Prayer nourished and consoled his spirit as he drank deep of the presence of God in all that lives. While at prayer, Elijah perceived the Blessed Mother holding the Christ Child in the immense light that surrounded the peaks of the mountain. The Divine Child and His Blessed Mother were encased in a dazzling cloud of illumination in the sky above Elijah, and the cloud brought a great brilliancy to the earth.

Through the divine gift of interior illumination, Elijah the Prophet recognized the Blessed Virgin Mary, the human mother carrying God in human form. Elijah saw the promised Messiah, who is the light of the world, in the arms of Holy Mary.

As the vision ended, a great and steady rain poured from the heavens, ending a drought that had brought death to much life and vegetation. Elijah and his followers understood this prophetic apparition of the Blessed Virgin Mary and recognized her presence as a sign portending the mystery of suffering and glory to be fulfilled in the life, passion, death, and resurrection of the Blessed Virgin Mary's Son, Jesus Christ. The Suffering Messiah was also recognized and foretold by Isaiah the Prophet.

The apparition filled Elijah's spirit with a new awareness. He recognized the abyss between God's sovereign, majestic holiness and human pettiness rooted in sin. The profound love and beauty that he experienced in the vision of the Blessed Mother with her Divine Infant gave him a keen awareness of God's intoxication with the human race. He realized that God has loved humankind into existence and, through the Promised One, redeems His beloved children from the effects of their sinfulness.

A number of holy men joined Elijah. They began to dwell in caves on Mount Carmel, calling themselves hermits of Our Lady of Mount Carmel.[6] There on the mountain they erected what some consider to be the first chapel on earth dedicated to the Mother of God. The spirit and power of Elijah led the men, in the company of angels, to a life that some saw as quite austere. They practiced the virtues of silence; constant prayer; and fasting from people, places, and things that might distract them from the presence of God in and around all that lives. They lived from day to day in extraordinary simplicity so that they could perceive the presence of God. They sought at all times to be consciously bathed in the sea of God's love.

Tradition affirms that Elijah did not die, that he traveled by chariot to an unknown place. It is believed that he will return in the end times (Malachi 3:1, 23). Throughout the ensuing centuries, Elijah's ascetic life of love and prayer would bear sweet fruit, for the crusaders brought some of the holy hermits of Mount Carmel back with them to Europe.

The Carmelites, as they came to be known, settled in England and France, and eventually all over the world. Their philosophy and commitment continue to the modern day. Canonized saints such as Saint Teresa of Ávila, Saint Thérèse of Lisieux, and Saint John of the Cross are numbered among their members. Several, including those just mentioned, have been privileged to experience apparitions of the Blessed Mother during their lives.

Only gradually is humanity realizing that authentic apparitions of the Blessed Mother concern everyone because her Divine Son is the center of the universe and human history.[7] The response of each person to such apparitions affects everyone else, and the planet, too. No one and nothing is exempt. When divine messages are sent to everyone in the entire world, everyone needs to do his or her part so that all may live.

The Blessed Mother proclaims that peace is God's way. Peace is the only way. Silence is God's response to rebellion. He departs from His enemies. As He withdraws, He withholds His blessings. When the protective hand of God does not rest upon His children, they experience the tortures of the damned. Peace, joy, and love flow only from the hand of God.

The Blessed Mother warns, especially in the twentieth century, that those who do not forgive, as God has commanded us to do, forfeit peace, joy, and love. To forgive, the Blessed Mother says, is to trust God. Vengeance is His alone, but God's vengeance cleanses. His vengeance purifies.

The Blessed Mother promises that God's ways bring the Kingdom of Heaven to earth for those who hear and obey His voice. He is the Lord of all creation. All the treasures of creation flow from God's heart of pure love.

Visionaries tell the world much about the Blessed Mother. She is a source of enlightenment for those who choose to avail themselves of her presence. She is the divinely appointed Mother of those who overcome death to rise with her Divine Son in a divine existence that is without end.

The purpose of human life is to become aware of truth. Enlightenment is the awakening and integration of the entire human personality into the reality of the world within and beyond the five senses. Death is unconsciousness of the human personality that eventually claims the human body also.

Before the world was made, the Blessed Mother was conceived in the Divine Mind of such a purity, such an exquisite perfection that no darkness could ever attach to her in any way.[8] Those who would be close to her come to that realization and share in her light.

The Blessed Mother is not divine. Rather, she is the living tabernacle of the Most High. Her Son Jesus is both human and divine. He is the light of the world. He is truth. His life, His ways bring human beings conscious awareness of the reality of God in the world, in our lives, in our hearts, in our own eternal now.

Do Not Be Afraid

Secrets of the spirit world are a mystery. God's children are becoming aware of the presence of the Blessed Mother in the world as they awaken to the reality of God in their lives. The Age of Mary arrives on the wings of the angels in her celestial court. She brings the divine light of God to earth. Her presence resonates now in the reservoir of human consciousness.

The Apostles in Jerusalem

The apostles and disciples of Jesus were in the upper room with the Blessed Mother when the fire of the Holy Spirit first descended upon them (Acts 2:1–4). The love and longing instilled into their hearts that day was a fire that would reach to the ends of the earth.

Early Christianity followed the paths of the ancient

Roman roads. Everywhere the apostles and disciples went, devotion to the Mother of God flourished.

In Jerusalem, nestled in the Kidron Valley at the foot of Mount Olivet, a church is built on the site of the tomb of the Blessed Virgin Mary. According to modern local lore, the Kidron Valley will be the site of the Last Judgment. Such belief has turned the area into a huge necropolis in which Jews, Moslems, and Christians alike choose to be buried.

There is a story that circulates in the area that Saint Thomas the Apostle arrived at the tomb where the Blessed Mother had been laid to rest three days earlier. Anxious to behold the Mother of his Savior one last time, Thomas helped the other apostles roll back the stone of the tomb. Nothing was found inside but the simple robes of the Blessed Mother and a magnificent garden of blooming lilies growing there in the darkness. Astounded, the apostles cried out as one: "Holy Mary, Mother of God, pray for us sinners now and at the hour of our death!"

At the conclusion of their prayer, it is said, the Blessed Mother appeared before them, clothed with the sun, with the moon under her feet, and on her head a crown of twelve stars as Saint John later described in Revelation 12:1. Overwhelmed with joy at the celestial splendor they were witnessing, and realizing they were once again in the mysterious presence of the Mother of God, the apostles fell to their knees.

Extending her arms to the apostles in a gesture of eternal motherly love, she spoke:

"Dear children of God, I am with you always. Love my Son. Serve my Son. Be like my Son."

Her words, like a lullaby in the recesses of their memory, erased the grief that tore at their wounded souls. Word of the apparition of the Mother of God to the apostles spread like a gentle breeze on a scorching day, and the followers of Jesus flocked to Mary's tomb. They, too, wanted to experience the joy of the Blessed Mother's presence.

The words of the angel Gabriel satisfied their longing: "Hail Mary, full of grace, the Lord is with you" (Luke 1:28). Elizabeth's grace-filled exclamation at the Visitation, "Blessed are you among women and blessed is the fruit of your womb!" (Luke 1:42), comforted their sorrows. "Jesus!" they prayed. Only Jesus could fill their hearts. "Holy Mary, Mother of God, pray for us sinners now and at the hour of our death. Amen," echoed from hearts that were waiting in joyful hope for the coming of the Lord Jesus. Catholics have prayed the Hail Mary ever since.

Though the apparition of the Blessed Mother to the apostles faded into history, the apostles were renewed in mind and heart. The power of the Holy Spirit continued to inspire and guide them. They had formed a church as they recited the first Hail Mary, and thereafter thus spoke of the Blessed Mother as the Mother of the Church.

In these times, all nations and religions have the right to offer worship in the sepulcher of the Mother of God in Jerusalem. The Greeks and Armenians have liturgies here. The Syrians, the Copts, and Abyssinians also have liturgies. The Muslims and Jews have a special place of worship for their religious ceremonies in this sanctuary. All on earth are welcome, for the Mother of Jesus is everyone's Mother.

Saint John the Apostle

Humanity was learning to drink of the compassion and tenderness of God as the Blessed Mother's presence continued to be experienced by the early Christians. Jesus had entrusted the care of His Blessed Mother to His beloved and exquisitely sensitive apostle John. After the Blessed Mother's dormition, he grieved her absence most deeply and prayed for her intercession with her Divine Son in the heavenly Kingdom.

It is believed that Saint John the Apostle frequently experienced apparitions of the Blessed Mother after her dormition, and most especially in his old age. He alone was permitted to see the heavenly Jerusalem. Near the end of his life, Saint John left for all times the description of the end times in the final book of the Bible, Revelation. He described the triumph of the Lamb on His throne. He gave the world the description of the woman clothed with the sun wearing a crown of twelve stars. He identified the army of angelic spirits and their work in the last days.

Miracles and shrines followed the apostles and extended throughout the immense Roman Empire and beyond. The catacombs, hiding place of the Christians during the bloody persecutions of the first three centuries, are filled with frescoes that represent the life and teachings of the Lord Jesus Christ and His Blessed Mother in thousands of shapes and forms.

Among the first teachings given by the apostles was a deep veneration for the Blessed Mother that they and their followers carried with them everywhere they traveled. As they honored the Mother of Jesus, all mothers and all women were included and elevated in her honor. The elderly, the sick, and the poor found meaning in their lives. Family life flourished. A gentleness of spirit seeped into the consciences of those who faithfully followed the Gospel messages of the Lord Jesus.

A Soldier Who Became Emperor of Constantinople

A blind, emaciated beggar and his starving dog plodded along a dusty road about ten miles outside of Constantinople in the year c. 455. Misfortune was their traveling companion. The dog died and the beggar was left without even a walking stick. After tripping over a stone he could not see, the blind man lay bleeding and dazed in the noonday sun.

Passersby heard only a haunting hollowness from his parched throat as he cried out: "Holy Virgin! Though I have never seen your image, I have always trusted in your protection. On the faith of your promises I left my home and family to undertake this journey. Please do not let me perish here without your help."

Some time passed. Leo, a soldier of the Roman army carrying dispatches of his commander to Constantinople, happened upon the unfortunate old man. Feeling some compassion for him, he offered to lead the old man along on his way. "Where are you going?" he asked.

"The Holy Virgin appeared to me in a dream and promised me that should I journey to Constantinople she would grant me the favor of seeing the crowning of the new emperor."

It was clear that the blind man was dying of thirst. The soldier, keenly touched by the helplessness of the old man, prayed: "O Queen of Heaven, this unfortunate has exposed himself to endless danger because he trusted in you. Do not let his faith prove deceptive." Suddenly he heard himself called by name. Startled, the soldier forgot the old man and hastened along the road. Then he heard his name called once again.

"Why are you so troubled? Here before you in the grove is a pond full of water."

Immediately he heard the bubbling water. There at the edge of the grove the soldier found a crystal clear pool, and remembering the miserable old man who lay dying on the road he prayed that death would not take the man before he could enjoy the water. Then the soldier heard the voice respond to his thoughts:

"Fear not. She whom the blind man invoked will not abandon him in his suffering. Because your soul is compassionate and your heart was open to the appeal of the less fortunate, and because you had confidence in my intercession and have honored me with persevering devotion, I have obtained for you the highest earthly dignity man can seek. You who have been faithful in small acts of love shall now be awarded the opportunity to serve my Son in great acts of love for your brothers and sisters. You will be proclaimed emperor and will sit on the throne where sat Constantine, who served me so faithfully. You will reign with glory

during seventeen years. In this very place your grateful heart will build a church, and my Son will be pleased to hear my divine motherhood invoked therein. He will draw multitudes of the faithful by the countless miracles and blessings worked in my name. This is the sign by which you and all my children may know that I am truly the Mother of God. I have chosen you to make that known because of the kindness of your heart. Please fill your helmet with water from this pond and take a handful of mud. Give the water to the old man to drink, and he shall regain his strength. With the mud anoint his eyes and he shall see. Go quickly to him for he touches the portals of death."

Everything happened just as the Mother of God promised. The blind man saw and the soldier was greatly rewarded for his obedience to God's will. When he became emperor Leo I, he built the Church of Our Lady of the Golden Fountain. It was widely renowned because of the numberless cures and blessings wrought there.[9]

Saint John Damascene

Saint John Damascene was the son of a wealthy and influential government official of Damascus. He was educated by a Sicilian monk who instilled in him a great love for prayer and a commitment to the ascetic principles of Christianity. When John ascended to his father's position, he used his high office to promote the faith of Jesus Christ.

The stress of wealth and power plagued his sensitive soul as he wrestled with the illusions and allures of a passing world. He finally resigned his position and gave his worldly possessions to the poor. Then he journeyed on foot to the Holy Land. In Jerusalem, John recommitted his life to Jesus Christ and worked his way to the monastery at St. Sabas. There he lived a life of prayer, labor, and obedience.

Officials in Damascus were enraged by John's public disdain for wealth and power. The people were intrigued by his choices and were actively seeking information about John's faith. Trumped-up charges were leveled against John's honesty to discredit him with the people. It is said that the caliph ordered John's right hand to be severed and hung up in the marketplace as an example to all. John was in torment as he heard the taunts and jeers of the crowd that had gathered to see the sentence carried out. In a powerful stroke of the executioner's sword, John's severed right hand fell to the ground. Then it was hung up in the marketplace for all to see.

In his disgrace, John turned to the tenderness and power of the Blessed Virgin Mary. He prayed: "O Holy Mother of God, Your Son knows all that is seen and not seen. You know of my innocence of all these charges. Heal me, holy daughter of our Father, Mother of God's Son, Spouse of the Holy Spirit, that I may write of the glories of Your Son."

The stump of John's right arm was slow to heal and he endured intense physical sickness. Though he was abandoned by friends and family, John continued to pray with faith more fierce than the burning pain that crept up his arm. His sleep was interrupted by the profuse sweats that accompanied his high fever.

As illness relentlessly assaulted his body, John fell at last into a deep sleep. The Blessed Mother appeared to him in a dream. Her gentle Mother's heart was filled with filial love as she promised:

> *"Your hand is whole. Let it be as you have asked. May your pen write swiftly."*

When John awoke, his hand was restored. Only a thin red line indicated the place where the executioner's sword had severed it. John was no longer sick. All sign of infection was gone. Health and zeal for God's glory now consumed this faithful son of the Blessed Virgin Mary.

Word spread through all of Damascus of the divine favor granted John by the Blessed Virgin. People flocked to see his restored right hand. Great conversions occurred because of the miracle. The caliph restored John's reputation to save his own. The writings of Saint John Damascene have been a source of inspiration ever since. He is included among the doctors of the Church.[10]

"Mary's Dowry"

Shortly before the Norman Conquest, during the reign of Saint Edward the Confessor, Richeldis de Faverches, Lady of the Manor of Walsingham, had a vision in which the Mother of God took her in spirit to Nazareth and showed her the dwelling where the Holy Family resided. The Blessed Mother requested of her that a shrine be dedicated in England to serve as a perpetual memorial of the Annunciation to Mary and the Incarnation of the Lord Jesus Christ. The Blessed Mother promised:

> *"Let all who are in any way distressed or in need seek me there in that small house that you maintain for me at Walsingham. To all that seek me there shall be given succor. The small house at Walsingham shall be a remembrance of the great joy of my Salutation, when Saint Gabriel the Archangel announced that I should become the Mother of God's Son through humility and obedience to His will."*

It is said that angels mysteriously transported and constructed the shrine of the Holy House of Nazareth at Walsingham. The king, Saint Edward the Confessor, entrusted England to Mary. He officially pronounced: "This is your Dowry, Holy Virgin." Later monarchs renewed the solemn dedication and Walsingham became one of the great places of pilgrimage in the Middle Ages, ranking behind only Jerusalem, Rome, and Santiago de Compostela. "Mary's Dowry" was famous as a place of prayer, grace, healing, miraculous cures, and reconciliation.[11]

Saint Simon Stock

Saint Simon Stock, a native of England, like most of his countrymen had deep devotion to the Mother of God. He became a member of the Order of Our Lady of Mount Carmel while on a pilgrimage to the Holy Land.

The Blessed Mother showed her love for England, her "Dowry," and for the Carmelite Order on July 16, 1251, at

Aylesford. The Mother of God, holding the Infant Jesus in her arms, appeared on that date to the Carmelite friar. She entrusted to Simon Stock the brown scapular, to be worn as a sign of consecration to God and to the Blessed Mother, with the words:

> *"My beloved son, receive this Scapular for your Order.*
>
> *It is the special sign of a privilege which I have obtained for you and for all God's children who honor me as Our Lady of Mount Carmel.*
>
> *Those who die devotedly clothed with this scapular shall be preserved from eternal fire.*
>
> *The Brown Scapular is a badge of salvation.*
>
> *The Brown Scapular is a shield in time of danger.*
>
> *The Brown Scapular is a pledge of peace and special protection, until the end of time."*

Many miracles are associated with the brown scapular of Our Lady of Mount Carmel, the use of which carries with it the pontifical blessing of Pope Benedict XIV. Several other Popes have granted spiritual privileges to those who wear the brown scapular faithfully.

The conditions attached to the privileges are:

- to observe exactly what has been prescribed regarding the material, color, and form of the brown scapular;

• to receive it from a person duly authorized to give it;
• to wear it constantly in the manner prescribed.

The blessings that are connected with wearing the brown scapular are extraordinary graces. They are available and offered to all people on earth.[12] The humble Blessed Mother invites. God's children are free to choose or reject her gifts.

God Himself donned the composition of human nature to manifest to us the love and respect with which He has endowed us. He made us stewards of all His creation. He gave us hope of eternal life with Him. In love, He has given us Himself, clothed in the flesh of His beautiful masterpiece, the Blessed Virgin Mary (John 1:14). And He has even given us His own Immaculate Mother.

The Eternal One brought His heart into the world through the Blessed Virgin Mary. She, with her Infant Son, brought a gift to humanity to wear as a sign of love and gratitude, the brown scapular.

CHAPTER THREE

Mother of Divine Grace

"Can a mother forget her infant,
be without tenderness for the child of her womb?
Even should she forget,
I will never forget you,
See, upon the palms of my hands I have
written your name. . . ."

ISAIAH 49:15–16

Manresa, Spain:
Saint Ignatius of Loyola, 1522

Ignatius of Loyola, born at Loyola Castle in 1491, grew
into a dashing young courtier who had influential friends
in the political and cultural centers of Europe. Handsome
and an excellent dancer, he was popular with the royalty of
his day. He chose to enter the military, and he became a
powerful and effective soldier. When Ignatius was thirty
years old, his right leg was brutally injured by a cannon
blast. As he lay on his deathbed, Saint Peter appeared to
him. Ignatius miraculously recovered his health but he was
left partially crippled, his leg badly deformed. Ignatius
had a quick wit and a marvelous sense of humor, and he

enjoyed court functions. He submitted to excruciating pain to have his injured leg repaired so that he could once again wear the tight-fitting hose that men of the aristocracy sported.

While recuperating from the leg surgery that was motivated by youthful vanity, Ignatius read two volumes: a Life of Christ and a Lives of the Saints. Suddenly his heart had new heroes. Ignatius burned with a zeal to live his life for the highest possible purpose. He thrilled to the example of Saint Francis of Assisi, who knew Christ so intimately. His heart pounded with fervor at the sublime sentiments that Saint Dominic espoused in his preaching. He, too, longed to know Jesus as they did.

"Who knows Him better than His Mother?" reasoned the ardent soldier turned prayer warrior. Falling to his knees, Ignatius prayed humbly and fervently to the Blessed Mother of Jesus. His autobiography describes a most extraordinary event that forever altered the course of his life:

> One night, as he [Ignatius of Loyola] lay sleepless, he clearly saw the likeness of Our Lady with the holy Child Jesus, and because of this vision he enjoyed an excess of consolation for a remarkably long time. He felt so great a loathsomeness for all his past life, especially for the deeds of the flesh. . . .[1]

Those who knew Ignatius well were astounded at the change in his outlook after the apparition. He'd had a vision that forever transformed his life. What really happened to him? Was his chamber suddenly filled with the glorious celestial light that surrounds the visual presence of the Blessed Mother and her Divine Son? Did the light of their presence lift the veil that shrouds life on earth? Ignatius embraced the morning of his conversion like a man who has fled the dungeon of darkness. His exuberance for the things of God was matched only by his devotion to the Blessed Mother of Jesus. Ignatius swore his fealty to her. He entrusted his life to the Mother of His Savior in exchange for her protection and constant intercession with her Child, whom Ignatius saluted as the King of Kings and Lord of Lords.

Ignatius traveled to the abbey of Montserrat, the great spiritual sanctuary of the Blessed Mother, in the vicinity of Manresa. There he spent the night. He chose not to sit or lie down during the night vigil. Rather, he either stood or knelt before the altar of Our Lady of Montserrat. He asked the Blessed Mother to take him under her special protection and to fill him with her humility and purity. He later spoke in his autobiography of arranging "to hang up his sword and dagger at Our Lady's altar in the church" of Montserrat, thereby setting aside his worldly possessions to embrace his new life in Christ. Ignatius came to the shrine in noble robes. He exchanged his fine garments with a beggar at Montserrat and donned the garments of a pilgrim.

The decision at Montserrat was final for Ignatius. There would never be any other woman in his life except the great Queen of Heaven and earth. From that moment, Ignatius traveled the high road of sanctity.

Embracing wisdom, Saint Ignatius taught that persons given to prayer may easily become too wedded to their own ideas. He prayed constantly for humility and loving reverence for the will of God. He worked assiduously to integrate the human need for work and for prayer.

Saint Ignatius gained mastery over his own naturally fiery temper and became renowned for his sweetness and gentleness. Yet he could speak with such severity in the face of injustice that his listeners trembled before him. Ignatius never lost his tranquillity. He found that peace flows from the river of love. God is love. Ignatius knew Jesus. He founded the Society of Jesus and his Jesuits have continuously influenced the course of human history.

Guadalupe, Mexico: Juan Diego, 1531

Juan Diego was a pious Native American convert to Christianity. On December 12, 1531, the Blessed Virgin Mary appeared at daybreak to the poverty-stricken fifty-seven-year-old Aztec Indian on Tepayac Hill. Though Tepayac was a barren desert, at one time it had housed a temple to the mother-goddess of the Aztecs.

Juan Diego, whose name in the Aztec tribe was Na-huatl, which means Singing Eagle, saw a woman of celestial beauty on the hill. She was beautiful, so beautiful and regal that Juan was overcome with shyness. He cast his eyes to the ground and joined his hands in prayer. Suddenly the Beautiful Lady stood before him surrounded by rays of light as bright as the noonday sun. The moon was beneath her feet. She wore a gown of crimson and gold, and a blue mantle bespangled with stars covered her head and cascaded down over her dress in graceful folds.

The Blessed Mother spoke in Juan's mother tongue:

"My dear little son, I love you. I desire you to know who I am. I am the ever-virgin Mary, Mother of the true God who gives life and maintains it in existence. He created all things. He is in all places. He is Lord of Heaven and Earth. I desire a teocali {church or temple} in this place where your people may experience my compassion. All those who sincerely ask my help in their work and in their sorrows will know my Mother's Heart in this place. Here, I will see their tears; I will console them and they will be at peace. So run now to Tenochtitlán and tell the Bishop all that you have seen and heard."[2]

Juan fell to his knees in tears of love and awe as he replied: "Noble Lady, I will do as you say." He arose and fled to Tenochtitlán (now Mexico City). There he found the bishop's palace and knocked at the door. The porter was much surprised to see such a humble person requesting a meeting with the bishop. Juan suffered some embarrassment, but finally he was permitted to see the bishop.

Bishop Zumárraga was a Franciscan who had great love for the Blessed Mother. He was deeply touched by the humility and awe of the Aztec convert who spoke of the Mother of Jesus with such reverence. The bishop listened patiently as Juan described the request of his Heavenly Queen for a church to be built on Tepayac Hill. He promised Juan that he would take his request under advisement and ended the interview. The bishop, however, was quite busy. Although he was impressed by Juan Diego, he had little regard for the uninhabited hill that was distant from everyone and everything.

As Juan returned home, he once again climbed Tepayac

Hill. There he found the Blessed Mother waiting for him. He fell in tears at her feet explaining that his mission on her behalf had failed. Holding his trembling hands in hers, the Blessed Mother soothed his anguished soul with the promise:

"My little son, there are many that I could send to the Bishop. But you are the one whom I have chosen for this assignment. One day all will know my love for you and all my little children. Tomorrow morning you must return to the Bishop and express once again my great desire for a church in this place."[3]

Juan Diego went obediently to the bishop's residence the next morning. There was little enthusiasm this time in the bishop's response. He demanded a sign from the Blessed Virgin to corroborate the story. Juan Diego returned to the hill and found the Blessed Mother waiting for him.

"My little son, am I not your Mother? Do not fear. The Bishop shall have his sign. Come back to this place tomorrow. Only peace, my little son."[4]

Juan Diego did not return to the hill the next day. His uncle had become mortally ill, and Juan Diego stayed to care for him. Two days passed, and, as death seemed near, Juan Diego headed to find a priest for his uncle. It was necessary to pass Tepayac Hill. Juan encountered the Blessed Mother there, waiting for him.

"Do not be distressed and afraid, my littlest son. Am I not here with you who am your Mother? Are you not under my

shadow and protection? Your uncle will not die at this time. There is no reason for you to engage a priest, for his health is restored at this moment. He is quite well. Go to the top of the hill and cut the flowers that are growing there. Bring them then to me."[5]

Juan Diego's heart was filled with faith in the Blessed Virgin's promises as he climbed the frost-covered hill on the freezing December morning. There he found, in full bloom, magnificent Castilian roses. Their exotic beauty had never before graced the arid soil of Tepayac Hill. As Juan Diego cut the beautiful roses, he noticed that they were drenched in summer dew. No frost had touched them.

Juan removed his *tilma*, or mantle, and used it to gather the huge array of blooming roses. When the flowers were safely in the tilma, Juan Diego carried them to the Blessed Mother. She rearranged the bouquet and said:

"My little son, this is the sign I am sending to the Bishop. Tell him that with this sign I request his greatest efforts to complete the church I desire in this place. Show these flowers to no one else but the Bishop. You are my trusted Ambassador. This time the Bishop will believe all that you tell him."[6]

Before long Juan Diego was standing before the bishop once again. This time the bishop had members of his staff with him. As Juan Diego recounted the request of the Mother of God for a great church on Tepayac Hill, his tilma opened and the full-blown Castilian roses fell before the astonished eyes of all. Suddenly the bishop was kneeling. "My Lady and my Queen!" he sobbed as he caressed the roses. Juan realized that all those in the reception salon were gazing in rapt wonder at his tilma. The full-length image of the Blessed Virgin was mysteriously and divinely imprinted upon the fabric.

Within six years, an estimated eight million Aztecs gazed at the image of the Blessed Virgin Mother of God on Juan Diego's tilma and came to embrace Christianity. There in the mysterious divine painting upon the poor cloth of Juan's tilma were the symbols of the old, pagan faith the Aztecs had treasured; but now they were seen in the illumination of revealed truth. They recognized her as the Virgin Mother bearing God within, for when the tilma is held properly, it is quite obvious that the Theotokos, the God-bearer, is full with her Divine Son.

The Aztecs gazed upon the tilma with such awe that word spread throughout the people like lightning across the sky. As far as is known in these times, the image of the Blessed Mother on Juan Diego's tilma is the only divine image of the Blessed Virgin Mary that exists on earth. It now hangs on display in the great basilica that was constructed on Tepayac Hill in Mexico City. Approximately seven million pilgrims come from all over the world each year to the great basilica of Our Lady of Guadalupe.

Ávila, Spain: Saint Teresa of Ávila, 1561

Teresa was born to a noble family in Ávila, Spain, in 1515. She and her older brother Rodrigo were devout children who dreamed of serving in the missions, where they could give their lives as martyrs for the faith. They were quite prayerful children who built little private grottos, where they prayed each day.

When Teresa was twelve years old, her mother died. In her grief, Teresa turned to the Blessed Mother and asked for her special protection and assistance. Her prayer was answered in a most gracious and generous way. No other known saint has enjoyed the seraphic heights of mystical union that Saint Teresa of Ávila knew during her lifetime. She is one of two women doctors of the Church.

An angel from the cherubim choir is described by Teresa:

> I beheld in his hands a long poniard of gold, at whose extremity was a slight spark of flame. From time to time he plunged this into my heart and buried it into my entrails; it seemed to me that he took them from me with this poniard, and left me filled and burning with the love of God. This wound, inflicted thus, caused me an indescribable martyrdom, and at the same time made me taste of perfect joy. There exists between God and the soul at that instant a union of love so perfect that it is impossible to describe it. I consider my sufferings as a glory in comparison with which all the other glories of the world are as nothing.[7]

At another time Saint Teresa described the following experience with the divine:

> The Lord desired that I see the vision in the following way: the angel was not large but small; he was very beautiful, and his face was so aflame that he

seemed to be one of those very sublime angels that appear to be all afire. They must belong to those they call the cherubim, for they don't tell me their names. But I see clearly that in heaven there is so much difference between some angels and others and between these latter and still others that I wouldn't know how to explain it. I saw in his hands a large golden dart and at the end of the iron tip there appeared to be a little fire. It seemed to me this angel plunged the dart several times into my heart and that it reached deep within me. When he drew it out, I thought he was carrying off with him the deepest part of me; and he left me all on fire with love for God.[8]

Saint Teresa enjoyed apparitions not only of the Blessed Mother but also of Saint Joseph. Teresa had great love for Saint Joseph, through whom Jesus was heir to the Davidic promise. She was given a vision of the glories and splendor of the Assumption of the Blessed Virgin Mary.

The saint's great work involved her tireless efforts to reform the Carmelite Order and, with it, the Christian world that had grown lax, luxury-craving, and slothful. Though Teresa had a deep devotion to the virtues of humility and voluntary poverty, she always retained a joyful sense of humor and was renowned for her quick wit. Accordingly, she told her nuns that on the Day of Judgment both majestic palaces and humble cottages would fall and she had no desire that the convents of her nuns should do so with a resounding clamor.

Saint Teresa of Ávila's writings have become a blueprint for the spiritual journey of a soul. Her splendid classic on prayer, *The Way of Perfection*, has been consulted by enlightened people for four hundred years. In its simplicity, it has been accepted as a work of sublime mystical beauty. In these times when many speculate about the end of the world, the secrets of Fatima, the ominous warnings from the apparitions at Rwanda and elsewhere in the twentieth century, her voice of wisdom echoes through the ages to instruct those who would be wise:

We are meditating on the nature of the world, and on the way in which everything will come to an end, so that we may learn to despise it, when, almost without noticing it, we find ourselves ruminating on things in the world we love. We try to banish these thoughts, but we cannot help being slightly distracted by thinking of things that have happened, or will happen, of things we have done and of things we are going to do. Then we begin to think of how we can get rid of these thoughts; and that sometimes plunges us once again into the same danger. It is not that we ought to omit such meditations, but we need to retain our misgivings about them and not to grow careless. In contemplation, the Lord Himself relieves us of this care, for He will not trust us to look after ourselves. So dearly does He love our souls that He prevents them from rushing into things which may do them harm just at this time when He is anxious to help them. So He calls them to His side at once, and in a single moment reveals more truths to them and gives them a clearer insight into the nature of everything than they could otherwise gain in many years. For our sight is poor and the dust we meet on the road blinds us; but in contemplation the Lord brings us to the end of the day's journey without our understanding how.[9]

Teresa was a woman of immense prudence. Though she was exceedingly cautious regarding supernatural favors such as visions and apparitions, she founded the Carmelite reform because of what she believed was an order from the Lord Himself.[10] In the modern day, the prudent cling to her discernment regarding visions, apparitions, and locutions, for she is one of the most revered doctors of the Church. Her wisdom shines in the advice she left future generations regarding visions and apparitions:

> The good or the evil does not lie in the vision but in the one who sees it and in whether or not she profits by it with humility; for if humility is present, no harm can be done, not even by the devil. And if humility is not present, even if the visions be from God, they will be of no benefit. For if that favor which should humble a nun when she sees she is unworthy of it makes her proud, she will be like the spider that converts everything it eats into poison, or like the bee that converts it all to honey.[11]

In reality, the choice is always ours regarding how we respond to the gifts God so dearly desires to give His children of the earth. God's love is constant. We can make His gifts either our poison or our honey.

The writings of Saint Teresa of Ávila, taken together, are a masterpiece, for she is a rare soul who truly experienced mystical union of the highest order. Such a union is the promise for all those who remain faithful to God's will. Her writings are a preview of what lies beyond the five senses. Those who long to sit at the feet of God gain much understanding of His ways from the works of Saint Teresa of Ávila. It is believed that at her death, on the feast of Saint Francis of Assisi, October 4, 1582, the Lord came personally with His Mother, Saint Joseph, and many other saints to gather her soul.

Paray-le-Monial, France: Saint Margaret Mary Alacoque, 1673

Born to devout, noble parents, Saint Margaret Mary is the special messenger of the Sacred Heart of Jesus whose life and mission were foretold by Saint Gertrude the Great more than 300 years earlier. When Margaret Mary was nine years old, her father died and she was sent to live briefly in a convent. There she received a love for the religious life that never left her, though her family was not keen on her choice and placed many obstacles in her way. She entered the Visitation Convent at Paray-le-Monial in 1671 and became a nun the following year. The Blessed Mother was constantly in her thoughts: she prayed continuously that she might receive the grace from the Mother of God to be pleasing to her divine Son, Jesus the Lord.

Saint Joseph and the wise men and shepherds of Bethlehem learned that those who approach the Blessed Mother find Jesus. Saint Margaret Mary learned that also. During a strange sickness that overtook her as a child, the

Lord manifested Himself. For the rest of her life, Saint Margaret Mary was the very privileged apostle of the Sacred Heart of Jesus. The Lord Jesus spoke to all succeeding generations through this saint when He manifested the intensity of unconditional love for His people contained in His Sacred Heart. His words, recorded in Saint Margaret Mary's diary, are:

"Behold this Heart which has loved humans so much that It has spared nothing, even to exhausting and consuming Itself, in order to testify to them Its love; and in return I receive from the greater number nothing but ingratitude by reason of their irreverence and sacrileges, and by the coldness and contempt which they show Me in this Sacrament of Love. But what I feel the most keenly is that it is hearts which are consecrated to Me, that treat Me thus."[12]

Saint Margaret Mary, like Saint Teresa of Ávila, witnessed an apparition of the Blessed Mother concerning the dogma of her Assumption into Heaven. She describes the vision:

On the feast of her triumphant Assumption, the Blessed Virgin Mary allowed me to see a crown which was composed of all her holy children whom she placed in her retinue before the Throne of God. She confided to me that the flowers that God wished to place upon her head were too deeply rooted in the earth. This vision allowed me to comprehend the dignity of detachment so that our thoughts may truly ascend to the ways of heaven.[13]

Jesus often appeared to Saint Margaret Mary manifesting His desire that God be the absolute ruler of the hearts of all His children. Jesus promised that if she was faithful to God's will, He would teach her to know Him. She comments:

I withdrew into a small courtyard, near the Blessed Sacrament, where doing my work on my knees, I felt myself wholly rapt in interior and exterior recollection, and at the same time, the Adorable Heart of my Jesus appeared to me brighter than the sun. It was surrounded by the flames of Its pure love, and encircled by Seraphim, who sang in marvelous harmony: "Love triumphs, love enjoys, the love of the Sacred Heart rejoices!" These blessed spirits invited me to unite with them in praising this Divine Heart, but I did not dare do so. They reproved me, telling me that they had come in order to form an association with me, whereby to render It a perpetual homage of love, adoration and praise, and that for this purpose, they would take my place before the Blessed Sacrament. Thus I might be able, by their means, to love It continually, and as they would participate in my love and suffer in my person, I, on my part, should rejoice in and with them. At the same time they wrote this association in the Sacred Heart in letters of gold, and in indelible characters of love.[14]

Three centuries earlier, Saint Gertrude the Great had been promised by the Lord Jesus that one day He would reveal His Sacred Heart to the world. God's time is not like our time. Three hundred and fifty-three years after His promise, that day arrived. Saint Margaret Mary describes it:

The Lord said to me:

"My Divine Heart is so passionately in love with human beings that it can no longer contain within itself the flames of its ardent charity. It must pour them out by means of you, and manifest itself to them to enrich them with its precious treasures, which contain all the graces they need to be saved from perdition. . . ."

Before disappearing, He asked for my heart, and I begged Him to take it. He did so, and put it into His own Adorable Heart, in which He allowed me to see it as a little atom, being consumed in that fiery furnace. Then drawing it out like a burning flame in the form of a heart, He put it into the place whence He had taken it, saying:

"Behold, My beloved, a precious proof of My love. I enclose in your heart a little spark of the most ardent flame of My love to serve you as a heart, and to consume you until your last moment. Until now you have taken the name only of My servant. From now on you shall be called the well-beloved disciple of My Sacred Heart. . . . If My people return even a little portion of My love, I will consider as naught all I have done for them. . . . They meet My love with coolness and rebuffs. Will you console and rejoice with Me by supplying as much as you are able for their in-

*gratitude? Fear not for behold in My Heart is all that is
wanting in humanity. I am their strength."*[15]

Jesus asked Saint Margaret Mary to communicate to
the world, from behind her cloistered Visitation Convent
walls, His desire that His people receive the Holy Eucharist on the first Friday of each month and make an act
of reparation to God for their ingratitude. He asked those
who are able to rise every Thursday night between eleven
and twelve o'clock and wait and watch with Him in expia-
tion for the sins of all humanity.

Jesus told Saint Margaret Mary that the weakness of
the apostles in the Garden of Olives was only a prelude to
the weakness of all God's children. He asked that souls entrust their hearts to His Sacred Heart. In response to that
request recorded in the diary of Saint Margaret Mary, millions all over the world have presented themselves before
Jesus in the Blessed Sacrament in adoration and reparation.

The Blessed Virgin Mary appeared to Saint Margaret
Mary and imparted the following mission for the Sisters of
the Visitation and the Fathers of the Society of Jesus:

*"Come, my beloved daughters of the Visitation, approach, for
I wish to make you the depository of this precious treasure, the
Sacred Heart of My Son Jesus Christ. You sons of the Society
of Jesus have a great part in this precious treasure; for it is
given to the daughters of the Visitation to make it known and
loved, and to distribute it to others. To the Fathers of the Society is given the commission to make the value and utility of
the Sacred Heart of Jesus understood. In proportion as you
shall console the Divine Heart of Jesus, the fruitful source of*

graces and blessings shall pour itself out so abundantly on the functions of your ministry, that you shall produce fruits above your hopes and labors; and the same for the perfection and salvation of each one of you in particular."[16]

The Lord Jesus Christ made the following promises to Saint Margaret Mary for all those who venerate His Sacred Heart all on fire with love for mankind:

- I will give them all the graces necessary for their state of life.
- I will establish peace in their families.
- I will console them in all their difficulties.
- I will be their assured refuge in life, and more especially at death.
- I will pour out abundant benedictions on all their undertakings.
- Sinners shall find in My Heart the source and infinite ocean of mercy.
- Tepid souls shall become fervent.
- Fervent souls shall advance rapidly to great perfection.
- I will bless the house in which the image of My Sacred Heart will be exposed and honored.
- I will give to ministers of the Gospel the power of moving the most hardened hearts.
- Persons who propagate this devotion shall have their names inscribed in My Heart, and they shall never be effaced from it.
- I promise that in the excess of the mercy in My Heart, its all-powerful love shall grant to those who receive the Eucharist on the First Friday of each

month, for nine consecutive months, the grace of final repentance; they shall not die under My displeasure, nor without receiving the Sacraments. My Heart shall be their secure refuge at the last hour.[17]

Saint Margaret Mary said that, at the conclusion of the promises of the Lord Jesus Christ to humankind, seraphim who surrounded Him sang, "Love triumphs, love rejoices. The love of the Sacred Heart gladdens." The seraphim then invited all those who love the Sacred Heart of Jesus to sing those words in adoration and praise with them daily.

The first Mass ever celebrated in honor of the Sacred Heart of Jesus occurred in the chapel of the Visitation at Dijon, France, on February 4, 1689. It was the first Friday of the month.

The Shrine of the Sacred Heart at Paray-le-Monial, France, draws people from all over the world who desire to sing with the seraphim before the throne of God. One of the massive silver lamps bears three medallions in enamel with the inscription:

To the Sacred Heart of Jesus
The Church in America
Consecrates the hearts of all her children, that they may
burn more
and more with His Divine Love.

On the reverse side, an angel with outspread wings carries the escutcheon and colors of the United States, while an American eagle, in an azure sky, bears aloft the motto that promises many hearts in one Divine Heart: E PLURIBUS UNUM.

CHAPTER FOUR

Seat of Wisdom

"You will receive power when the Holy Spirit comes upon
you, and you will be my witnesses in Jerusalem, throughout
Judea and Samaria, and to the ends of the earth."

ACTS 1:8

Rome, Italy: Alphonse M. Ratisbonne, 1842

Twenty-eight-year-old Alphonse Ratisbonne was a wealthy
Alsatian from a prominent Jewish banking family. Alphonse loathed the Catholic Church, which he felt was an
institution of madness.

Before his marriage, Alphonse chose to enjoy a year of
travel. Along his journey, Alphonse visited Rome, where
he greatly enjoyed the antiquities. Here he met a former
schoolmate, M. Gustave de Bussieres, whose father, the
Baron de Bussieres, was a convert to Catholicism from
Protestantism. Filled with the zeal of the Holy Spirit, the
baron spoke endlessly about his newfound faith. Ratisbonne was appalled. He found such overbearing discussion
of religion tasteless and irritating.

One glorious evening, as Ratisbonne dined in the splendor of de Bussieres's home, the baron offered Alphonse a

Miraculous Medal of the Blessed Virgin Mary. "How absurd!" thought Alphonse. Nevertheless, since his manners were impeccable, he accepted the medal as a memento for his fiancée. The baron then pounced upon him. "You must repeat the Memorare morning and evening!" he insisted. That evening Alphonse left the palace of the baron with a copy of the Memorare composed by Saint Bernard of Clairvaux, which he promised to transcribe forthwith and return. Alphonse himself describes what happened to him:

> What was this irresistible impulse which made me do that which I would not? O Providential Guidance! There is then a mysterious influence which guides a man on the road of life. I had received at my birth the name of Tobias, along with that of Alphonse; I had forgotten the first name; but my invisible agent [guardian angel] did not forget it. Here was the true friend which Heaven had sent me; but I did not know him. Alas! there are many Tobiases in the world who do not know that celestial guide, and who resist his voice![1]

No matter how hard Alphonse tried to forget the words of the Memorare, they kept running through his mind: "Remember most gracious and loving Mother of God, that never was it known that anyone who fled to your protection, implored your help, or sought your intercession was left unaided. Inspired by this confidence, I turn to you, O Virgin of virgins, my Mother. To you do I come; before you I stand, sinful and sorrowful. O Mother of the

Word Incarnate, despise not my petitions, but in your mercy, hear and answer me. Amen."

On January 20, the baron asked Alphonse to enter a church with him en route to a formal lunch. Alphonse could not refuse. While his host retreated to the monastery to arrange for the funeral of a friend, Alphonse was suddenly alone in the chapel of Saint Michael the Archangel. There in the splendor of his solitude, Alphonse saw a small ball of light, which suddenly exploded into thousands of fragments of dazzling brightness that shattered his illusions and pierced his heart with the love of the Blessed Virgin Mary. In the celestial light she stood before him, surrounded by the pulsating rays of the sun. Alphonse described his experience:

When I looked up, the whole building around me seemed to have disappeared. I could only see one chapel, which had, as it were, gathered all light unto itself, and there, in the midst of the light, standing on an altar, beautiful and majestic, was the Blessed Virgin Mary as represented on the Miraculous Medal. I was drawn towards her as by an irresistible impulse. . . . She did not speak but I understood everything. . . . I could not give an idea in words of the mercy and liberality I felt to be expressed in those hands. It was not only rays of light that I saw escaping thence. Words fail to give an idea of the ineffable gifts that flow from those hands of our Mother! The mercy, the tenderness, and the wealth of Heaven escape thence in torrents on the souls of those whom Mary protects.[2]

So shocked was the baron when he returned to find his guest prostrate on the floor of the chapel that he canceled his luncheon with high-ranking diplomats to kneel and pray beside the ecstatic Ratisbonne. Shortly thereafter, a meeting with Pope Gregory XVI was arranged. Alphonse was enthralled to see the portrait of the Immaculate Conception as represented by the Miraculous Medal that was one of the Pontiff's treasures. But Alphonse was heard to sigh: "No human depiction can capture the beauty of our Mother who dwells in Heaven. Her love is beyond the world and she pulls her children into her world of love."[3]

The thinking of Alphonse Ratisbonne was so radically changed that he combined his natural love of antiquities with the zeal of his newfound faith and headed for the Holy Land. There he was able to acquire the land beside the ancient arch of Ecce Homo. Alphonse became a priest and founded the Congregations of the Work of Our Lady of Zion.

Between the years 1859 and 1864, on the site of the public trial of Jesus Christ before Pontius Pilate, archaeological teams were assembled to remove the ruins in order to construct a convent for the Sisters of Zion. Here Jesus was condemned to death, took up His cross, and began the journey to Calvary for crucifixion. The archaeological discoveries produced by the excavations of Alphonse Ratisbonne include a pavement bearing traces of games played by Roman soldiers. The depicted "king's game," played with dice, could have been used with Jesus as its subject as described in Matthew 27:27–30 and Mark 15:16–20. The soldiers used to choose a prisoner, mock him as a fake king, and then put him to death. The restorations begun by Ratisbonne are considered by many to be among the most interesting sites in the Holy Land.

Forty years after the apparition of the Blessed Mother, Alphonse Ratisbonne died in Jerusalem. Those who were present at his death said that he again saw his heavenly Mother and died with such a radiance that all present were lifted to new heights of faith and hope and love for the Blessed Mother whom God has given to all His children.[4]

La Salette, France: Maximin and Melanie, 1846

High in the French Alps, near Grenoble, is the tiny hamlet of La Salette. Sparsely populated, the village is a quiet sanctuary protected by towering mountains. There in the crisp autumn air, fourteen-year-old Melanie Mathieu and eleven-year-old Maximin Giraud were spending the day tending a small herd of cattle.[5] It was September 19, 1846. The unwanted children were completely unaware that Heaven had designs on their lives, and through them, on the world.

France had survived its great revolution. Though contemporaries proclaimed the times as the Age of Reason, history is less generous. The French Revolution has been called the Age of Insanity. France survived, but ever so gradually belief in the lovely, simple blessings of life were crushed by the engine of political aggrandizement, greed, avarice, and a host of other negative impulses that were destroying French family life. The graciousness and dignity of mutual respect, service, and abiding love were slowly crumbling into indifference, self-indulgence, and indolence.

In the bright afternoon sun, Melanie and Maximin saw a brilliant light below them in a large ravine. As the children gazed in amazement at the light, they began to see in its interior a most Beautiful Lady who was weeping in profound grief. The children drew as near as they dared. Then they heard the Beautiful Lady call to them:

"Come to me, my dear children. Do not be afraid. I have come to tell you something of great importance."

The children noticed that the beautiful, extremely sad Lady wore a dress of white radiance, studded with pearls, and a gold-colored apron. She wore a wreath of roses around her headdress, which was a high cap, bent slightly forward in front. Her slippers were tipped with roses. Melanie observed the strange necklace the Beautiful Lady wore. Attached to it were a crucifix with a hammer on one side and pincers on the other.

There is much mystery surrounding the messages of La Salette. The generally accepted version includes the following:

"Dear little children, I entreat my Son constantly for all of you. Will you not listen to your Mother's voice? My Mother's heart bleeds for each of you. I love you so much! Do not bring more suffering upon yourselves.

"Dear little children, return to God. Only in God do you experience peace, joy, and love. Only in God, in His ways, in His ordinances is happiness attainable. God has given you six days to work, but you take seven. Many people swear. They profane God's name.

*"I come to warn you that a great famine is coming.
Nothing can grow without the blessing of God. When the
harvest is spoiled, realize you yourselves have caused this.
God's justice is love. He will permit the adults to atone for
their sins by hunger. Children under seven will be afflicted
with seizure and die in their homes.*

*"If God's people awaken to His presence and His
ways, the rocks will become piles of wheat and the potatoes
will sow themselves. You must say your prayers, my little
children, both in the morning and at night. Pray more.
Pray at least one Our Father, one Ave, each day if you can
do no more. Do not devour food like hungry dogs. Fast and
abstain for the love of God so that he may fill you with
health. Make my words known to everyone in the world."*[6]

A spring of water was discovered in the place where
the Blessed Mother appeared to the children, and miracles
of physical healing began to be associated with the water.
Pilgrimages began. An order of sisters was founded by the
bishop to assist the pilgrims from all over Europe who
came to the site. Within five years, the Church approved
the apparition.

It was the unmistakable healings attributed to the waters of the spring that flowed from the site of the apparition
that fueled national belief in the veracity of the apparition at
La Salette. Several blind people regained their sight when
they bathed their eyes in the water of the spring. Cripples
found that they could walk after visiting the spring, and people with intestinal maladies were cured when they drank the
water. Pilgrimages to the site of the apparition continue.[7]

The visionaries, Melanie and Maximin, claimed that

the Blessed Mother gave each of them a secret.[8] They steadfastly refused to disclose their secrets for five years. Dreadful prophesies attributed to the apparition at La Salette fed popular notions of divine wrath. Finally, after much intervention by certain cardinals and bishops, the children were induced to write their secrets for Pope Pius IX.

It was said that when the Pontiff read Maximin's letter containing the secret, he responded: "Here is all the candor and simplicity of a child."[9] When he read Melanie's secret, however, his face changed and reflected great emotion. He stated: "There are scourges that menace France, but Germany, Italy, all Europe is culpable and merits chastisements. I have less fear from open impiety than from indifference and from human disrespect."[10]

Several years later, the superior of the Missionaries of La Salette, a religious order formed to serve pilgrims at the site of the miraculous spring, had a private audience with the Pope during which he asked about the secrets of La Salette. The Pope replied: "You want to know the secrets of La Salette? Ah, well here are the secrets of La Salette: if you do not do penance, you will perish."[11]

Melanie's background was so humble that thinking people were impressed with the depth and vocabulary that she used when she finally published her secret. In 1879, a brochure entitled "The Secret of La Salette and the Apparition of the Very Holy Virgin on the Mountain, 19 September 1846," bearing the imprimatur of Monsignor Zola, bishop of Lecce, Italy, was distributed by Melanie.[12] The following excerpts are from that brochure:

"Melanie, what I am about to tell you now will not always be a secret. Some Priests and ministers of my Son, by their wicked lives, by their irreverence and their impiety in the celebration of the holy mysteries, by their love of money, their love of honors and pleasures, become cesspools of impurity. . . . Woe to those dedicated to God who by their unfaithfulness and their wicked lives are crucifying my Son again. The sins of those dedicated to God cry out towards Heaven and call for vengeance, for there is no one left to beg mercy and forgiveness for the people. There are no more generous souls, there is no one left worthy of offering a stainless sacrifice to the Eternal God for the sake of the world.

"In the year 1864, Lucifer together with a large number of demons will be unloosed from hell; they will put an end to faith little by little, even in those dedicated to God. They will blind them in such a way, that, unless they are blessed with a special grace, these people will take on the spirit of the angels of hell; several religious institutions will lose all faith and will lose many souls.

"Evil books will be abundant on earth and the spirits of darkness will spread everywhere, a universal slackening in all that concerns the service of God. . . .

"The Vicar of my Son will suffer a great deal, because for a while the Church will yield to large persecution, a time of darkness, and the Church will witness a frightful crisis. The true faith of the Lord having been forgotten, each individual will want to be on his own and be superior to people of the same identity. They will abolish civil rights as well as ecclesiastical, all order and all justice will be trampled underfoot and only homicides, hate, jealousy, lies and dissension will be seen without love for country or family.

"The Holy Father will suffer a great deal. I will be with him until the end and receive his sacrifice. The mischievous will attempt his life several times to do harm and shorten his days, but neither he nor his successor will see the triumph of the Church of God.

"All the civil governments will have one and the same plan, which will be to abolish and do away with every religious principle, to make way for materialism, theism, spiritualism and vice of all kinds. Several cities will be shaken down and swallowed up by earthquakes. People will believe that all is lost. Nothing will be seen but murder, nothing will be heard but the clash of arms and blasphemy.

"The righteous will suffer greatly. Their prayers, their penances and their tears will rise up to Heaven and all of God's people will beg for forgiveness and mercy and will plead for my help and intercession. And then Jesus Christ, in an act of His justice and His great mercy, will command His angels to have all His enemies put to death. Suddenly, the persecutors of the Church of Jesus Christ and all those given over to sin will perish and the earth will become desert-like. And then peace will be made, and man will be reconciled with God. Jesus Christ will be served, worshipped, and glorified. Charity will flourish everywhere. The Gospel will be preached everywhere and mankind will make great progress in its faith, for there will be unity among the workers of Jesus Christ and man will live in fear of God."[13]

Controversy developed surrounding the secrets of La Salette. There are many views.[14] Interest in those secrets does not abate. They remain an inducement to watchfulness, prayer, and obedience to the will of God.

A beautiful basilica now welcomes pilgrims who come to La Salette. Those who experience difficulties have a great lesson from the Mother of God at La Salette. Faithfulness begets faithfulness. Blessings beget blessings. The offspring of virtue are peace, joy, and abiding love.

Lourdes, France:
Saint Bernadette Soubirous, 1858

Troubles continued to brew in France. Widespread unemployment, disease, and moral breakdown touched nearly everyone, including the citizens of Lourdes, a town nestled high in the Pyrenees. Four years after the Catholic Church promulgated the dogma of the Immaculate Conception of the Blessed Virgin Mary, eighteen apparitions were experienced in Lourdes by a sickly, emaciated young girl of eleven. The daughter of a sporadically employed father and a mother who was forced to compensate for her husband's considerable shortcomings, Saint Bernadette Soubirous seemed to many an unlikely candidate for favors from heaven. Her family was not respectable. She had no outward indication of piety. In fact, she was so uneducated that she had not yet been taught her catechism.[15]

The Blessed Virgin Mary imparted three secrets to Bernadette at Lourdes. Bernadette guarded them carefully. She carried them with her to her grave.

Saint Bernadette Soubirous describes her first apparition, which occurred on the Thursday before Ash Wednesday, February 11, 1858:

> Suddenly I heard a great noise, like the sound of a storm. I looked to the right, to the left, under the trees of the river, but nothing moved. I thought I was mistaken. . . . Then I heard a fresh noise like the first. I was frightened and stood straight up. I lost all power of speech and thought when, turning my head toward the grotto, I saw at one of the openings of the rock a rosebush, one only, moving as if it were very windy. Almost at the same time there came out of the interior of the grotto a golden colored cloud, and soon after a Lady, young and beautiful, exceedingly beautiful, the like of whom I had never seen, came and placed herself at the entrance of the opening above the rosebush. She looked at me immediately, smiled at me and signed to me to advance, as if she had been my Mother. All fear had left me but I seemed to know no longer where I was. I rubbed my eyes, I shut them, I opened them; but the Lady was still there continuing to smile at me and making me understand that I was not mistaken. Without thinking of what I was doing, I took my Rosary in my hands and went on my knees. The Lady made a sign of approval with her head and herself took into her hands a Rosary which hung on her right arm. . . . The Lady let me pray all alone; she passed the beads of her Rosary between her fingers but she said nothing; only at the end of each decade did she say the "Gloria" with me.[16]

The Beautiful Lady appeared seventeen more times to Bernadette in the grotto at Massabielle attired in a simple white gown with a long blue sash at the waist and wearing a flowing white veil. The Beautiful Lady wore no shoes, but golden roses on her feet matched the chain of her glimmering white rosary. She asked Bernadette to pray much for poor sinners.

One day the pastor of the town asked Bernadette to inquire about the identity of the Beautiful Lady. Sometime later, the shivering child stood knocking at the pastor's door as the rain and wind bit at her thin frame. Finally the priest opened the door. Bernadette was terrified, for she had no understanding of the words she was about to communicate on behalf of her heavenly visitor as she sputtered, "The Beautiful Lady said, 'I come from Heaven. I am the Immaculate Conception' "[17] Stunned, the priest awoke. He said, "Please come in! Can you ever forgive me for doubting your visions of the Mother of God?"

During one of her apparitions, obedient little Bernadette responded to the Beautiful Lady's request for penance and humiliations on behalf of poor, rebellious sinners. Kneeling, Bernadette dug in the mud of the grotto and even ate some of the mud. "She's insane," some onlookers hooted. "What do you expect?" others scorned. But as the child dug deeper into the mud, a bubbling sound was heard. Then a trickle came out of the mud. Soon miraculous waters gushed from the site of the apparition.

The Blessed Mother asked Bernadette to communicate her request for a chapel on the site of her apparitions at Lourdes where the sick could come bearing lighted candles as a sign of their faith and hope in God's love and mercy.

The sick began almost immediately to come to these waters of Lourdes. For over one hundred and fifty years, people have traveled from all over the world to bathe in the miraculous waters given by the Beautiful Lady at Lourdes. Great and miraculous healings continue to occur, even in these times. Crutches, wheelchairs, hearing aids, braces, and prostheses that are no longer needed are on display at Lourdes. They are a testimonial to the healings that have occurred in the miraculous waters.

And Bernadette? She spent her short life in a convent at nearby Nevers where today visitors may see her incorrupt body preserved by divine grace for more than 100 years. It rests encased in glass under the main altar. The Beautiful Lady had told her:

"I do not promise you happiness in this life, but in the next."

Saint Bernadette's visions, however, brought blessings to her family and extraordinary, ongoing renewal to the town of Lourdes. The healing waters rejuvenated the exhausted inhabitants through the love energy brought to them by the pilgrims who congregated there in ardent faith. Modern-day Lourdes remains one of the most sought-after places of healing on earth.[18]

The apparitions at Lourdes demonstrate the effect of conscious awakening to divine life within and around all that lives. Those who are able to drink of that life enter into the rhythm of eternity. The synergy of human creativity with the Source of life is living peace, joy, love, wholeness, and abundance.

The message from Lourdes is once again the Gospel

message: love; heartfelt prayer, especially the meditations of the Rosary, which illuminate the life of Christ; and loving cooperation with the will of God are the path that frees the world from darkness, from blindness to God's presence in and about all that lives. Synergy between God and His people creates new life in its fullness.

Pontmain, France: 1871

The Blessed Virgin Mary has shown herself to be Mother Most Faithful to her children in France. Once again she appeared there as fear and even terror overtook her French children during the war of 1870. Paris was surrounded by Prussian invaders on September 18, bombarded beginning December 27, and finally the people were starving. Prayer, their only hope, was offered to God constantly by the frightened people of France.

Pontmain, situated on the borders of Brittany, is an ancient town that boasts the ruins of a fortress castle. The people of this principally agricultural area have remained God-fearing and devout throughout the centuries. On the evening of Tuesday, January 17, 1871, twelve-year-old Eugène Barbedette stood transfixed as he saw the heavens open. There in the brilliance of the millions of shining stars he beheld *"Une Grande Belle Dame,"* a most Beautiful Lady who smiled at him in a gaze of eternal love.

She wore a dark blue dress that was adorned with golden stars. Her dark blue silk slippers were fastened with golden ribbons that formed rosettes. On her head she wore a black veil and a golden crown with a red band.

Eugène called to his ten-year-old brother Joseph, who also saw the Beautiful Lady in the sky. When the children exclaimed to their parents that they saw a celestial apparition, the mother and father strained to see what kept their sons in such rapt attention. Finally the mother suggested that the family kneel there and pray five Our Fathers and five Hail Marys.

Soon others from the village gathered. Some said that they saw three strange stars in the sky. Nine-year-old Jeanne-Marie Lebossè and her eleven-year-old sister Françoise exclaimed that they too saw the Beautiful Lady. A sickly boy, age six, and a tiny girl, age two, also exclaimed that they saw the apparition.

At that exact moment, far away in the Church of Our Lady of Victory in Paris, a novena to obtain the cessation of hostilities through the intercession of the Blessed Virgin Mary was beginning.

A small red cross formed over the Blessed Mother's heart at Pontmain. By now about eighty people had gathered to listen to the children's description of the apparition. All the villagers saw the three stars, which were in a triangular formation. They began to pray the Rosary. Then the children spoke the letters they saw forming in the sky: MAIS PRIEZ, MES ENFANTS (But pray, my children).

By now, the Prussian invaders had reached Laval. Would their village be next? The people at Pontmain began to sing the Litany of the Blessed Virgin Mary. Then the children called out the letters they saw in the sky: MON FILS SE LAISSE TOUCHER (My Son allows Himself to be persuaded).

The excited people continued to pray with a heightened fervor. Then the four children exclaimed that they saw a large red crucifix, bearing the figure of Jesus Christ, near the Blessed Virgin. They saw the Blessed Mother take the crucifix in her hands and present it to the children. The people sang now with great inspiration. Then the cross disappeared, leaving only the Blessed Virgin Mary standing before the amazed eyes of the children. Soon her presence too became dim to their eyes and they no longer were able to see the beautiful Blessed Mother of Jesus. The people would never forget. The world too would always remember their night.[19]

Our Lady of Hope is a treasure of the French people, for ten days after her apparition in Pontmain, on January 27, 1871, a full armistice was signed, ending the war. Jesus indeed had allowed Himself to be persuaded to rescue His faithful, praying children. Apparitions of Our Lady of Hope are a harbinger of those wonderful times when God reigns in the hearts of all His people. The people at Pontmain found the key to God's mercy: prayer with the heart.

Knock, Ireland: 1879

Devotion to Mary, the Mother of God, is a vital component of the faith in Ireland. Saint Patrick entrusted his ministry there to her maternal intercession and asked for her continued presence among the Irish whom he loved so much.

Saint Patrick built the great abbey at Trim in Meath. He dedicated the abbey church to the Mother of God, naming it Our Lady of Tryme. This sanctuary of the Blessed Mother became one of the most famous pilgrimage places in Europe. Many miracles are associated with the faith of the people who flocked to the shrine imploring the assistance and intercession of the Mother of Jesus Christ. The Irish people have never wavered in their devotion to the Blessed Virgin Mary.

God rewards faithfulness. On August 21, 1879, the Lord sent His Blessed Mother to Knock, in County Mayo. She was accompanied by Saint Joseph and Saint John the Evangelist. Many people attribute the sanctity of family life that remains strong among the Irish people to the special grace the vision at Knock represents.

Knock is an ordinary village of hardworking, God-fearing farmers. As evening came, a steady downpour began. Few people were out, but those who were suddenly noticed a celestial light that emanated from the gable end of the village church. An elderly woman saw the light and paused to gaze at it. In a moment of exhilaration she cried out: "The Blessed Virgin!" and ran towards the vision with her arms outstretched. A man ran through the streets shouting, "Come quickly! The Blessed Virgin is here at the church!" Several people assembled. They exclaimed, "Look! There's Saint Joseph! And Saint John the Evangelist too!" The phenomenon lasted about two hours.

On January 6, 1880, and again on February 10 and 12 of the same year, more apparitions occurred. All the visions were the same. The Blessed Mother stood in the center of the wall of celestial light. She wore a long gown, and on her head she had a crown of exquisite brilliance that dazzled like pulsating rays of the sun. Her hands, raised to the height of her shoulders, were extended to the people and at the same time lifted toward heaven. Saint Joseph stood on her right and Saint John the Evangelist on her left. To the left of the group was an altar with a large cross. At the foot of the cross was a lamb. There were angels surrounding the cross in adoration. People have subsequently referred to Our Lady of Knock under her ancient title, Queen of the Angels.

Large numbers of people saw the apparitions at Knock. No one was surprised that the blessing had come to Ireland, for the Blessed Mother is venerated there with steadfast devotion and commitment. Saint Joseph has always been revered in Ireland. Saint John the Evangelist understood love. The Irish people know love. Knock is a sign of that love.

Pilgrims thronged to the shrine from all over Europe, and the rest of the world too. Many healings and miracles have been documented at this shrine that honors family life.

Peace is the merciful Heart of Jesus. Those who seek peace seek God. Those who seek Him find Him. He sends His Mother to our times, to our civilization, to our consciousness clothed in divine motherhood and divine power. The Queen of the Angels is accompanied by Saint Joseph and Jesus. They come with the celestial army of angels. Those who love hear her voice. The Queen of Angels is gathering the flock of her Son.

PART TWO

Cause of Our Joy

The world recognizes the voice of the Blessed Mother, for it is recorded in Scripture. Her message is constant. Her instruction is divinely simple:

"Do whatever He tells you."

A maternal voice from Heaven sounded that truth once again as the Blessed Mother spoke to the shepherd children at Fatima, Portugal, in 1917. People still speak with awe about the cosmic miracle of the sun she brought to Fatima to assure the people of her presence there.

Jesus promised that He comes to give life in abundance. The Gospel messages of Jesus Christ bring peace, joy, and abiding love. The process is painfully slow, for humans learn slowly. God is patient. From generation to generation He allows us to struggle in pursuit of truth. Jesus identified Himself and His ways as truth. Few recognized Him during His human life. Since His Resurrection, multitudes know Him. All people must respond to truth when it personally confronts them.

The twentieth century began with upheaval in the political systems of the world's nations. War has afflicted the century in a seemingly never-ending escalation of confrontation among the nations and regions of the world. Perhaps the only positive value of evil is that people do get sick of chaos and despair.

Everyone who encounters evil needs faith and hope in the value of individual human life and the providential power of God's love. He does promise to bring good out of evil. Auschwitz was an unprecedented horror, yet the blood of the martyrs of the concentration camps gave birth to the modern State of Israel.

Apparitions of the Blessed Mother at Fatima, Portugal, gave messages from Heaven that were intended to prevent the terrors of war. Few responded. World War II brought warfare as the nations of the world had never fathomed. The Korean War frightened much of the world. Then Vietnam. War goes on and on.

And so do apparitions of the Blessed Mother. From the hills of Garabandal, Spain, to Akita, Japan, to Cuapa, Nicaragua, apparitions and messages are great harbingers of future times. They contain seeds of new life that are still germinating.

The Gospel of the Lord Jesus Christ is illuminated by apparitions that manifest the universality of human dignity rooted in God, our Creator. The following apparitions are a glorious preview of His Kingdom of love.

"And how does this happen to me, that the mother of my Lord should come to me?"

Luke 1:43

CHAPTER FIVE

Comforter of the Afflicted

Fatima, Portugal:
Lucia, Francisco, and Jacinta, 1917

In the Fatima region of Portugal early in the present century, little hamlets nestled half-hidden in valleys or on the mountain slopes. White stucco houses with tile roofs provided shelter for families whose livelihood depended on shepherding and farming the land by hand. Life was hard and as consistent as the weather.

The Catholic faith was strong in Fatima. People knew the Ten Commandments. Everyone had rosary beads and many people used them.

As for Portugal, the monarchy was gone and a republic had been in place since 1910. The regime quickly demonstrated an antireligious bias: Minister of Justice Afonso Costa confidently assured the more politically "enlightened" that within two generations religion would be totally eliminated in Portugal.

Freedom was interpreted to mean no God and no king. Monasteries and convents were closed by order of the republic.

The rural families of Fatima tended their flocks and worked the land. In 1915, eight-year-old Lucia dos Santos, born March 22, 1907, was the youngest of Maria Rosa and Antonio dos Santos's six children. Antonio's sister, Olimpia de Jesus, and her husband, Manuel Pedro Marto, lived nearby with their seven children. Their youngest were seven-year-old Francisco, born on June 11, 1908, and five-year-old Jacinta, born on March 11, 1910. Both families were relatively well-to-do. They owned their grazing land, their flocks, and their farming land. The youngest children had the responsibility of caring for the family flocks.

At that time Lucia did not yet know how to "count the years, nor the months, nor even the days of the week."[1] She and three other little girls were tending sheep on Mount Cabeço. Lunch was finished and the girls faithfully recited the Rosary as they always did after eating.

Lucia saw a strange cloud, whiter than the snow that hung over the valley below them. But Lucia realized the cloud was more than a cloud. It was transparent, all light, and in the form of a huge angel. When Lucia later shared her story at home about the angel, her mother belittled her. "Foolish girl!" she chided, and the older children quickly began to taunt their youngest sister.[2]

On another occasion, Lucia once again saw the angelic form hovering over the village of Fatima as she tended her flocks high in the surrounding hills. This time she said nothing for fear of being mocked. As the year ended, Lucia saw the mysterious cloud in the form of a great angel of light a third time as it covered the skies of Fatima.[3]

In the spring of 1916, Lucia and her two younger cousins, Francisco and Jacinta, were playing merrily while tending their herds of sheep at Chousa Velha, a field owned by Lucia's parents and located east of Mount Cabeço. A drizzle sent the children scampering up the mountain to a large, roofless stone niche located behind an olive grove owned by Lucia's godfather, Anastacio.[4] When the rain stopped, the children sat at the entrance of the niche to eat their lunch and then to pray the Rosary. Later they began to play a little game with the small stones that surrounded the entrance of the niche.

Suddenly the children heard a powerful wind that shook the surrounding trees and vegetation. They looked up. Lucia saw with amazement that the immense rays of light resembled the angelic form that she had seen three times before in the translucent cloud hovering over Fatima. Silently, the immense light drew close to the children. In the center of the light the children observed a great angel of immense power and glory. The beauty of the angel was beyond the ability of the children to describe. They stared at the celestial being in absolute awe. In her memoirs, translated as *Fatima in Lucia's Own Words*, Lucia wrote of the encounter:

> As it drew closer, we were able to distinguish its features. It was a young man, about fourteen or fifteen years old, whiter than the snow, transpar-

ent as crystal when the sun shines through it and
of great beauty. On reaching us, he said:

"Do not be afraid! I am the Angel of Peace. Pray with me."

Kneeling on the ground, he bowed down until
his forehead touched the ground, and made us repeat these words three times:

*"My God, I believe, I adore, I trust and I love you! I ask
pardon of You for those who do not believe, do not adore,
do not trust and do not love you."*

Then, rising, he said:

*"Pray thus. The hearts of Jesus and Mary are attentive to
the words of your prayers."*

His words engraved themselves so deeply
on our minds that we could never forget them.
From then on we used to spend long periods of
time, prostrate like the Angel, repeating his
words, until sometimes we fell, exhausted. I
warned my companions, right away, that this
must be kept secret and, thank God, they did
what I wanted.

Some time passed and summer came. . . . One
day we were playing on the stone slab of the well
down at the bottom of the garden belonging to
my parents. . . . Suddenly, we saw beside us the
same figure, or rather Angel. . . .

"What are you doing?" he asked. *"Pray, pray very much! The most holy hearts of Jesus and Mary have designs of mercy on you. Offer prayers and sacrifices constantly to the Most High."*

"How are we to make sacrifices?" I asked.

"Make every possible sacrifice. Offer it to God as an act of reparation for the sins by which He is offended, and in supplication for the conversion of sinners. Above all, accept and bear with submission, all the suffering which the Lord allows in your lives. In this way you will draw down peace upon your country. I am the Guardian Angel of Portugal."

Months passed. Lucia recounts:

A considerable time had elapsed. . . . we went to pasture our sheep . . . on the slope of a hill. . . . As soon as we arrived there, we knelt down, with our foreheads touching the ground, and began to repeat the prayer of the Angel: "My God, I believe, I adore, I trust and I love You." I don't know how many times we had repeated this prayer, when an extraordinary light shone upon us. We sprang up to see what was happening, and beheld the Angel. He was holding a chalice in his left hand, with the Host suspended above it, from which some drops of blood fell into the chalice. Leaving the chalice suspended in the air, the Angel knelt down beside us and we repeated three times:

"Most Holy Trinity, Father, Son and Holy Spirit, I offer You the most precious Body, Blood, Soul and Divinity of Jesus Christ, present in all the tabernacles of the world, in reparation for the outrages, sacrileges and indifference with which He is offended. And through the infinite merits of His most Sacred Heart, and the Immaculate Heart of Mary, I beg of You the conversion of poor sinners."

Then, rising, he took the chalice and the Host in his hands. He gave the Sacred Host to me, and shared the Blood from the chalice between Jacinta and Francisco, saying as he did so:

"Take and drink the Body and Blood of Jesus Christ, horribly outraged by ungrateful men! Make reparation for their crimes and console your God."

Once again, he prostrated on the ground and repeated with us, three times more, the same prayer: "Most Holy Trinity . . ." and then disappeared.

We remained a long time in this position, repeating the same words over and over again. When at last we stood up, we noticed that it was already dark. . . .⁵

Winter came to the village. The souls of the three shepherd children were filled with the prayers of the Rosary and the Angel of Portugal. Who could guess that the Queen of Angels would soon be sent seven times to the three shepherd children of Fatima with a plan of peace for the world?

The First Apparition at Fatima

On Sunday, May 13, 1917, Lucia, Francisco, and Jacinta were leading their flocks towards Cova da Iria, a grazing field in the parish of Fatima, near Aljustrel. Suddenly, great flashes of light frightened them. Then Lucia and Jacinta saw a Beautiful Lady in the light who was "more brilliant than the sun." She spoke to them, but only Lucia heard:

> *"Fear not, I will not harm you. I am from heaven."*

Lucia, summoning all her courage, asked, "What do you want?" The Beautiful Lady from heaven said:

> *"I ask you to come here for six consecutive months, on the 13th day, at this same hour. I will tell you later who I am and why I have come to you. I shall return here again a seventh time."*

Lucia timidly asked, "Dear Beautiful Lady, may I go with you to heaven? And Jacinta and Francisco too?"
The Beautiful Lady responded:

> *"You all will come to heaven with me. Francisco must pray many Rosaries."*

Francisco, at this time, could only see the miraculous light, but he could hear Lucia speaking to a presence in the light. The Beautiful Lady from Heaven said to Lucia:

"Let him pray the Rosary. In that way he too will be able to see me."

Francisco immediately began to pray his Rosary. After one decade, he too saw the Mother of God. It was then that the Beautiful Lady from Heaven spoke again:

"Do you want to offer yourselves to God, to endure all the sufferings He may allow, as an act of reparation for the sins by which He is offended and as a supplication for the conversion of sinners?"

The three little children responded, "We will do as you ask."

The Beautiful Lady from Heaven then opened her hands and great streams of light radiated upon the children. Lucia later spoke about that moment:

"This light penetrated us to the very depths of our heart, and allowed us to see ourselves in God, Who was that Light, more clearly than we see ourselves in a mirror. Then we were moved by an inner impulse, also communicated to us, to fall on our knees, while repeating, 'Most Holy Trinity, I adore you. My God, My God, I Love You in the Most Blessed Sacrament.' "

The parting message of the Beautiful Lady from Heaven to the children was:

"Say the Rosary every day to earn peace for the world and the end of war."

Little Jacinta, describing the conclusion of the fateful apparition, said, "When she went back to heaven the doors seemed to shut so quickly that I thought her feet would get caught."[6]

The Second Apparition

The second apparition at Fatima occurred on June 13, 1917. No more than fifty people were present. Lucia's mother was certain that her daughter was lying about the vision of the Beautiful Lady from Heaven. She punished her severely, and Lucia suffered intensely. Lucia's father, who had a penchant for wine, distanced himself from the controversy in his family about the heavenly gifts that his daughter claimed. Jacinta's and Francisco's father, however, believed his children. He protected them and blessed them tenderly. Still, many people in the village discounted the children's stories of celestial visions.

The Beautiful Lady from Heaven kept her promise. She once again appeared in that glorious, mystical light that envelops "the woman clothed with the sun." On that warm June day, the Beautiful Lady from Heaven taught the three children this prayer to add to each decade of the rosary:

ROSARY PRAYER OF OUR LADY OF FATIMA
Oh my Jesus, forgive us our sins,
save us from the fires of hell,
lead all souls to heaven,
especially those most in need of thy mercy.

The Mother of God then made a special request of the three children: she asked them to learn to read. The

Blessed Mother told Jacinta and Francisco that she would take them to Heaven soon. But to Lucia, the Blessed Mother said:

"You will remain on the earth for a long time. My Son Jesus desires to use your life to make me known and loved. He wills now to establish devotion to my Immaculate Heart in the world."[7]

In the name of her Divine Son, the Mother of God then made a promise to the world through the three children visionaries that came to be known as the first secret of Fatima:

"I promise salvation to those who embrace devotion to my Immaculate Heart. Their souls will be loved by God as flowers placed by me to adorn His throne. These souls will suffer a great deal but I will never leave them. My Immaculate Heart will be their refuge, the way that will lead them to God."

Lucia's memoirs describe her vision: "She opened her hands and pierced our hearts with the light that streamed from her palms. It seems then that the first purpose of this light was to give us a knowledge of a special love for the Immaculate Heart of Mary just as on two other occasions it gave us a knowledge of God and the mystery of the Holy Trinity. From that day on we felt in our hearts a deeper love for the Immaculate Heart of Mary."[8]

The Third Apparition

The date was July 13, 1917. The weather was cool and the wind was brisk even though it was summer in Europe. World War I was raging.

The village of Fatima was named after a Muhammadan princess who in turn bore the name of Muhammad's daughter, Fatima. Her castle was the last major stronghold of ancient Islam in central Portugal.[9] Christians, Moslems, and Jews worship and adore the one true God in whom all things are made. In the village of Fatima, the wedding of prayer, fasting, almsgiving, and pilgrimage that are central to each faith found resonance in the three little shepherd children who were claiming that the Blessed Mother intended to appear to them for the third month in a row.

That day, thousands of pilgrims had gathered in front of the small tree in the Cova da Iria where the two previous apparitions had occurred. The large crowd was restless. The words of the *Ave* echoed as rosary beads slipped through the fingers of people of all ages and levels of faith.

Lucia had described the Blessed Mother as being "all light, crystal clear, dazzling light, gleaming most brilliantly, like a crystal of great beauty through which the sun's rays glisten." There were those who wondered if the apparition was really that of an angel, for the children had spoken about the great Angel of Portugal, known as the Angel of Peace, who had visited them before the Blessed Mother's first apparition to them.

There were also a few cynics waiting to be convinced

of the spiritual event. Of course, the sick, the injured, and the dying were there too, for miracles are always possible.

A fine, cool breeze was blowing. The people fell silent, for suddenly there was a buzzing sound, and everyone noticed a small cloud moving in above the oak tree. The three children fell into ecstasy. Their eyes peered into the luminous cloud that hovered over the tree. Lucia and Jacinta saw and heard the Mother of God. Francisco only saw the vision.

Lucia, in her memoirs, described her vision. She saw the Mother of God in the mystical light. She heard this message:

> *"Do not offend the Lord our God anymore, because He is already so much offended. I desire you to come back here on the 13th of next month. To obtain peace in the world, continue to pray the Rosary every day in honor of the title God has given me, Our Lady of the Rosary. In these times, only under that title can peace be obtained. Sacrifice yourselves for sinners. Say often, especially when you offer some sacrifice: 'My Jesus, it is for the love of You, for the conversion of sinners, and in reparation for sins committed against the Immaculate Heart of Mary.' I desire you to come back here on the 13th of each month and in October I will tell you who I am and what I ask. I will then perform a miracle so that all may believe."*

The Mother of Jesus Christ, at that moment, spoke of a divinely obtained cosmic miracle that would be granted so that all might believe.

Then the Beautiful Lady opened her hands. Rays of

light poured from her palms and appeared to penetrate the earth. Lucia in her memoirs recounts:

> Our Lady showed us a large sea of fire which seemed to be beneath the earth. Plunged in this fire were the demons and the souls who were like embers, transparent and black or bronze colored, with human forms which floated about in the conflagration, borne by the flames which issued from it with clouds of smoke, falling on all sides as sparks fall in great conflagrations, without weight or equilibrium, among shrieks and groans of sorrow and despair, which horrified us and caused us to quake with fear.
>
> The devils were distinguished by horrible and loathsome forms of animals, frightful and unknown, but transparent and blank. This vision vanished in a moment. Providentially, our good heavenly Mother had promised us in the first apparition to take us to heaven. Otherwise, I think we would have died of fright and horror.

Lucia recounts that the Blessed Mother then imparted to the three what has been referred to as the second secret of Fatima.

> We then looked up at the Blessed Mother, who said to us so kindly and so sadly:

> *"You have seen hell where poor sinners go. To save them, God wishes to establish in the world devotion to my Immaculate Heart. If what I say to you is done, many souls will be saved and there will be peace in the world.*[10]

The war will end but, unless people cease to offend God, another, even worse, will begin. . . . When you see the night lit up by an unknown light, then know that it is the great signal that God gives you that He is about to allow mankind to choose punishment for its crimes by war, hunger, persecution of the Church and the Holy Father.

"To prevent this, I shall ask for the consecration of Russia to my Immaculate Heart and a Communion of reparation on the first Saturday of each month. If my appeal is heard, Russia will be converted, and there will be peace. Otherwise, its errors will spread about the world, promoting wars and the persecution of the Church.

"The good will suffer martyrdom. The Holy Father will suffer grievously. Several nations will be annihilated.

"Finally my Immaculate Heart will triumph. The Holy Father will consecrate Russia to me and the earth shall enjoy a period of peace. In Portugal, the faith shall always be maintained."[11]

A third secret was entrusted to the three shepherd visionaries on that date. The contents were never officially disclosed, though the apparitions that would come later in the century at Akita, Japan, contain and promulgate the third secret of Fatima.

Capuchin Father Christopher Rengers offers this interpretation of the July 13 vision of hell disclosed by the three children of Fatima: "The children, by special illumination saw self-love, undisguised and naked, consuming itself from within. They heard every jealousy, pride, greed, lust and the assorted choir of all the vices, shouting and shrieking and screaming in the disharmony and harshness of their own intimate natures. They saw the final state of those called to love who make a final, unchangeable choice not to love. They saw the disorder of sin, undisguised by its usual trappings, as it is in its essence."[12]

The Blessed Mother may well have been showing the three visionaries a preview of the wars that would come to the inhabitants of different regions of the earth before the twentieth century would end.

The hell of war is that it is born out of the actions and decisions of human beings who refuse to engage in and accept peaceful means of resolution. Before war breaks out among people, it festers and breeds within their hearts, their families, their cities, their nations, and then finally among nations. War is the lived expression of the condition of the hearts of human beings who do not yet know how to love and serve one another for the glory of God and the joy and well-being of one another.

History shows that few responded to the July 13, 1917, message from heaven. The "unknown light," promised as a sign preceding World War II, occurred on January 25–26, 1938. The international newspapers referred to it as an aurora borealis.

A youth in Ireland was an eyewitness to the strange light. He said it was such an ominous and mystical light that it knocked him off his bicycle. As he lay in the dust he promised the Lord he would become a priest should God spare him whatever punishment that ominous light portended.

Only years later, when he was indeed a priest, did the young man learn the messages of Fatima and the Blessed Mother's prophecy of the "unknown light." He scoffed, "An Aurora Borealis! Oh the pride of men. How it blinds us all to truth." That priest, now a well-known monsignor, works tirelessly to spread the messages of the Blessed Mother. He says, "Ireland alone could have prevented World War II. The problem is, we didn't know about Fatima in time!"[13]

The great secret given to the children at Fatima in 1917 is that peace and the Immaculate Heart of Mary are very much intertwined in God's plans for humankind.[14] Little Jacinta, who died soon after the visitations, began to speak of war as hell on earth. She saw hell as God's justice and the Immaculate Heart of Mary as His mercy.[15] Among her final words were: "Oh if I could only put into everybody's heart the burning fire I have inside me which makes me love the hearts of Jesus and Mary so much! The Heart of Jesus wishes to be honored together with the Immaculate Heart because God has entrusted peace to her."[16]

As virtue reigns among people, peace is a way of life. The more humanity recognizes the value of virtue, as expressed in the Gospel, the more peace the world experiences.

The Fourth Apparition

By August 13 the crowd had grown to nearly 15,000 people. This time there were no visionaries, for they were in jail. Once again the little cloud was seen to hover over the oak tree in the Cova da Iria in Fatima. There were sounds of explosion and a trembling like an earthquake. Then came the mystical light.

An eyewitness said: "As we walked around . . . our faces were reflecting all the colors of the rainbow—pinks, reds and blues. . . . The trees suddenly seemed to be made not of leaves but of flowers. The ground reflected these many colors and so did the clothes we wore."[17]

The crowd became angry that the children had been seized and imprisoned by local officials. The children were in fear for their lives. Officials threatened to boil them in oil, but no punishment or threat elicited the secrets from the visionaries.

The Fifth Apparition

By August 15, the visionaries were freed and returned to their village. The Blessed Mother appeared to the three children that day in the area of Valinhos. Lucia describes the message of the Blessed Mother in her memoirs:

> *"I want you to continue going to the Cova da Iria on the 13th, and to continue praying the Rosary every day. In the last month, I will perform a miracle so that all may believe."*

Lucia inquired what to do with donations.

> *"Have two litters made. One is to be carried by you and Jacinta and two other girls dressed in white; the other one is to be carried by Francisco and three other boys. The money from the litters is for the Feast of Our Lady of the Rosary, and what is left over will help towards the construction of a chapel which is to be built."*

Lucia then asked that the sick be cured.

"Yes, I will cure some of them during the year. Pray. Pray very much, and make sacrifices for sinners. So many souls go to hell because there is no one to pray and make sacrifices for them."[18]

Then the Blessed Mother began to rise and disappeared from their sight.[19] The children of Fatima never recovered from the awesome awareness the Blessed Mother gave the people of the world with those parting words of her August apparition. Even today, more than seventy-five years after such divine wisdom was shared once again with humanity at Fatima, many people with disabilities and dysfunctions of all kinds suffer the loneliness of hell because there is no one to pray and make sacrifices for them. If many enter hell because no one prays and makes sacrifices for them, it stands to reason that as prayers and sacrifices increase, as thinking people become aware of divine truths, the number of isolated, abandoned souls will decrease proportionately.

The three little visionaries of Fatima sought solitude to pray. After their August 15 apparition, play time became prayer time. Prayer seemed to be their only pleasure.

They began to wear a heavy rope under their garments because it caused pain that they could offer to Jesus for the conversion of sinners. Their memory of the vision of hell was so acute that suffering became a blessing because the Beautiful Lady had taught them the value of penance. Such knowledge is a divine grace.

Only those who pray understand penance. The materialist has no appreciation of penance, which is sacrificial love. Penance does not involve deriving pleasure from pain in the form of masochism. Penance, self-sacrifice flows from love, as the sisters who died in Zaire caring for those with the Ebola virus taught us and the Marines who rescued Captain O'Grady demonstrated.

The Sixth Apparition

By now the behavior of the visionaries left little doubt in their neighborhood that their apparitions were from a divine source. The three children were so markedly different than before their messages from heaven that few questioned the divine grace with which they were blessed. Crowds grew by September 13, 1917. Estimates were that the number had swelled to 30,000 people.

An eyewitness of the September 13 apparition, Monsignor Quaresma, vicar-general of the diocese, said in his journal:

> At midday there was complete silence. One only heard the murmurs of prayers. Suddenly there were sounds of jubilation and voices praising the Blessed Virgin. Arms were raised pointing to something in the sky. "Look, don't you see? Yes, yes, I do. . . ."
>
> There had not been a cloud in the deep blue of the sky, and I too raised my eyes and scrutinized it in case I should be able to distinguish what the others, more fortunate than I, had already claimed to have seen. With great astonishment I saw, clearly and distinctly, a luminous globe, which moved from the east to the west, gliding slowly and majestically through space.

My friend also looked, and had the good fortune to enjoy the same unexpected and delightful vision. Suddenly the globe, with its extraordinary light, disappeared. Near us was a little girl dressed like Lucia and more or less the same age. She continued to cry out happily: "I still see it. I still see it! Now it's coming down!" Monsignor Quaresma was later heard to say: "That globe I saw was Our Lady!"[20]

Those near Lucia heard her ask: "Dear Beautiful Lady, what do you want of me?" Although Francisco enjoyed the privilege of seeing the Beautiful Lady, he could not hear her words. Only Lucia and Jacinta saw and heard the Beautiful Lady respond:

"Let the people continue to say the Rosary every day to obtain the end of war. In the last month, in October, I shall perform a miracle so that all may believe in my apparitions. If they had not taken you to the town to prison the miracle would have been greater. St. Joseph will come with the Baby Jesus to give peace to the world. Our Lord will also come to bless the people. Besides, Our Lady of the Rosary and Our Lady of Sorrows will come."[21]

Saint Joseph, who has always been considered by Christians as the patron of happy deaths, was named in the August apparition. Tradition has stated that Saint Joseph will emerge as a powerful figure in the end times. The Blessed Mother promised that he would come to Fatima in October, with the Christ Child, to bring peace to the world.

The Seventh Apparition

By October 13, the press was aware of the promised cosmic miracle. The *O Dia* of Lisbon carried this description:

> For days prior to the thirteenth, groups of pilgrims traveled toward Fatima. They came on foot, buskins on their brawny legs, food bags on their heads, across the pine groves where the windmills rotate. A slow and swaying gait swung the hems of their skirts from side to side and waved orange kerchiefs upon which sat their black hats. . . . People from everywhere whom the voice of the miracle had reached, left their homes and fields, and came on foot, by horse or by carriage. They traveled the highways and the roads, between hills and pine groves. For two days these came to life with the rolling of carriages, the trot of the donkeys and the voices of the pilgrims. . . . Water dripped from the caps and broad-brimmed hats onto the new jackets of their suits for seeing God. The bare feet of the women and the hobnailed shoes of the men sloshed in the wide pools of the muddy roads. They seemed not to notice the rain. . . . A murmur drifting down from the hills reached us. It was a murmur like the distant voice of the sea lowered faintly before the silence of the fields. It was the religious songs, now becoming clear, intoned by thousands of voices. Over the plateau, over a hill, or filling a valley, they were a wide and shuffling mass of thousands upon thousands of souls in prayer.[22]

Great flashes of light signaled the beginning of the final apparition of the Mother of God at Fatima. Lucia, besieged by the crowds, asked the Beautiful Lady about cures for the sick who were present in large numbers. Her memoirs give us the response of the Blessed Mother:

"It is necessary that they amend their lives and ask pardon for their sins. Some will be cured and others will not."

Lucia describes the apparition in her memoirs:

Her face became grave as she continued:

"Let them offend Our Lord no more, for He is already much offended."

And opening her hands she made the light emerging from them ascend to where the sun ought to be. And while it was arising, her own radiance continued shining towards the sun.

Saint Joseph appeared in the sky. It was the moment for the great cosmic miracle of the sun. The sun shook, and spun so fiercely that it seemed to explode and come tumbling down toward the people, who were terrified. But it stopped, suddenly, and then went back to its normal position in the sky. It gave off colors of indescribable beauty, which shone down on the earth and all of the people gathered at Fatima. This miracle was seen, not only by the 50,000 people in the Cova da Iria, but also by people within a radius of at least thirty miles.

The poet Alfonso Lopes Vieira, working at noon on the verandah of his home thirty miles away in San Pedro de Muel, saw the phenomenon and in surprise called for his wife and her mother to come and see. At Alburitel, nine miles from Fatima, the schoolteacher, Delfina Pereira Lopes, ran with the children into the street. There, others prayed and shouted and cried, thinking the world was coming to an end.

The Baron of Alvaiazere, an attorney of Ourem, had come to the Cova da Iria for diversion. He was braced against the force of collective suggestion. He later wrote: "I knew it was necessary to be on my guard, not to allow myself to be influenced. I only know that I shouted, 'I believe, I believe, I believe, I believe,' and that tears fell from my eyes, wondering, ecstatic before this manifestation of divine power."[23]

Lucia wrote in her memoirs, at the request of her bishop, about the miracle of the sun during the final apparition at Fatima:

Here you have, Your Excellency, the reason why I shouted that they should look at the sun. My purpose was not to bring the attention of the crowd to the sun, because I didn't notice them. I was not even aware of their presence. I did so, moved by an inner force which impelled me to act thus. When Our Lady disappeared in the immense distance of the sky, next to the sun we saw Saint Joseph holding the Child Jesus and Our Lady dressed in white with a blue mantle. Saint Joseph and the Child seemed to be blessing the world, making the sign of the cross. Shortly after this vision had vanished,

I saw Our Lord and Our Lady who reminded me of Our Lady of Sorrows. Our Lord was blessing the world as was Saint Joseph. This vision vanished too, and it seemed to me I again saw Our Lady in a form resembling that of Our Lady of Mount Carmel.[24]

The visionaries later told the people that Saint Joseph and the Child Jesus were both dressed in red. They spoke of a white dress with a blue mantle which the Blessed Mother wore. Such is her attire as Our Lady of the Holy Rosary.

Saint Joseph came with the Child Jesus to "bring peace to the world." His role in God's plan is not only as intercessor, but as model for husbands and fathers. The sacrificial love of Joseph for the Blessed Mother, her sacrificial love for him, their mutual sacrificial love for the Christ Child are the dynamics that bring peace.[25]

Francisco was given the least significant part of the apparitions at Fatima, for while he saw the Mother of God seven times, he never heard any messages.

Francisco learned from Lucia the words the angel had spoken to him as he gave him the chalice to drink:

"Take and drink the Body and Blood of Jesus Christ who has been horribly outraged by ungrateful men. Remedy their crimes and console your God."

Francisco took upon himself the mission of consoling the Lord God. He sought solitude so that he was free to think of the Lord and pray constantly. Francisco began to live in silence, even around his family. When he was not in the fields with his flocks, he could be found in the church. A favorite hiding place for him, away from the eyes of the curious, was in the darkened confessional.

Francisco prayed the prayers given to him by the Angel of Peace and the Mother of God. He continuously prayed the Rosary with profound intensity during all the remaining days of his life on earth.

The worldwide influenza epidemic invaded Fatima in the fall of 1918. Both Jacinta and Francisco became sick and developed pneumonia. Francisco prayed the Rosary until he no longer had the strength to hold the beads. On April 3, he received his first and last Holy Communion from the hands of the village priest after his first sacramental confession. Then he received the sacrament of the sick. Jacinta, quite ill herself, was present. Before Francisco received Holy Communion, she said to her brother, "Give my love to Our Lord and to His Blessed Mother. Tell them I will suffer all they wish to convert sinners and to console the Immaculate Heart of Mary." The next morning at ten o'clock Francisco died with a smile on his face.[26]

Jacinta longed to join her brother in the Kingdom of God. The child had never recovered from the horror of the vision of hell that she had endured. She prayed and sacrificed constantly so that fewer souls would be lost.

The bishop of Leiria, João Pereira Venâncio, said of Jacinta, "She is the most richly endowed [of the three visionaries] with the gifts of grace."

Jacinta continued to receive private apparitions of the Blessed Mother throughout her illness. The Blessed Mother disclosed to her that she would be taken far away from home, that she would undergo lung surgery without anesthetic, that she would die alone in a hospital far from any family members. The brave little visionary endured all to save souls and to share the suffering that ungrateful people cause the Immaculate Heart of Mary. She trusted that the Blessed Mother and her Divine Son would come for her when her time of suffering was over.

As Jacinta was taken from her home to a hospital in Lisbon, she said to her cousin Lucia: "We shall never see each other again. Pray for me until I go to Heaven, then when I am there, I will appeal on your behalf. Never tell the secret to anyone, even if they kill you. Love Jesus and the Immaculate Heart of Mary very much and make as many sacrifices as you can for poor sinners."[27]

The Blessed Mother continued to appear to Jacinta while she was in the hospital. The nurse who cared for Jacinta wrote some of the messages that she says Jacinta shared with her:

The sins of the world are very great. The priests should only busy themselves with the affairs of the Church and with souls. The disobedience of priests and religious to their superiors and to the Holy Father are a great offense in the eyes of the Lord. If people knew what eternity is, they would do their utmost to mend their ways.

Certain fashions will be introduced that will offend Our Lord very much. Many marriages are not holy; they do not please Our Lord and they are not of God.

If the government of a country allows the

Church to exist in peace and gives liberty to our holy religion, it will be blessed by God.[28]

On February 10, 1920, Jacinta endured surgery without anesthetic for the removal of two ribs. She was heard to say: "Patience, for we must all suffer if we want to go to Heaven!"[29]

On February 20, at 10:30 P.M., little Jacinta Marto died alone. No one doubts that the Blessed Mother and her Divine Son were there to claim the little nine-year-old whose heart of sacrificial love was now all theirs.

Lucia endured at Fatima alone. To her fell the task of explaining, of defending, of remembering exactly the details of the great apparitions that she and her cousins witnessed for the world.

In May 1921, Lucia went to live in a convent. In 1925, the Blessed Mother and the Christ Child appeared to Lucia at Pontevedra, Spain, in the convent where Lucia was a postulant. On this occasion, the First Saturday Devotion of Reparation to the Immaculate Heart was requested of the entire world by the Lord Jesus.

In 1929, the Blessed Mother appeared to Lucia to announce the time for the consecration of Russia to her Immaculate Heart. Lucia, by then a nun, communicated this request to her confessor, her bishop, and the Holy Father.

The history of Marian apparitions indicates that those who approach Mary receive her Divine Son, Jesus. So it is for Lucia of Fatima. She sometimes sees or hears the Lord Jesus Christ, as well as His Blessed Mother. The Lord Jesus made the following request of Sister Lucia, the sole living visionary of Fatima, when he appeared to her as the Child

Jesus accompanying His Blessed Mother on December 10, 1925:

> *"Have compassion for this very sweet heart of My Mother, which is continually wounded because of the ingratitude of God's people and because she has so few who console her with personal acts of love."*[30]

The Portuguese bishops subsequently consecrated Portugal to the Immaculate Heart of Mary and Portugal was spared involvement in World War II. It was not until October 31, 1942, that Pope Pius XII consecrated the universal church and the world to the Immaculate Heart of Mary. At that time, World War II was raging. The war ended in 1945.

Lucia took solemn final vows at the Carmelite convent at Coimbra, Portugal, on May 31, 1949. Her name in Carmel is Sister Mary of the Immaculate Heart.

Pope Paul VI renewed the consecration of the world to the Immaculate Heart of Mary in 1964, at the Second Vatican Council. Once more he publicly made the consecration at Fatima during a pilgrimage celebrating the fiftieth anniversary of the apparitions of the Mother of God to the three children.

Lucia communicated to church authorities, however, that a "proper consecration" of the world to the Immaculate Heart of Mary occurred only in October 1984, when Pope John Paul II acted in concert with the bishops of the world. She said her source for that statement was the Lord Jesus Christ.

Bishop Paola Hnilica, S.J., secretly consecrated Russia

and the world to the Immaculate Heart of Mary inside the Kremlin in 1984. Illuminating the role of the Blessed Virgin Mary in human affairs at the end of the twentieth century, the Bishop wrote in 1994:

> The Mediatrix of All Graces, the Coredemptrix who was and who remained beneath the cross of her Son, has revealed at Fatima in this century of ours the only remedy for conquering evil in the world, every kind of evil: the devotion to and consecration to her Immaculate Heart! In her Immaculate Heart is, in fact, our only refuge: in it is revealed to us the maternal tenderness of God.

A terrible warning was given at Fatima:

"Several entire nations will be annihilated."

Today humankind has the means of annihilating the planet.

The third secret of Fatima was never publicly disclosed. Fifty-six years later, at Akita, Japan, the Blessed Mother gave a secret to her children on October 13, 1973, the anniversary of her great cosmic miracle at Fatima. The presiding bishop of Akita, the Most Reverend John S. Ito, announced that he believes the following message given in his diocese is the actual third secret of Fatima, communicated as a divine warning once again for the entire world.[31]

"If people do not repent and better themselves, God the Father will allow a terrible punishment of their own making

to fall upon them. All humanity will be involved. It will be a punishment greater than the deluge, such as has never been seen before on earth. Fire will fall from the sky and will wipe out a great part of humanity, the good as well as the bad, sparing not even priests. The living will be so desolate that they will envy the dead. The only arms that will remain for you will be the Rosary and the Great Sign left by my Son."[32]

Of great significance is the fact that the apparitions at Akita were the first Marian apparitions to be fully approved by the Church in more than fifty years.

The great promise of Fatima rests in the powerful words that the Mother of God left for our times: "In The End, My Immaculate Heart Will Triumph, The Holy Father Will Consecrate Russia to Me and a Period of Peace Will Be Granted to the World" (July 13, 1917, at Fatima, Portugal).

CHAPTER SIX

Gate of Heaven

"I will put enmity between you and the woman,
and between your offspring and hers;
He will strike at your head,
while you strike at his heel."

GENESIS 3:15

Garabandal, Spain: 1961 to 1965

From the days of Saint James the Apostle, who legend says brought the Gospel to Spain, the faith has always remained strong among the Spanish people. On June 18, 1961, in the little mountain village of San Sebastian, four young girls were enjoying the warm Sunday evening when suddenly they were startled by a strong flash of light.

A small, powerfully built angel appeared before Conchita, Maria Cruz, Mari Loli, and Jacinta. His hair was short and he was attired in a shining white garment. The girls perceived the angel as masculine because of his build. They saw him for a moment, and then the angel disappeared. Not one of the four girls had the least doubt that she had seen an angel from Heaven. They spoke freely about the appearance of the angel, and their news was greeted with mixed reactions. Some people laughed. Some were impressed. Some even scorned the four little girls.

The children returned to the place of the angel sighting the next day. But they saw nothing. Conchita asked to see the angel once again as she said her bedtime prayers. Suddenly she heard a voice say, "Don't worry. You shall see me again."[1] On Wednesday, June 21, the angel appeared again to the children as they knelt at the site praying. There were eyewitnesses with them and word spread quickly to surrounding villages about the apparition of the angel. For the next six days, the angel continued to appear to the children. The girls reported that the angel smiled at them but did not speak.

Each succeeding day, the crowds of spectators grew. On June 24, when the angel appeared, he was standing or resting upon a sign. The girls did not know what the sign meant. On July 1, the angel spoke to the children for the first time. He told them that the Blessed Virgin Mary would appear to them the next day as Our Lady of Mount Carmel.

As the angel had announced, on July 2 the Blessed Mother, accompanied by two angels, appeared to the four girls for the first of more than 2,000 apparitions that would occur during a two-year period. Visionary Conchita's diary describes the angels as twins. She says they even were dressed alike. Conchita identified one of the angels as Saint Michael the Archangel, but she did not know the name of the other angel. Conchita noticed a large eye that gazed at the girls as they experienced the apparition. She later said that it was probably the eye of God.[2]

The girls began to tell the large crowds that gathered

each day that the apparitions of the Blessed Mother were much more significant than the presence of the angels. The four girls told the people that the Blessed Mother looked young, though she was older than they. Her dress was white; she wore a cloak of blue. They said that she also wore a crown of twelve stars and that her hair was chestnut color and was parted in the center. The visionaries told the crowds that the Blessed Mother held a brown scapular in her outstretched hand.

The stories of the four visionaries of Garabandal are unique. They said that the Blessed Mother would sometimes come to them holding the Infant Jesus. According to the seers, the Blessed Virgin would actually hand the Infant to one or another of the girls to hold and cuddle. The visionaries claimed that they were quite playful with the Blessed Virgin, sometimes even taking the crown from her head and joyfully passing it from one to the other. The visionary Conchita described the apparition as follows:

> The Blessed Virgin appears with a white dress, a blue mantle and a crown of blue, golden stars. Her feet are not visible. Her hands are wide open with the scapular on the right wrist. The scapular is brown—*marron*. Her hair is long, dark brown and wavy, and parted in the middle. She has an oval-shaped face, and her nose is long and delicate. Her mouth is very pretty with rather full lips. The color of her face is dark, but lighter than that of an angel: it is different. Her voice is very lovely, a very unusual voice that I can't describe. There is

no woman that resembles the Blessed Virgin in her voice or in anything else.

Sometimes she carries the Infant Jesus—El Niño—in her arms. He seems very tiny, like a new-born baby with a little small face. His complexion is like that of the Blessed Virgin. He has a tiny little mouth, rather long hair and small hands, and a dress like a tunic, that is blue.[3]

During the following two years, the Blessed Mother appeared daily in the village of Garabandal. Her messages, delivered through the four young visionaries, incorporated much that has been disclosed through the former apparitions of the Blessed Mother. They stress prayer and penance as means of mystical union. They emphasize the immense value of the Eucharist as divine nourishment. The messages also request prayer in front of the Blessed Sacrament as a means of growth in divine intimacy.

Devotion to the angels was also emphasized at Garabandal. The Blessed Mother asked that the Rosary be recited continuously as an expression of love for God and acceptance of the pattern He has presented through Jesus' life, death, and resurrection. The visionaries asked all to pray for their own dead.

The Blessed Mother spoke as Queen of Prophets at Garabandal as she promised that Saint Michael the Archangel would bring the girls her final message six months later. On the exact date foretold by the Blessed Mother, Saint Michael the Archangel did appear to the girls. The experience is recorded on a videotape that captures the mysterious placement of a white Communion Host on Conchita's tongue by an invisible hand.[4]

The Blessed Mother, as Mother of the Church, prophesied imminent dangers threatening the priesthood and the Eucharist. She spoke of a time when belief in the real Presence of Jesus in the Eucharist would wane; she also spoke of confusion within the Church and exhorted intellectuals as well as nonintellectuals to gather the seeds of truth from prayer. The Blessed Virgin Mary gently spoke of God's great desire that His people live in holiness on the earth. She discussed the sacrificial commitment required by priests for holiness to flourish among the clergy in the Church.

The ecstasies of the four children of Garabandal lasted from as little as three minutes to as long as nine hours. During the ecstasies, their bodies were numb to pin punctures, loud noises and flashing, and high-intensity lights in their open eyes. The four were, to the visible world, frozen in space and time. They claimed, however, that they were traveling in the heavens, the galaxies, and across the earth with the Mother of God. They said they were totally aware of each other and the Blessed Mother and the places she wanted to take them. During the time of their ecstasies, however, their bodies were seen as rigid, hands folded in prayer, eyes riveted above at an object invisible to all others.

The visionaries were unaware that they were separated from their bodies as they enjoyed the privileges of the celestial world. (That spiritual phenomenon is known as bilocation—the capacity to be in two places at one time. Certain of the saints have been known to experience such ability. In this century, Padre Pio, the Capuchin Franciscan stigmatist of Italy, is said to have experienced bilocation.)

The apparitions at Garabandal also involved inexplicable phenomena like telepathy, incredible speed (eyewitnesses saw the ecstatic visionaries suddenly transported through the air at high speed), imperviousness to weather conditions, inexplicable weight increases (the visionaries' bodies were so heavy during the apparitions that they could not be lifted from the ground), synchronized gestures, Conchita's reception of the Eucharistic Host from an invisible hand, and other extraordinary occurrences that were seen by all the onlookers.

The visionaries, when interrogated later, claimed they were fully aware of their Heavenly Mother and her plans for them during the apparitions. The unusual experiences of these visionaries are captured on video and warrant analysis by those with interest in such phenomena.[5]

Conchita's apparitions lasted two years longer than those of the other three girls. She encountered some unexpected difficulties in the early days of her apparitions. Because she was the leader of the small group of visionaries, Conchita was removed from her home and brought to Santander to be investigated by a diocesan commission. One of the commission members threatened that she would be confined to an insane asylum and her family sent to jail if she failed to admit that her apparitions were illusion. He promised she would be considered for admission to a college if she signed a document admitting that she had lied about the apparitions.[6] Conchita says she was confused about the contents of a paper she signed stating that her visions might not be "real."[7] The diocesan commission disbanded with the receipt of Conchita's statement. Conchita was then permitted to return home.

Later, on two more occasions, Conchita and the other visionaries lost confidence in the authenticity of their visions and retracted them. By that time, however, so many others had witnessed the paranormal phenomena surrounding the visions that few regarded the children as anything other than authentic visionaries.

The four young girls continued to experience apparitions, although the patterns changed. The visions began to occur at any time during the day or evening. Onlookers were able to observe various paranormal phenomena during the visions that lent credibility to their supernatural origins.

The apparitions of the Blessed Mother were always preceded by three separate, distinct interior calls that alerted the girls before the Blessed Virgin Mary appeared. Conchita describes the calls in her diary.[8] No matter where the girls were in the village when their call would come, each of the four would run to the site from wherever she was in the village. Only the visionaries heard the interior call that alerted them to proceed to the place of the apparition.

Though the apparitions at Garabandal have not been approved by the Church, they remain under diocesan investigation. The messages from these apparitions are somewhat apocalyptic. The sun dances at Garabandal even today, as vast numbers of pilgrims have learned.

The "miracle of the sun" was first witnessed by 50,000 pilgrims at Fatima in 1917. The cosmic miracle was and is repeated later in the century, not only at Garabandal, but also at Medjugorje, Bosnia, beginning in 1981. This phenomenon continues to be reported around the world at various places, especially Marian Conferences that have been organized in various parts of the world, during prayer groups requested by the Blessed Mother, and sometimes at moments of high stress in individual people's lives.

The messages of Garabandal are as follows:

1. *A Warning for All Mankind.* The seers claim this will be some kind of spiritual awakening by which each person will be able to see himself or herself in the light of divine truth.

2. *A Great Miracle.* This miracle will occur in the pines of Garabandal and it will leave a permanent sign which can be photographed but not touched. Will it be a pillar of light like the Jews followed out of Egypt to the Promised Land? No one seems to know yet.

3. *Punishment?* If humanity responds positively and responsibly to the great miracle and to the permanent sign with ongoing conscious awareness of the presence of God in all that lives, there will be no global catastrophe but a world of great peace, love, and joy.[9]

Cairo, Egypt: 1968

The Holy Family resided in exile in Egypt until the death of Herod the Great. In the year 1968, people in Egypt were once again hosting the Holy Family under most mysterious circumstances.

Tradition teaches that Saint Mark the Evangelist brought Christianity to Alexandria, Egypt. In early 1968, some of the relics of Saint Mark were finally returned to Egypt, and the evening of April 2, 1968, brought an amazing and dazzling apparition to the vicinity of Cairo.

Atop Saint Mary's Coptic Orthodox Church in Zeitoun, a mysterious and beautiful woman clothed in garments that shone like the noonday sun was seen by a group of transport workers who were in front of the church. Visionaries gathered around crying out "Mary!" and "Mother of God!" Then the vision vanished.

One of the people who saw the apparition was Farouk Mohammed Atwa. He had a gangrenous finger that was to be amputated the following day. His finger was healed as he gazed at the image of the Beautiful Lady. Other inexplicable cures in the area were also attributed to the mysterious presence of the Blessed Mother atop the church at about 8:30 P.M. that Tuesday.

A week later, the same vision was once again sighted. The Blessed Mother began to be seen regularly after that. As many as 250,000 gathered to see the vision. The street was no longer passable for traffic and had to be closed to accommodate the curious and devout alike who crowded into the available space to await the apparition. The crowds were becoming so large that trees had to be chopped down. Even a garage was demolished to provide more space with a view of the roof of the church.

Each evening the apparition was preceded by immense flashes of light and the mysterious arrival of a flock of white doves flying in pairs. After this flight of the birds, sudden explosions of stars in the sky excited the crowds of onlookers, who remained in silent awe. The light would intensify above the church to such luminosity that all eyes were riveted upon the place of the apparition. Gradually the Beautiful Lady from Heaven would become visible in the light.

The Blessed Mother had a beauty that eyewitnesses found difficult to describe. They kept repeating the same word: "beautiful." They said that she smiled at some. She also waved. She often turned slowly and lovingly to view the entire crowd. A few swooned in shock as they saw her face for the first time. Some cried: "We believe!" Others were quiet with amazement. All seemed to know that she was the Mother of Jesus.

Many, if not most, of the people on any given evening were not even Christians, as Islam is the dominant religion in Egypt. Yet the Muslims saw her, and realized that she loves them exactly as they are. Few at the time tried to analyze what the apparition meant. On some evenings the Blessed Mother was accompanied by Saint Joseph and the Infant Jesus.

The Patriarch of the Coptic Church, Kyrillos VI, publicly announced that there was no doubt whatsoever that the Mother of God was appearing on the roof of Saint Mary's Coptic Church. He gave no explanation for his belief, saying that such explanations are unnecessary. A spokesman for the local Protestant denominations said that he had no doubt that the apparition was in fact the Blessed Mother. A secular official, the director of information, asserted that the Blessed Mother was appearing. On May 5, 1968, Kyrillos VI, referring to the Queen of Angels as "Mary, the Mother of Light," declared the Zeitoun apparitions authentic.

The visions continued over a three-year period. People of all faiths saw the numerous apparitions, which lasted an average of two hours each time. It was also reported that appearances of the holy angels and Mary and Joseph with the Baby Jesus were witnessed by the thousands of visionaries who gathered to view the extraordinary apparitions. During the appearances, Mary never spoke.

People of all faiths prayed together as they awaited the evening apparitions. Though the Blessed Mother spoke no words that have been recorded, her presence at Zeitoun to so many people, over such a long period of time, is considered a message of the universality of the love of God for each person on earth.[10] The different faiths of the people seeing the apparitions is perceived as a clear sign that all prayer is precious to God, for He is Father of everyone. Prayer with the heart is the universal language of love.

Akita, Japan: 1973 to 1984

A convent at Yuzawadai, on the outskirts of Akita, Japan, is the site of a series of extraordinary apparitions approved by the Roman Catholic Church.[11] Sister Agnes Katsuko Sasagawa is a member of the Servants of the Eucharist, a small group of women gathered together, in a house situated on a hill outside Akita, to lead a life of prayer. They live a strict vow of poverty, having abandoned all their earthly goods in order to consecrate themselves totally to God.[12]

The interior of the convent is paneled with light-colored wood that matches a beautiful, world-famous statue of Our Lady of All Nations.[13] The parquet floor is of a golden shade. There is a large fireplace made of two colors of Japanese brick and adorned with a high mantel. Above the mantel hangs a picture of Pope John Paul II alongside a picture of the Immaculate Heart of Mary and the Sacred Heart of Jesus encased in a beautiful mother-of-pearl frame.

The lifestyle of the women has been the object of criticism and calumny in Japan, where industry, output, and accomplishment are the norm.[14] They have been reproached for the amount of time they spend on their knees in adoration of the Blessed Sacrament.

At age nineteen, Agnes suffered paralysis as the result of a medical mistake during a routine appendectomy. For sixteen years she spent much of her time in the hospital and underwent multiple surgeries. When she discovered Christianity, she related deeply to the sufferings of Jesus Christ, who gave His life that others might see truth.[15]

In 1969, Agnes contracted a virus. She lapsed into a coma. A priest was summoned to administer the sacrament of the sick. Eyewitnesses heard Agnes respond to the prayers of the priest in Latin, though Agnes had never studied the language. Her only recollection of her three days in the coma is a strange story of preparation for later events.

She saw a Beautiful Lady in a field that was filled with flowers. The Beautiful Lady extended her hand and invited Agnes to approach her. But living skeletons rose up and grasped at Agnes. Agnes saw crowds of them fighting with one another as they struggled to obtain pure water from a flowing stream. The more they fought with one another, the weaker they became. The skeletons fell into a river of foul water, and they screamed in terror. Her heart filled with compassion for these distraught people and she began to pray for them. As she prayed for the people, she awakened from the experience. The Beautiful Lady was standing beside her at her hospital bedside. They prayed the Rosary together. After the first decade, the Beautiful Lady recited a prayer:

> *"Oh my Jesus, forgive us our sins,*
> *Save us from the fires of hell,*
> *Lead all souls to Heaven,*
> *Especially those in most need of Your mercy."*

The words of the prayer remained engraved in Agnes's memory. She continued to pray the Rosary, with the prayer added after each decade. A priest heard the prayer and wrote it down. Later he wrote to Agnes to tell her of his discovery that the Rosary prayer she taught him is the very one taught by the Blessed Mother to the three children of Fatima. The prayer was not yet translated into Japanese; Agnes could not have known it previous to her vision. Agnes recovered from her illness and she would see the Beautiful Lady again to prepare her to deliver messages for the world.

On March 16, 1973, Agnes suffered permanent, incurable loss of hearing. After rehabilitation and learning to lip-read, she went to live at the Convent of the Servants of the Eucharist on May 12, 1973.

Sister Agnes was alone at the convent on June 12, 1973, while the other sisters attended an afternoon conference in a nearby community. She had permission to open the tabernacle door for Eucharistic Adoration. In her own words she describes what occurred that day:

> As my hand touched the door of the Tabernacle, an overwhelming light from inside the Tabernacle suddenly shone forth. I was filled with shock and fear. I immediately prostrated myself with my face upon the floor. Many ideas not of my own making crossed my mind as I lay on the floor in front of the Tabernacle in that strange, powerful light. My body was immobile. This condition lasted at least an hour. When the powerful light ended, I asked myself many questions as I lay on the floor. The experience was so overwhelming that I could not arise for some time.

Sister Agnes spoke of her strange experience to no one. The next evening as she prayed with the other sisters in community, the same phenomenon occurred. She was instantly overcome by a supernatural light. Sister Agnes was absolutely certain that the Lord Jesus Christ, truly present in the Eucharist, manifested His divine Presence and power to her in that moment.[16] She went prostrate in front of the tabernacle and remained in that posture for "a long time." In describing this experience to the author in 1991 she said, "His Presence was so real that I wanted to remain with Him forever." She confided with so much obvious joy that it was quite evident the intervening years have not dimmed her gift.

Sister Agnes began to experience the light phenomenon frequently. Sometimes she saw red flames that seemed to consume the immense rays of light that poured from the tabernacle. At other times, Sister Agnes saw the tabernacle itself all aflame. She said that in those circumstances she would immediately fall prostrate before the divine power manifested both as total love and total power. She explained that prostrating herself was the only possible human response. She defines the act of prostration as "total adoration."

Sister Agnes saw the light and the flames with her eyes; she was quite certain that her experiences were not interior illuminations. She actually saw the tabernacle as fire that consumes but does not burn. Her gift was a subjective phenomenon. No one else in the community saw what she did at the time.

Friday, June 29, was the feast of the Sacred Heart of Jesus. Sister Agnes was assigned to Eucharistic Adoration from 9:00 to 10:00 A.M. She knelt on the straw mat and took her rosary in her hands. In that moment, a person appeared beside her. She describes the experience:

> The person who suddenly appeared on my right in the Chapel was the Beautiful Lady who appeared at my side in the hospital and taught me the Rosary Prayer from Fatima. I felt a deep prayer intensity. We prayed the Rosary together. When I said the words: "Our Lady of the Most Holy Rosary, pray for us," the Beautiful Lady smiled and then I could no longer see her.

Sister Agnes's diary[17] explains:

> Following was the time of silent prayer. Suddenly, I saw the blinding light. I immediately prostrated

myself in adoration and when I lifted my eyes, I saw a soft light which enveloped the altar like a mist or a dense smoke in which appeared a cohort of angels turned towards the Blessed Sacrament whose pure and clear voices proclaimed "Holy, Holy, Holy." When they finished, I heard a voice on my right praying the prayer composed for our order by the bishop:

"Most Sacred Heart of Jesus, truly present in the Holy Eucharist,
I consecrate my body and soul to be entirely one with Your Heart
Being sacrificed at every instant on all the altars of the world
And giving praise to the Father,
Pleading for the Coming of His Kingdom.
Please receive this humble offering of myself.
Use me as You will
For the glory of the Father
And the salvation of souls.
Most Holy Mother of God,
Never let me be separated from your Divine Son.
Please defend and protect me as your special child.
Amen."

The Beautiful Lady continued to appear to Sister Agnes. On July 5 a painful wound in the form of a cross formed in the palm of Agnes's right hand. By three o'clock in the morning, the pain in her right hand was so intense that Sister Agnes got out of bed to change the bandage. Then she heard the sweet voice of the Beautiful Lady:

> *"Do not fear. Pray, not only for your own sins, but in reparation for the sins of all humankind. The Sacred Heart of Jesus is wounded by the ingratitude and injuries of the world. The Blessed Mother's wound is much deeper than yours. Let us go to the chapel together."*

At that moment Sister Agnes saw a huge angel, radiant with white light. She remembers that she prayed fervently as she followed the angel to the chapel. Before entering, Sister Agnes asked, "Who are you?" The angel responded:

> *"I am your Guardian Angel. I am assigned to you from all eternity to guide you and care for you."*

The guardian angel and her charge then entered the chapel and knelt near the statue of the Blessed Mother. From the area of the statue, Sister Agnes, who was clinically deaf, heard a clear voice that was as gentle as a warm wind, as sweet and mysterious as the sounds of a harp, as distant as eternity and as close as her heart:

> *"My daughter, you have been most obedient. You have abandoned everything to follow me. Is your deafness causing you much trouble? You will soon be cured. Be certain of that. Be patient. This is the last trial. Does the wound in your hand hurt you? Pray in reparation for the sins of humanity. Each of the sisters in this house is precious to me. Say the prayer of the Servants of the Eucharist very*

well. Now let us pray together the prayer composed by your faithful Bishop.

"Most Sacred Heart of Jesus, truly present in the Holy Eucharist,
I consecrate my body and soul to be entirely one with Your Heart
Being sacrificed at every instant on all the altars of the world
And giving praise to the Father,
Pleading for the Coming of His Kingdom.
Please receive this humble offering of myself.
Use me as You will
For the glory of the Father
And the salvation of souls.
Amen.

"Pray much for the Pope, the Bishops and the priests. Tell your Superior what I have communicated to you this day. Very soon he will ask you to pray thus:

"Lord Jesus Christ, Son of the Father,
Send Your Spirit over the earth.
Make Your Spirit dwell in the hearts
Of all the people
That they will be delivered
From corruption, disasters and war.
Amen."

At 5:10 A.M. the voice stopped. Though the angel had disappeared, the right hand of the statue of the Blessed

Mother, a replica of the statue of Our Lady of All Nations from Amsterdam, was bleeding.

On July 12 the hand of the statue bled again. The bishop, who was aware of the phenomena at the convent, came to see the bleeding statue. Sister Agnes's wound by now was deeper in her right palm. By July 27 the pain was nearly unbearable. She retreated to the chapel in desperation. The angel was there. Addressing Agnes, the angel said:

"You have been suffering. Preserve carefully the memory of the blood of the statue of the Blessed Mother and engrave it on your memory. The bleeding statue is God's way of asking you for conversion, for peace; to make reparation for the ingratitude of humanity and for the outrages committed in front of God. Pray for the conversion of all sinners, while adoring the Sacred Heart of Jesus and His Sacred Blood."

As the Angel finished speaking, all Agnes's pain stopped. The blood stopped flowing from the wound in her hand. Her hand was healed. The angel prayed with Sister Agnes in front of the Blessed Sacrament. Once again Agnes heard a clear voice from the area of the statue. She recognized the voice of the Blessed Mother:

"My daughter, do you love the Lord? If you love Him, please listen to what I say to you. Inform your superior of my request. In the world, many people afflict the Lord. I seek souls to console Him. To assuage the sorrow of the Eternal Father at His children's disobedience, which gives rise to His mighty justice, I, with my Son, await those souls who will expiate with their suffering and their spirit

of renunciation for these sins of ingratitude. My Son and I unite with us generous souls as a gift to our Father.

"*The Eternal Father is quite prepared to allow the world's peoples to experience the consequences of their spirit of disobedience and rebellion to His Divine Plan. I with my Son have often intervened in the affairs of the world to mollify the natural justice of God which allows humanity to bear the consequences of their own choices. Our intervention has delayed the calamities that people have created for one another and for the planet. My Son offers all His suffering on the Cross, along with mine, and all the victim souls who unite their sufferings and penances to God as a gift of love.*

"*Prayer, penance, courageous sacrifice mitigate the consequences of evil behavior. I ask your community to live in strict poverty so that the ingratitude and outrages of many may be touched by your spirit of reparation. As you recite the Prayer of the Servants of the Eucharist be fully conscious of its meaning. Put it into practice and offer it in reparation for sins. Ask everyone in the entire world, according to their position, to say this prayer as a sin offering. Offer yourselves entirely to the Lord.*

"*Souls all over the world who are willing to pray and sacrifice for others out of love for God are being gathered together. As the Century closes this will become more evident. Be faithful and fervent in your prayers to console the Heart of God.*"

On October 13, 1973, the anniversary of the cosmic miracle of the spinning sun at Fatima, Sister Agnes was once again praying in front of the Blessed Sacrament. From the area of the statue she again heard a voice:

"Listen carefully to what I say to you and inform your superior. If humanity does not repent and improve, the Eternal Father will allow a terrible punishment to befall all humankind. This punishment will be worse than the flood or any that has ever been seen before. A fire will fall from the sky and annihilate large numbers. Neither priests nor the faithful will be spared. The survivors will be in such desolation that they will envy the dead.

"The only weapons that will remain will be the Rosary and the Sign that the Eternal Father will leave. Pray the Rosary every day. The devil's attack will be the most intense against those who have consecrated themselves to God.

"The loss of so many souls will deepen the grievous sorrow in my heart. If sins grow and become more accepted there will be no pardon for them."

[Only sins for which a person repents are pardoned. Those who deny that sin is sin do not repent. Hence they are not pardoned.]

On January 4, 1975, the guardian angel spoke to Sister Agnes a last time:

"Do not be surprised to see tears flow from the eyes of the statue of the Blessed Virgin. Every soul which is converted and consecrated is precious to her. She shows her sorrow to you by means of the statue to enliven your faith, which is enfeebled. Now that you have had all these signs, speak courageously and spread the messages and prayers you have for the glory of her Son, Jesus."

Episodes of weeping continued to be observed. This phenomenon with the statue was of immense interest to others outside the convent walls. Secular officials, such as the mayor of Akita, and experts in psychology, medicine, and various technologies also witnessed and examined the phenomenon. The bishop, other members of the clergy, and a diocesan commission examined the tears that flowed from the statue of Our Lady of All Nations.

Theories to explain the phenomenon were brought forth. Among them was "ectoplasm." After ten years of investigation by experts this was absolutely ruled out.

The bishop made repeated journeys to Rome for consultation with the Sacred Congregation of the Doctrine of the Faith about the matters at Akita. From January 4, 1975, until September 15, 1981, the statue wept 101 times.

Sister Agnes Katsuko Sasagawa was provisionally diagnosed as cured of her deafness. Later, after severe trials, the cure was diagnosed as permanent and complete, as the Blessed Mother promised. The permanent cure happened in the following way. On September 21, 1974, Sister Agnes's guardian angel had appeared to her with a message:

Today or tomorrow, begin a novena, one of your choice, and then two more. During the time of these three novenas made before the Lord Truly Present in the Eucharist, your ears will be opened during adoration and you will hear. The first thing that you will hear will be the chant of the Ave Maria which you are accustomed to singing. Then you will hear the sound of the bell ringing for the Benediction of the Most Blessed Sacrament. After the Benediction you will ask the one who directs you to have a Canticle of Thanksgiving sung. Then it will be known that your ears hear again. At that moment your body also will be healed and the Lord will be glorified.

The first healing occurred just as the angel said on October 13, 1974. The permanent cure happened as the Blessed Mother promised on Pentecost Sunday, May 30, 1982. Her guardian angel has not appeared to her since.

At Akita, the Blessed Mother warned that if humanity does not turn away from its sinful ways, fire will fall from the heavens. The power of the fire will be so intense that all who live will experience the scorching light of truth. The desolation of desolations will be the absence of God. The living will envy the dead who have already passed over to God. Those who believe, who are already filled with love, who know how to pray, how to access the power of the angels, how to dwell in the conscious presence of God have nothing to fear. Love begets love.

The Bishop of the diocese has approved the apparitions and messages of Akita as worthy of belief. He has solemnly recognized their supernatural character after mature reflection and detailed examination.

Many city officials witnessed the miraculous statue as it wept 101 times. Akita officially acknowledged the miraculous nature of the events at the convent.

Sister Agnes speaks of God's great unfathomable love for all His children. The Sisters at Akita are gracious and generous to pilgrims, as my husband and I discovered during a visit to the convent. Our first night there, my husband and I were summoned from our sleep by a quite tall sister who insisted that we go to the "baths" even though it was sometime during the night. I had no desire to go to the baths, since the straw floor mat was actually beginning to feel comfortable after our arduous three-week journey through the Philippines.

My husband remarked, "Don't bother to argue with a nun. They usually get their way. Let's get this 'bath' finished so we can try to get back to sleep."

We followed the tall sister through the long, silent corridors to a set of steep, winding stairs. We continued to follow her down the flight of stairs to a ground-floor chamber, where we were shown a "bath" that was approximately thirty-six feet long, two feet deep, and three feet wide. The water looked somewhat dirty. I was quite hesitant. The nun, whose face we do not remember seeing, said, "God wants you to enjoy His mineral waters. This is His gift to you tonight."

My husband assured the nun that we would comply and bade her good night. The water was a fizzing liquid. All our weariness disappeared in the quiet gurgling of the hot mineral waters. How lovely are the baths at the convent of Akita!

After the baths, we slept on our floor mats with such contentment that my husband and I both experienced the heavenly peace that comes from profound religious experiences. I had a most interesting dream:

> It was as if the heavens opened up in front of me. The Blessed Mother was attired as Queen of Heaven and earth. She was holding a beautiful

small sheared lamb with her right hand and a scepter with her left hand.

God our Father, glorious and all-powerful King of all creation, was attired in a most splendid robe and a magnificent crown. There was a small dove over his right shoulder. He was gazing at the Blessed Mother and the lamb. Then the Blessed Mother disappeared and an angel began presenting the lamb to God our Father.

Then the scene of God the Father and the dove disappeared. In its place was the sorrowful face of Jesus looking at the earth.

Then I saw a wounded lion lying at the feet of a medium-sized angel. The angel was bending over the lion, as if ministering to it.

Then I heard a voice say: "The lion is all mankind who do not yet live the messages of the Blessed Mother." (I was given to understand that the fore-going visual scene refers to the Scripture about the lion lying down with the lamb.)

Then I saw a nuclear explosion mushroom cloud high in the sky. Below it was Our Lady of Medju-gorje and below her was the planet earth.

Several hours later, a pilgrim who wishes to re-main anonymous experienced the following during early-morning adoration of the Blessed Sacrament with the sisters:

I perceived the presence of the Blessed Mother holding the Infant Jesus with her left hand. With her right hand she held His hand and they pointed toward the crucifix on the wall.

The Blessed Mother was very beautiful. Her skin was the color of French vanilla ice cream with a deep, rich texture like satin. She was dressed in gold. I could not see the Infant's face or garments to remember, though at the time I was aware it was Jesus in her arms. Then I saw interiorly that the Blessed Mother gives Jesus to those people in the world who ask her for Him.

During the Hosanna of the Mass, I heard the voice of a young man singing with such exquisite sweetness that my heart was seared. When I looked to see him, there was no one there. Then I realized that those who would have been privileged to hear Jesus sing during His life on earth would have heard the sounds of Paradise in their fullest.

Truly there are exquisite graces that abound at the convent of Akita. Later, as we visited with the Mother Superior, we thanked her for sending the tall nun to take us to the baths. She was astounded. "No one came to take you to the baths last night. All the sisters were asleep in the cloister!" she earnestly informed us. We insisted. Then the Mother Superior said, with her eyes twinkling, "Observe the nuns of our convent. They are all present. Do you see a tall sister?" We quickly scanned the nuns' smiling faces, and their heights. The tall nun who had escorted us to the baths the night before was not there. Or was she?

The Mother Superior then told us about the mysterious baths at the convent of Akita. Early in the days of the foundation of the convent, an angel told the sisters about a spring that God our Father desired His children to use as a bath of healing. The sisters dug in the ground at the site shown to them by the angel. Gushes of therapeutic mineral waters flowed forth, and an indoor bath was built to contain the sacred waters. Before the appearance of the tall nun, we did not know about the baths at Akita.

Sister Agnes Sasagawa's eyes glistened as she remarked, "The Blessed Mother always gets her way!" She spoke with a profound simplicity that surprised no one.

The sisters told me that when the guardian angel appeared to Sister Agnes, he encouraged them to read chapter 3, verse 15 in the book of Genesis. The guardian angel identified the Blessed Mother of Jesus as the woman spoken of in that verse, and announced that the mission of the Blessed Virgin Mary at Akita is to crush the head of Satan.

Sister Agnes and the other sisters at the convent in Akita said that the gifts and messages of the Blessed Mother and the guardian angel at Akita are for everyone on earth. The guardian angel explained that if people are made aware of the seriousness of the messages they will repent and reform their lives. Every guardian angel of each person on earth is standing by waiting to assist the people of these times in their courageous journey out of darkness into the light of truth.

The messages and miracles of Akita are a wake-up call

to all those who slumber in fear and uncertainty. Chastisements are, after all, self-made. We bring them upon ourselves. Guardian angels always tell us that obedience to the will of God brings peace, joy, abundance, and abiding love for everyone.

CHAPTER SEVEN

Queen of the Holy Rosary

There are different kinds of spiritual gifts but the same
Spirit; there are different forms of service but the same Lord;
there are different workings but the same God who produces
all of them in everyone. To each individual the manifestation
of the Spirit is given for some benefit.

1 CORINTHIANS 12:4–7

Betania, Venezuela: since 1976

Venezuela, one of the wealthiest countries in Latin America, is rich in religious custom as well. The Blessed Mother
is revered there. Tradition holds that she first appeared in
Venezuela to the chief of the Coromato tribe on September 8, 1652, asking him and all his people to be baptized.
The chief responded by throwing his spear at the apparition.
The Blessed Mother continued to appear to him on later
occasions. It was not until the chief was bitten by a poiso-
nous snake that he capitulated to the wishes of the Beautiful
Lady from Heaven. He was baptized on his deathbed and
directed that the whole tribe follow his example.

In the parish of Our Lady of the Holy Rosary in Betania, Venezuela, about a two-and-a-half-hour drive from

Caracas, many thousands have claimed to see, and continue to report, apparitions of the Blessed Mother as Our Lady of Lourdes, Our Lady of the Miraculous Medal, or Our Lady of Sorrows. In Betania, it is the presence of the Blessed Mother that is important. Her presence is the message. The apparition site of Betania has been formally approved as authentic by the Roman Catholic Church.

Estimates of upwards of a quarter-million people in Betania are reported as visionaries. They say they have seen or are seeing apparitions of the Blessed Mother at the grotto. Extraordinary photos are turning up in the possession of visitors from everywhere. They depict an image of the Blessed Mother in various phenomenal ways.[1]

The first apparition occurred on March 25, 1976, in the grotto of Betania, near the waterfall and spring which many since then have found to possess healing qualities.[2] The Blessed Mother appears at Betania in various ways, but most frequently as Our Lady of Lourdes, attired in white garments and with a blue sash at her waist. The apparitions are usually preceded by a great flash of light, and are accompanied by the sweet perfume of roses. Sometimes great flocks of blue butterflies are seen by the pilgrims as the apparition occurs.

Many of those who congregate at the grotto have been heard to exclaim that they see multitudes of angels surrounding the apparition of the Blessed Mother. Many have testified that a "person" approaches to help them, or to answer a grave concern that has brought them to the grotto. Then, just as suddenly, the "person" disappears. A question that is frequently asked at Betania: "Was the 'person' an angel in corporeal form?" Many sick and injured people have claimed physical cures—of everything from cancer to paralysis—at Betania.

The Blessed Mother identified herself and her mission at Venezuela:

"My dear little children, I am the Blessed Virgin Mary, Mother and Reconciler of people and nations. I come with my Son Jesus in my arms to reconcile each of you. Forgive one another. Love one another. Serve one another. Pray for the Church. Pray for priests. Return to the Sacraments, dear little children. Confess your sins while the sun shines. Sacrifice yourselves for the conversion of sinners and for peace in the world. All of you are children of God. All are loved. Love one another in His name. Pray the Rosary, dear little ones, that you may find the path of my Son. Peace, little children. Only peace."[3]

The ordinary of the diocese of Los Teques, presiding Roman Catholic Bishop Monsignor Pio Ricardo, S.J., is a theologian who earned his doctorate in psychology. On November 21, 1987, after consultation with Rome, he officially declared a pastoral instruction: "Having studied the apparitions of the Virgin Mary at Betania and having prayed assiduously to God for spiritual discernment, I declare that in my judgment the aforementioned apparitions are authentic and are supernatural in character."[4]

Such official recognition of the supernatural character of the apparitions in Venezuela is remarkable. Extraordinary phenomena have accompanied these public apparitions of the Blessed Mother, including luminous signs in the sky such as a spinning sun, and involving various stars and other solar objects.

The Blessed Mother often appears quite unexpectedly, bathed in light. No one seems to know when the apparitions will occur or who will see the Blessed Mother. An apparition can happen at any time at Betania. People speak of the sudden smell of roses. They mention hearing an invisible choir. Often, too, pilgrims see blue butterflies of incredible beauty and color. The Blessed Mother has said that the butterflies are a sign of her presence.[5]

Many pilgrims claim to have been cured of terminal illnesses at Betania. Authenticating documentation is accepted by the diocese from those interested in publicizing their cures.

A Roman Catholic priest celebrated Mass at the grotto in 1992 for a large group of pilgrims who had come to Betania hoping to catch a glimpse of the Queen of Angels. To the shock of the pilgrims and the priest, the Host he consecrated turned into pulsating, bleeding heart muscle in clear view of all those at the Mass. The miraculous Host continues to bleed type AB human blood and is in the possession of the local Archbishop.[6] (It is important to note that the Holy Eucharist is never considered "flesh" in the sense of human flesh. Rather, it is the essence, the body and blood, soul and divinity of Jesus Christ.)

Many years ago, the apparitions in the grotto of Betania were prophesied by the Blessed Mother to a Venezuelan visionary, Maria Esperanza Medrano de Biancini, born on November 22, 1928. She is married to an aristocratic Italian who operates an oil business in Venezuela. They are the parents of seven children and the grandparents of many more. Maria Esperanza began seeing the Blessed Mother when she was a small girl, six years old. This apparition was not her first: the sickly child first saw Saint Thérèse of Lisieux when she was five years old. The saint, popularly known as the Little Flower, tossed a pink rose to the five-year-old. Roses and rose petals have since been part of the mystical signs that surround Maria Esperanza.

Few who know Maria doubt her extraordinary spiritual gifts. Witnesses from every continent have seen many of the phenomena, including clairvoyance, the ability to predict the future, stigmata (physically bearing in her body the wounds of Christ), transfiguration (the witness is looking at Maria yet seeing another), healing powers, the mysterious reception of the Eucharist, and the mysterious emission of flowers and sweet odors from her body.[7]

The Blessed Mother appeared to Maria Esperanza when she was fourteen years old. At that time the Blessed Mother began to prepare Maria for the apparitions in Betania that she said would begin on March 25, 1976.[8] Maria's family was aware through the years that the Venezuela apparitions were promised for March 25, 1976. No one was surprised, therefore, when the Blessed Mother appeared to Maria in Betania near the waterfall of the grotto. As she held a rosary, the Blessed Mother began to explain the purpose for her later public apparitions at Betania that would begin on March 25, 1984:

"I am the Mother and Reconciler of all people and Nations. Pray the Rosary fervently. Recognize that the Rosary can placate the thirst for revenge that haunts hu-

manity's heart. It can assuage the craving for material possessions that stalks humanity. Experience the reality that I live among you."

People of all races, levels of belief, faiths, and nations have seen the Blessed Mother at Betania, Venezuela. One eyewitness of the apparitions has said: "It was as if the whole vision penetrated into every part of me and saturated every pore of me. I felt such deep peace. The apparition of the Blessed Mother was so beautiful that I have no words to explain it."[9]

At her apparitions in Betania, the Blessed Mother has promised all people on earth who turn to her:

"I am your Mother. I will be your refuge."

An Interview with Visionary Mary Esperanza Biancini

Q. Has the Lord Jesus or His Blessed Mother ever spoken to you about the Triumph of the Immaculate Heart that was promised by the Blessed Mother at Fatima in 1917?

A. That triumph means that good will triumph over evil. There is much war now. There will be more unless God intervenes. In the 1950s, when I was a young girl, I had visions of the peoples of the east and the west luring each other into brutal war. I saw that the hand of the Creator will stop it. There cannot be another world war. . . . The situation in the world is critical now. In 1994 conversion of people is not complete. There are those in various countries who want to attack other nations. They look for any pretext to ignite a war. Enslaved nations will be free one day. In the meantime we must all pray much.

Q. When will the Triumph of the Immaculate Heart occur?

A. It is my belief that by the year 2004, the fulfillment of this promise will be with us.

Q. Is there more pain for the world that you know about?

A. Yes. There will be difficult international political moments. They will erupt very fast. I have traveled all my life to spread the message of the Blessed Mother to help bring about peace in the world. Everyone who helps to spread Our Lady's messages helps to bring peace upon the earth.

Q. Those who help spread Our Lady's messages are really angels of God's mercy. Maria, do you know exactly what the Triumph of the Immaculate Heart will be?

A. It will be the triumph of the principles of Jesus Christ. People all over the world are learning that nothing else makes sense. It will include harmony among all nations. These days we live now are God's gift of divine mercy. When you realize the evil in the world, yet experience the love of God that we have in the Blessed Mother's apparitions to people of all faiths all over the world, it is easy to recognize God's divine mercy.

Q. Do you know anything about the Second Coming of Jesus Christ that is foretold in the Gospels?

A. Yes.

Q. Is the Second Coming of Jesus Christ going to occur in the immediate future—the next few years?

A. Jesus has told us that only the Father knows the day and

the hour. The apparitions of the Blessed Mother all over the world are preparing people for the coming of her Son.

Q. How will His coming occur?

A. First of all, people need to know Our Lord. He is so humble, so filled with tenderness. Jesus Christ will come in every sense. The world has gone crazy. [*Tears. Weeping.*] Many claim now to be Jesus. They are false prophets. Jesus is alive. Jesus is with us in the Eucharist. Who has eyes to see Him? Who has ears to hear him? [*More sobbing and many tears.*] Two things will happen at the same time. He will show Himself in a very interesting way so that people will realize that He is there. We will also be able to see Him. Many things are going to happen all over the earth. He is going to manifest Himself in many ways. Grace is preparing souls so that He may bring order to their ideas, prepare their minds to comprehend His presence. Little by little the truth is going to spread. Now there is just a small group of people, but they bear the fire of truth. More and more people are seeing truth.

Q. Will the angels be involved in the Second Coming of Jesus Christ?

A. Yes, in a most important way. The angels are already involved.

Q. Does the Blessed Mother have a special message for me to share now?

A. Yes. Our Lady gives this message for you to share with everyone. She speaks to everyone.

"My little child, I give my heart to you. I will continue giving my heart to you always. My little child, I take you

by the hand. I lead you to My Divine Son Jesus. During the difficult hours, stay within the supreme will of Our Father. My Son and I affirm such little ones during their journey on the earth.

"I am here with you now so that all may become apostles of the ways of my Son. I am here to help you walk serenely in the laws, the might, power, light and the hope of our Heavenly Father. His positive forces, the holy angels and the grace of the Holy Spirit allow His chosen children to feel the delight of His presence.

"This is the great time of human seeking for an encounter with our Heavenly Father in my Divine Son Jesus. All of you cry out for justice, for the renewal of faith. To accelerate, to hasten the uniting of all people and nations, it is necessary to follow God's will and accept His divine plan of love given by my Son Jesus.

"Attend devotedly the Sacrifice of the Holy Mass. Participate at the Eucharistic table which is the center and culmination of the whole life of the human community. Those who dwell in silence before the Eucharistic Presence of Jesus become children of the light. They will be able to sow goodness. They will acquire the disposition of living the Gospel.

"Little children of mine, I love you so much. Be very humble. Stay united. Meditate and pray. Follow the rules of God and you will be healed from within. In this way you will come to a deep intimacy and sharing with My Divine Son, your brother."

Q. Maria, I have heard that if we are not like Jesus, we will not be able to find Him to choose Him.

A. Many have, do, and will miss the time of their visitation. The Blessed Mother asks us to live the life that Jesus taught. Do all for Jesus. Be living examples of God's children. Then we will all know real love. Jesus has infinite love for every soul. His Sacred Heart will never change. He awaits all.

Cuapa, Nicaragua: 1980

According to the 1990 census figures, an estimated 202,000 Nicaraguans reside in the United States. Most came to the United States in the 1980s when they fled Nicaragua during the brutal war between the Sandinistas and the contras.[10]

Before the war began, the Blessed Mother appeared six times to a native Nicaraguan, Bernardo Martinez, with warnings and messages from heaven for the people of Nicaragua. From October 8 until October 13, 1980, the Blessed Mother appeared in Cuapa to Bernardo Martinez, who was then about fifty years old, in poor health, without money, and out of work.

Life in Nicaragua was fraught with poverty and uncertainty. An earlier earthquake had caused substantial property and financial damage. Political woes threatened the internal structure of the country. Bernardo was depressed and sometimes even wished he was dead. Many others shared his feelings.

In May 1990, Bernardo Martinez came from Nicaragua to share his testimony at the first Pittsburgh Marian Conference, held at Duquesne University. He was one of several respected visionaries from around the world who gathered there to speak publicly about personal messages and visions of the Blessed Mother. Since he spoke no English, he offered his public witness through translators.

Bernardo is a large-boned man with steel-gray hair. He wore a plaid cotton shirt and navy trousers. He looked sturdy, strong, and quite healthy, like many of the local Pittsburgh men in the audience. His story is well known now. The official messages and statements about his apparitions are disseminated by the office of Monsignor Pablo Antonio Vega, Prelate Bishop of Juigalpa, and, in the United States, by the Nicaraguan Community in Exile. The story of his apparitions follows.

On May 8, 1980, Bernardo was close to the breaking point physically and emotionally. Being out of work was bad enough, but he was also ill and had no means of caring for himself or his family. To cheer himself, he went to the river to fish. When it began to rain, about one o'clock in the afternoon, Bernardo decided to sit under a tree and wait for the rain to stop. He dozed a bit, then awakened with a start. He felt frightened, but he was not certain why. He decided to pray the Rosary. By three o'clock, he gathered his fish and set off toward his home. Later, at the request of his bishop, he described what happened to him:

> Suddenly I saw a lightning-flash. I thought and said to myself: "It is going to rain." But I became filled with wonder because I did not see from where the lightning had come. I stopped but I could see nothing; no signs of rain. . . . I saw another lightning-flash, but that was to open my vi-

sion and she presented herself. . . . I saw that she blinked . . . that she was beautiful. . . . There was a cloud . . . it was extremely white . . . it radiated in all directions, rays of light with the sun. On the cloud were the feet of a very Beautiful Lady. Her feet were bare. The dress was long and white. She had a celestial cord around the waist. Long sleeves. Covering her was a veil of a pale cream color with gold embroidery along the edge. Her hands were held together. . . . I felt no fear. I was surprised. . . . I saw that she had human skin and that her eyes moved and blinked. . . . My mind was the only thing that I could move. . . I felt numb . . . everything immobilized. . . . She extended her arms and from her hands emanated rays of light stronger than the sun. . . . She spoke with sweetness . . . softer than I have ever heard any woman speak:

"I am the Mother of Jesus. I come to you from Heaven to ask you to pray the Rosary every day with your family, especially your children. I wish you to make this message known. It is important that children, as soon as they reach the age of reason, pray the Rosary daily with their parents. Say the Rosary every day at the same time with biblical meditations, as soon as all the household chores are finished. Nicaragua has suffered much. Nicaragua will suffer more. You, and all God's people in this country, will continue to suffer unless you change. Do not be afraid. I will help you. Tell believers and nonbelievers that the world is threatened by grave dangers. Please spread this message to all the people."

Bernardo felt quite intimidated. Suddenly recovering his voice, he replied, "I have many problems. Who would listen to me?"

The Beautiful Mother of Jesus from Heaven responded to his pain:

"Our Lord has selected you to give the message. Not everyone can see me. People will see me when I take them to Heaven. They should pray the Rosary as I ask."

Bernardo then described: "She looked upward toward Heaven and the cloud that held her slowly elevated her. As she was in a ray of light, when she reached a certain distance, she disappeared."

The second time that Bernardo saw the Blessed Mother, she pointed toward the sky and it seemed to open. Then she showed him a scene from the early days of the Church:

I saw a large group of people who were dressed in white and were walking towards where the sun rises. They were bathed in light and were very happy; they sang. I could hear them but I could not understand the words. It was a celestial festival. It was such happiness . . . such joy . . . which I had never seen before. . . . Their bodies radiated light. I felt as if I were transported. In the midst of my admiration I heard the Blessed Mother tell me:

"Look. These are the very first communities when Christianity began. They are the first catechumens; many of them were martyrs."

Bernardo was not exactly sure whether a martyr was one who openly professed his faith or a person who was killed for his faith, so he did not know how to respond truthfully when the Blessed Mother asked him:

"Do you wish to be a martyr?"

He describes:

> In that instant I did not know exactly what the meaning of being a martyr was . . . but I answered yes. After that I saw another group, also dressed in white, with some luminous rosaries in their hands. The beads were extremely white and they gave off lights of different colors. One of them carried a very large, open book. He would read, and after listening they silently meditated. They appeared to be as if in prayer. After this period of prayer in silence, they then prayed the Our Father and ten Hail Marys. I prayed with them. When the Rosary was finished, the Blessed Mother said to me:

> *"These are the first ones to whom I gave the Rosary. It would please God if you would all pray the Rosary that way."*

Then Bernardo saw others in the procession. He described the last group he saw:

> It was a huge procession of people dressed as we dress in these times. It was such a huge group that it would be impossible to count them. It was like

an army in size, and they carried rosaries in their hands. I desired to join them. But I looked at my hands and saw them dark, without light. All those in the procession radiated light. Their bodies were beautiful. I asked the Blessed Mother to allow me to join those, dressed like me in the procession. She responded:

"No. You are still lacking. Tell people what you have seen and heard. I have shown you the glory of Our Lord. You people will acquire this glory if you are obedient to Our Lord, to the Lord's Word; if you persevere in praying the Holy Rosary and put into practice the Lord's Word."

On September 8, Bernardo saw the Beautiful Lady from Heaven. He had quite a surprise. He describes:

I saw her as a child. Beautiful! But little! She was dressed in a pale, cream-colored tunic. She did not have a veil, nor a crown, nor a mantle. No adornment, nor embroidery. The dress was long, with long sleeves, and it was girdled with a pink cord. Her hair fell to her shoulders and it was brown in color. The eyes, also, although much lighter, almost like the color of honey. All of her radiated light. She looked like the Lady, but she was a child. I was looking at her amazed, without saying a word, and then I heard her voice as that of a child . . . a child of seven . . . eight . . . years. In an extremely sweet voice she gave the message; totally identical. . . . She said:

"It is enough for you to give the message to others because for the one who is going to believe that will be enough, and the one who is not going to believe, though he should see me, is not going to believe."

Bernardo asked the Blessed Mother if she desired that the people of Cuapa build a church or a basilica to honor her.

"The Lord does not want material churches and temples to be built to honor Him. He wants each of you to be a living temple in which He is invited to dwell. In you is the gratification for the Lord. Love each other. Restore yourselves as sacred temples of the Lord! The Churches and temples are you, each of you!"

The final vision of the Blessed Mother to Bernardo in Nicaragua occurred on October 13, 1980. The date marked the sixty-third anniversary of the final apparition of the Blessed Mother at Fatima, Portugal, when the great cosmic miracle of the sun shocked 50,000 eye-witnesses.

A group of approximately fifty people went to the site of the preannounced apparition with Bernardo. They arranged the flowers that they'd brought atop a pile of rocks and knelt down on the ground to pray the Rosary. Since it was a Monday, everyone joined in reciting the Joyful Mysteries. As they finished the Rosary, a large, luminous circle formed over the ground in front of the group. Everyone saw the light that came from the sky, a single ray, like a powerful spotlight that illuminated the circle in front of them. Then the people noticed that a circle had also formed in the sky. They shouted: "It's like a ring around the moon or a ring around the sun, but it's not the moon or the sun! What is it?" The circle began to radiate all the colors of the rainbow. It was exactly three o'clock in the afternoon. A soft rain fell gently, like a refreshing breeze, but no one was wet. The ground, too, remained dry as the glorious colors from the circle in the sky performed an intricate dance for everyone to see. Bernardo explained what followed:

> All of a sudden a lightning-flash, the same as the other times, then, a second one. I lowered my eyes and I saw the Blessed Mother. This time the cloud upon which she stood rested over the flowers we had brought. She is so beautiful! She extended her hands to us and rays of light reached all of us. . . . I could hear some of the people crying.

Bernardo implored the Blessed Mother to allow others to see her too. She replied:

> *"Not everyone can see me."*

Bernardo persisted. He said:

> Blessed Mother, let them see you so they believe. Many do not believe. They tell me it is the devil who appears to me. They tell me the Blessed Virgin Mary is dead and turned to dust like any mortal. Let them see you, Blessed Mother!

She did not answer. She raised her hands in the pose you see in the statues of Our Lady of Sorrows. Her face became sad, it became very pale. The color of her dress and mantle and veil turned to gray. She began to weep. When I saw her tears, I too began to cry. I trembled to see her like that. I said to her: "Blessed Mother, forgive me for what I said to you. You are angry with me. Forgive me! Forgive me!" She then answered me, saying:

"I am not angry with you, nor will I be angry."

I asked her: "Why are you crying?" She told me:

"It saddens me to see the hardness of those persons' hearts. Please pray for them so that they will change."

I could not speak. I continued to cry. I felt my heart being crushed. I was so sad that I thought I was going to die from the pain. I felt responsible for the Blessed Mother's sadness because I had insisted so strenuously that she show herself to others. I could not endure her pain. I continued to cry. Then she gave me the message:

"Pray the Rosary. Meditate on the mysteries. Listen to the Word of God spoken in them. Charity is a way of life that builds up humanity and the world. Love each other. Pardon each other and make peace. Do not ask for peace unless you make peace.

"Fulfill your duties. Put the Word of God into practice. Seek ways to please God. Help others as a way to please God. In that way you will be pleasing to God. Do not ask God constantly for things that are unimportant. Ask God to increase your faith so that you have the strength to carry your own cross.

"The sufferings of this world, and these times, cannot be taken away from you. Such is the way of the world. There are problems with the husband, with the wife, with the children, with the brothers and sisters. Talk, communicate with one another so that your problems will be resolved in peace. Do not turn to violence. Never turn to violence. Ask instead for faith in order that you will have patience.

"You shall no longer see me in this place."

Bernardo was shocked to hear her farewell. He began to shout: "Don't leave us, my Mother! Don't leave us, my Mother! Don't leave us, my Mother!" He then heard her beautiful voice once again:

"Do not be grieved. I am with you even though you do not see me. I am the Mother of all of you. I am the Mother of all sinners. Love one another. Forgive each other. Make peace, because if you do not make peace there will be no peace. Do not turn to violence. Never turn to violence. Nicaragua has suffered a great deal since the earthquake and will continue to suffer if you do not change. If you do not change, you will hasten the coming of the Third World War. Pray, pray, my son, for all the world. Grave dangers threaten the world. This mother never forgets her chil-

dren. I have not forgotten what you suffer. I am your Mother who never forgets her children. I am with you though you do not see me. I am the Mother of all sinners. I am with all of you, especially in your suffering. Love each other. Pardon each other.

"Please pray this prayer knowing it is pleasing to my Son: 'Most Holy Virgin, you are my Mother, the Mother of all sinners. Help me, my Mother, help my family, my country, my world. Amen.' "

Bernardo concluded his report of his apparitions:

She was elevated as if the cloud were pushing her . . . she disappeared. I am no more than a decayed cane through which this message is passed. In my ignorance, I say it poorly. . . . The Holy Virgin tells us to make peace and the peace is Jesus Christ. I will never cease repeating the message. For as long as my tongue has movement I will shout it to the four winds.

On November 13, 1983, the local bishop, Monsignor Vega, published his approval of the apparitions at Cuapa, Nicaragua.

San Nicholás, Argentina: 1983 to 1990

A city that bears the same name as Santa Claus, San Nicholás, Argentina, is now serving as host city to the Blessed Virgin Mary and her Son Jesus. They began appearing there on September 25, 1983, to a local woman,

Gladys de Motta, while she knelt on the floor praying the Rosary. She described the Lord and His Mother "transfigured by a living light."[11] The Blessed Virgin, attired in a blue dress, held her Son in her arms and carried a rosary in her hand.

Several weeks earlier, the visionary and some neighbors had noticed rosary beads hanging from her bed, lighted up like a neon rosary. They'd decided to pray the Rosary together daily after that unexpected sign. Gladys also prayed the Rosary privately. Then she had her first apparition.

Gladys's messages from the Blessed Virgin Mary are permeated with biblical citations. The messages indicate Jesus' Mother insists that God's people know and understand the Word of God in these times. The messages of the Blessed Mother from San Nicholás, Argentina, are of international significance; they impact every town, village, and hamlet on earth. The world is awakening to the presence and messages of the Blessed Mother and her Divine Son Jesus in the city of San Nicolás, Argentina.

The visionary, Gladys de Motta, is the wife of a retired metalworker. She has two daughters and several grandchildren. She completed only the fourth grade and her reading skills are poor. Before her apparitions, Gladys had never written even a simple letter. Since mid-November of 1983, when Gladys's apparitions became a daily occurrence, Gladys has received and written more than 1,800 messages from Heaven.

On October 7, 1983, the feast of the Holy Rosary, Gladys felt a tingling sensation in her arms and an impulse in her heart that notified her of an impending divine visitation. She composed herself, closed her eyes, and saw the light that announces an apparition. In the intense light, Gladys saw the living, breathing Mother of God before her, holding a large rosary. Gladys describes: "I saw her and asked her what she wanted of me. Then her image faded away and a chapel appeared. I understood that she wanted to be among us." The Blessed Mother appeared to Gladys from 1983 until 1990, identifying herself as Our Lady of the Rosary.

Gladys received her apparitions in a different manner than the visionaries at Medjugorje, Bosnia, or those in Rwanda. Marian scholar René Laurentin explains that at Medjugorje and Rwanda, "the visionaries cease to see and to hear what surrounds them after the beginning of the apparition. A brilliant perception of another world obscures the world here below. Gladys's perception is tangible, real, surrealistic. But she frees herself from the external world, simply by closing her eyes."

Gladys's apparitions were not mere internal, subjective vision. Father Laurentin comments: "For Gladys the Blessed Virgin is real, living. She has touched her. She has felt the firmness and warmth of her body, not through ordinary perception, but according to a more direct, more existential way, no less real, but surrealistic. It commands a linking of coherent reactions—a listening, and a response in a very real intimacy. At times those around her perceive a sweet smell of roses and a feeling of warmth."

On November 15, 1983, the Lord Jesus Christ began to speak to Gladys and to give messages through her to the world. He said:

"I am the Sower. Gather the harvest. It will be great."

The next day, the Blessed Mother of Jesus said:

"I am the Patroness of this region. Assert my rights."

Gladys asked the Blessed Mother if she desired a chapel or a basilica. The Blessed Mother responded:

"I desire to be near you. Water is a blessing. Place my shrine near the river. Holy Scriptures say: They will make me a sanctuary and I will dwell in the midst of them. *Please carry out my request."*

The Blessed Mother advised Gladys:

"Do not forget the sanctuary, because it is a sanctuary of the Lord. Time will pass away, but it will remain."

The following day, the Blessed Mother's Divine Son spoke again to His people with great joy:

"Glorious days await you. You will rejoice in Me, My beloved children."

During her apparitions in 1983 and 1984, the Blessed Mother continued to ask for a special sanctuary, a basilica, to be built at the site of her apparitions on the banks of the Paraná River and located in a field known as the Campito. The curious were fascinated to notice that on two different occasions, during the apparitions of Gladys, a sudden ray of light was visible, marking the exact location for the construction of the sanctuary.

The official title of the Blessed Mother disclosed to Gladys is Our Lady of the Rosary of San Nicholás. In response to that title, Our Lady said:

> *"My wish is to be among you, to fill you with blessings, with peace, joy, and to bring you closer to God our Lord."*

By 1984, Gladys began to understand the place of physical and moral sufferings for humans in the spiritual ascent to union with God. Silence became for Gladys a personal interior sanctuary in which she listened for the voice of the living God within. It is said she rarely speaks now.

Gladys discerned a divine invitation to become a victim soul for the love of God. On Friday, November 16, 1984, she experienced some of the sufferings of the passion of Jesus. Evidence of nail wounds showed on her wrists. They have renewed during Advent and Lent ever since. Blood flows from the wrist wounds only on the Fridays of Lent. On Good Friday, a little after 3:00 P.M., additional injuries manifest themselves on Gladys's feet and her shoulder. A transfixion occurs in her side as a wound opens up without a flow of blood.

The Blessed Mother invited Gladys to undertake extreme fasts. During Advent of 1984, Gladys ate no solid food at all, taking only grapefruit juice and tea and coffee with milk. She said that she did not experience hunger or discomfort. She does not lose weight or become ill in any way from her strict fasts. The Blessed Mother explained on January 11, 1989:

*"This Mother always seeks the good of her children. I ex-
pect of them prayer, fasting, conversion. They will find salvation if they do not flee from God, if they accept God.
Many souls lack peace. If the soul searches for peace, it will
find God."*

From the beginning, as Gladys experienced her apparitions, she—and those with her—noticed a great aroma
of roses. Only years later, on June 27, 1987, did the
Blessed Mother explain to Gladys the meaning of the sudden scent of roses:

*"Those who experience the perfume of my roses walk
with me."*

Dramatic healings of the sick have occurred in connec-
tion with the apparitions. In 1984, a seven-year-old boy,
Gonzalo Miguel Godoy, was dying of a brain tumor that
had left his right side totally paralyzed. After administer-
ing the Last Rites of the Church and first Holy Communion to the boy, the chancellor of the diocese, Father Ariel
David Busso, placed Gonzalo under the protection of Our
Lady of the Rosary of San Nicholás. Within a month, Gonzalo was completely and miraculously healed.

A book of testimonies is on display in the sanctuary
that was built to honor the apparitions of Our Lady of the
Rosary of San Nicholás. It contains nearly 200 pages of
statements of claimed miraculous healings attributed to
the intercession of Our Lady of the Rosary of San Nicholás.
A team of medical specialists has been assembled to study
and verify these reported miraculous cures.

Pilgrims come to San Nicholás from all over the world. The prayer intensity is remarkable. Sacramental confession is considered a vital part of the prayer graces given there. Many of those who avail themselves of the opportunity for reconciliation (sacramental confession) report that they have subsequently experienced a unique and personal awareness of the real Presence of Jesus in the Eucharist.

The bishop of San Nicholás, Monsignor Domingo Castagna, assembled a commission to investigate the supernatural elements of the apparitions. The commission members included a psychologist, two graphologists, and a team of psychiatrists from the School of Psychology at the Jesuit University of Salvador. All the studies have been positive. The bishop personally leads pilgrims to the beautiful sanctuary, which is nearing completion.

On November 25, 1986, Archbishop Jorge M. López went to San Nicholás to venerate the Blessed Virgin of the Most Holy Rosary. He wrote later of the reason for that visit: "I was a pilgrim like the others . . . in order to show my support and my approval of the principles and directions of my dear bishop of San Nicholás, Msgr. Domingo Salvador Castagna, on the subject of the apparitions and the messages of the Most Holy Virgin to Mrs. Gladys de Motta, living in this city. . . ."

A special medal has been struck and is widely distributed; it bears the image of Our Lady of the Rosary on the front and the symbol of the Holy Trinity on the back. Those who wear the medal claim many blessings and graces which they believe are the result of wearing it.

Urgency and the imminent return of Jesus are the underlying themes of the apparitions and messages in Argentina. According to experts, the messages indicate that God desires to renew the covenant with His people through the Blessed Mother of Jesus, His own Ark of the Covenant. God created her to be, with her consent, His dwelling place among His people. Mary, the divinely created Ark of the Covenant, is now in the midst of God's people, who are invited to follow her out of the desert of evil to the promised land of God's heart.

Gladys experienced sixty-eight visions and messages from the Lord Jesus Christ. On June 15, 1984, He told her:

> *"Those who listen to My words will find salvation. Those who put them into practice will live forever. Those who hope in God do not hope in vain."*

On October 4, 1985, Jesus told her:

> *"A nation that prays and respects My Word will live in peace. I protect such a nation."*

On March 12, 1986, Jesus said:

> *"If this generation does not listen to My Mother, it will perish. I ask everyone to listen to her."*

On November 19, 1987, Jesus shone with a dazzling light as He solemnly announced:

> *"Today I warn the world, for the world is not aware: Souls are in danger. Many are lost. Few will find salvation un-*

less they accept Me as their Savior. My Mother must be accepted. My Mother must be heard in the totality of her messages. The world must discover the richness she brings. The children of sin will grow up in sin if their unbelief increases. I want a renewal of the Spirit, a detachment from death, and an attachment to life. I have chosen the heart of My Mother, so that what I ask will be achieved. Souls will come to Me through the means of her Immaculate Heart."

On November 17, 1989, Jesus said:

"My light wants to illuminate all nations, for it is the true light. All those who receive it will be called true children of God."

In December 1989, Jesus showed Gladys the work of the creation of the world. Then He said to her:

"In the past the world was saved by the Ark of Noah. Today my Mother is the Ark. It is through her that souls will be saved, because she will lead them to Me. He who rejects My Mother rejects Me. Many are those who allow the grace of God to pass these days."

The Blessed Mother told Gladys that two-thirds of the world's people live without any conscious awareness of God. She explained that her apparitions are a gift of God's love to His children. The Blessed Mother said that we witness the world on the brink of destruction and that the world as we know it is passing away. On December 18, 1988, the Blessed Mother told her:

"I address all humanity: The Lord does so much for you! Do not prevent the Lord from entering into your life. Recognize that He is speaking to you. I myself call each of you. I am waiting.·. . . I desire that you pray and meditate. The rays of light from my Immaculate Heart are God's love for you. He sends me to you because He desires to save as many of His people as awaken to His presence and His ways. Every soul must prepare so as not to be imprisoned eternally by darkness."

The messages of the Blessed Mother in Argentina offer profound insight concerning the special times in which we live, and the mission of the Mother of God. On August 24 and 25, 1988, the Blessed Mother promised:

"I am above all a Mother. I am beside my children, watching over them. My Mother's heart goes toward all corners of the earth. I console and protect each heart that seeks my protection. I am the Mother of All Ages. I am the Mother of all God's Children. I am the Mother of Christ. Blessed are they who take refuge under my mantle in my Immaculate Heart.

"In my Immaculate Heart there is enough purity to purify the whole world. In my Immaculate Heart there is enough love to sweep away all the hatred of the ages accumulated in hardened hearts. In my Immaculate Heart there is enough light to enlighten every soul ever created and the entire creation.

"Do not be ashamed of sin. My Son is the Savior of sinners. Be ashamed of not loving God. Be ashamed of not trusting God."

On May 24, 1989, the Blessed Mother said:

"I am the door of Heaven and the help of people on earth. I am your Heavenly Mother who descends to my children of the earth to give you safety and protection. I am the Anchor grasped by the humble, the destitute, the lost who go to seek God. I ask you for courage and surrender. Come out of the dark. Abandon yourself in the arms of your Heavenly Mother. Glory be forever to the Lord."

On August 7, 1988, the Blessed Mother asked Gladys to tell the world:

"Pray for all the children of the Universe. For those in need of bread, for those who are deprived of love, and above all of the word of God. The one who is compassionate with a child is compassionate with God. The one who gives love to a child gives love to God. The one who reveals the word of God to a child is truly a child of God. May the Lord be praised."

On January 31, 1984, the Blessed Mother showed Gladys a large saloon filled with drunken young people. Then she explained:

"These young people are calamities. They are human spoils. Children of effective parents do not come to these places, for God's will is not respected here, nor in places such as these. None is seeking the Lord in this place. Pray for the young people of the world who have not found God. Pray for those who, ill-advisedly, behave shamefully. The

Lord can rescue them because He is merciful and loves His children. Read Galatians 6:2–10."

On September 13, 1986, the Blessed Mother said:

"The earth, polluted because of the evil one and his rebel cohorts, shall be cleansed by the grace of God from this day forward. This requires honest attitudes, purity of heart, and surrender to the Lord. He sends to you His own Mother, for I am Queen of the Angels.

"It is my Immaculate Heart that asks His children to return to Him. It is my Immaculate Heart that speaks to you. It is my Immaculate Heart where Jesus desires to see humanity. Cleansed, you will see life. Glory be to the Lord of all Creation."

On September 29, 1989, the Blessed Mother said:

"Today you have the special protection of the archangels. They fight intrepidly as messengers of God against evil under all its forms. . . . They defend souls against the perils of the devil. They open a path of light for the soul in the midst of darkness. They restore health of body. In harmony with the Holy Spirit, they prepare the soul with a heightened desire for salvation."

On August 31, 1985, the Blessed Mother sent this message to God's faithful children from San Nicholás:

"Do not look for rest day or night. It is necessary to evangelize."

In Argentina, on March 26, 1988, Our Lady of the Most Holy Rosary of San Nicholás announced the imminent return of her Divine Son Jesus:

> *"The coming of the Savior is imminent. As the Gospel says, no one knows the date or the hour, but the hour will come, and it is certain that the soul of the Christian must be prepared for that hour. Even the stones will be witnesses to it. That is why I, His Mother, want you to make known the Word of My Son."*

The last public message of Our Lady of the Holy Rosary of San Nicholás occurred on February 11, 1990.

On the twenty-fifth of each month, the same day as the first apparition, a large procession fills the streets of the area during the hour preceding a special Mass presided over by the bishop. In gratitude, the believers of San Nicholás prepare for the coming of the Lord.[12]

CHAPTER EIGHT

Mother Most Admirable

"There is nothing concealed that will not be revealed, nor secret that will not be known. Therefore, whatever you have said in the darkness will be heard in the light, and what you have whispered behind closed doors will be proclaimed on the housetops. I tell you, my friends, do not be afraid of those who kill the body but after that can do no more. I shall show you whom to fear. Be afraid of the one who after killing has the power to cast into Gehenna [hell]; yes, I tell you, be afraid of that one.

"Are not five sparrows sold for two small coins? Yet not one of them has escaped the notice of God. Even the hairs of your head have all been counted. Do not be afraid. You are worth more than many sparrows.

"I tell you, everyone who acknowledges me before others the Son of Man will acknowledge before the angels of God. But whoever denies Me before others will be denied before the angels of God."

LUKE 12:2–8

Holland: 1945 to 1959

All over the world experts study the possibility that the fulfillment of the revelation of God's plan for His people is contained in the messages of the Lady of All Nations.[1] In the spring of 1945, beginning on March 25, the messages were delivered in Holland and in Germany to a simple, unmarried office worker, about forty years old, from the city of Amsterdam.

World War II was raging. The people of Holland still speak of the winter of 1945 as the "hunger winter," for many did not know how they could endure in the face of such hardship. The amazing series of apparitions and messages that came to Amsterdam from Heaven are only now being understood.

Quite unexpectedly, the seer saw a brilliant light. She described the experience:

> I . . . suddenly saw a light coming . . . I saw the light coming nearer. The wall disappeared before my eyes, with all the rest that was standing there. There was, instead, one sea of light and an empty space. It was neither sunlight nor electric light. I can't explain what sort of light it was. . . . Out of it I suddenly saw an image move forward, a living figure, a female form. She was clad in white and wore a blue sash. She stood with her arms lowered, and the palms of her hands turned outward, towards me. As I stared, a strange insight, a strange feeling came over me; I asked myself, what is this? And even now I don't understand how I dared to think it: I thought, it must be the Blessed Virgin, it can't be anything else. . . . Then, all at once, the person began to speak to me. "Repeat what I say." . . . When the Lady had told me all she wanted me to say after her, she withdrew very slowly. Only after that, the

light too disappeared, and I saw everything around me in the room as it had always been.[2]

Some experts who have studied the apparitions which occurred from March 25, 1945, until May 31, 1959, say the heretofore obscure messages of Amsterdam point to a "Second Advent," a "New Beginning," or a "New Era" of peace, tranquillity, and unity among people and nations.[3] The visionary, Ida Pederman, experienced the presence of the Blessed Virgin Mary as her own Eternal Mother: The Beautiful Lady's smile of love for her penetrated to the depths of her comprehension. The Beautiful Lady spoke to Ida about the times and events that would unfold around the world.[4] She told the visionary:

"I who am all tranquillity have come from Heaven. In all tranquillity I shall return to Him who has sent me."[5]

The Beautiful Lady identified herself as Mary, the Mother, or the Lady, of All Nations and All People. More than fifty apparitions occurred, concluding on May 31, the feast of the Visitation, in 1959.

The Mother of All People spoke with deep compassion of those who had become so engrossed in the affairs of the world that their spirits were suffering. She told the visionary:

"I have already come upon this earth in many forms."

She disclosed that God has sent her to the earth as the Mother of All People, to lead all nations to the lovely morning beyond the darkness of violence, disbelief, materialism, and despair.

In the fifty-first vision of Ida, the Mother of Jesus Christ said:

"I have constantly, in a veiled fashion, foretold these times. Very well, peoples of the earth, these times have arrived."

The Lady of All Nations disclosed at Amsterdam:

"God the Son came in accordance with the will of the Father. Now it is Spirit who will come into the world; and I have been sent so that this event may be prayed for."

The visionary says that from out of the immense light she saw the clear outline of the Blessed Virgin Mary as the Mother of All People. Mary's hands were outstretched. Dazzling, glorious rays of light emanated from her palms. She stood upon a globe with a life-size cross at her back.

This description of the Blessed Mother as the Lady of All Nations has been the subject of many images: paintings, icons, and statues that are now in churches, convents, rectories, homes, schools, hospitals, and offices throughout the world. One such statue, in the chapel of the convent at Akita, Japan, wept tears and blood during the apparitions and messages to Sister Agnes that are described in Chapter 6 of this book.

The Mother of All People, whose Son Jesus fulfilled the laws of Moses without disturbing eternal doctrine, spoke at Amsterdam about the various religions of the world to the visionary:

"The doctrine is good, but the laws can and must be changed. . . . You must be in step with the times. . . . Let a movement be set on foot to mobilize the laity."

The Lady of All Nations stressed the need for learning disciplines that are in keeping with modern enlightenment, including theology, philosophy, psychology, sociology, science, art, and literature. Her messages are an invitation to discard the accretions that obscure the dignity, beauty, holiness, and preciousness of all God's creation, especially humanity.

The central theme of the apparitions in Holland and Germany expresses a divine call for unity among all people on earth under God. The Blessed Mother said:

"The Lord and Master wishes to bring spiritual unity to the peoples of this world. It is for this that He sends Myriam {Mary}, and He sends her as the Lady of All People."

The Lady of All Nations spoke of

"a new Era when all peoples will acknowledge the Kingship of Jesus Christ . . . to the end that all people may be one in Jesus Christ."

She showed the visionary the churches of England, Armenia, and Russia bound together by one cord. The Pope was shown to be instrumental in this unification.

The messages of the Lady of All Nations indicate that the unity of all peoples of the world will come in the full flowering of the mystery of God's plan. She points to a springtime, a new world filled with peace, joy, and abiding love.

The Lady of All Nations leaves little doubt that the advent of the Lord Jesus, in ways that we yet do not comprehend, is imminent. She said:

"When the time of the Lord Jesus will arrive, you will see that the false prophets, war, disputes will disappear. Now this time is going to come and there will be peace, true peace. Peoples of the world, this true peace is the Kingdom of God, and it is closer than ever. Let these words be clearly understood."

The Lady of All Nations spoke about the outpouring of the Holy Spirit to accomplish this great work of unification. When the light of truth shines on earth, Satan will be driven from the nations. Even now, Satan and all his violence is being unmasked.

The Blessed Mother spoke to this generation in Holland and Germany about her role in these times:

"The Mother of All People as the Lady of All Nations has now received the power to come to drive out Satan."

She who is the Queen of Humility has come to drive the proud and mighty spirits of human degradation and despair from the earth through the power of human prayer.

The following prayer has been approved for all nations by the church and is widely circulated among people of every faith, race, and nation:

Lord Jesus Christ, Son of the Father,
Send now Your Spirit over the earth.
Let the Holy Spirit live in the hearts of all peoples,
That they may be preserved from corruption, disaster and war.
May the Mother of All Peoples, who once was Mary,
Be our advocate. Amen.

The final apparition occurred on May 31, 1959. The following are excerpts from the visionary's description of what she saw and heard.

From my window I suddenly saw a great light in the sky. I was amazed and shouted to my relations, "Look! There!" pointing into the air. It was a light, but so intense that it was impossible to gaze upon it. I could not look into the powerful light and covered my eyes with my hands. Yet I was compelled to look at it. It seemed that the sky was torn apart—it really was a tearing apart of the sky! Then I suddenly saw the Lady! She was enveloped in dazzling glory. I had never before seen her in such splendor! I saw nothing but the dazzling Lady at the center of this immense, inexplicable glory.

I cannot possibly describe this heavenly, powerful, splendid sight. I saw no sheep, no Cross, only the Lady, with rays of dazzling glory about her!

She wore a crown. Never before had I seen her wear a crown. I saw no gold or diamonds, yet I know very well that it was a crown; she now wore a crown. Its gold and diamonds were made of light. It sparkled with light more brilliant than the rarest diamonds and the finest gold. The Lady herself was one explosion of immense, extraordinary light. She was heavenly, glorious! I cannot explain with only words.

Below this glorious manifestation of the Lady was the ordinary, blue sky. Beneath the sky was the top portion of the globe. This was completely black. Then I saw the Lady moving her finger from one side to the other and shaking her head as if in disapproval and warning. And I heard her say: "Do penance."

Then something very strange happened. From the dark globe there rose up a vast number of human heads. Gradually, from the depths of the globe all kinds of people ascended to the surface of the hemisphere. I pondered this scene, thinking, "How is it that there are so many races and nations of people?"

The Lady then extended her hands in blessing over all these people, and the sadness left her face. I heard, "Make amends to Him."

Suddenly the Lady disappeared. In her place, I saw an immense Host. It was an enormous Host but quite a normal one like those we see in church.

Then a chalice appeared in front of the Host. It was made of magnificent gold. The chalice then toppled over towards me. I saw thick streams of blood pouring from the chalice upon the globe and spilling over the earth. It was a very distressing sight and I became filled with horror.

Suddenly the bloody vision melted into a brilliant, dazzling Sacred Host. It shone so brightly that I felt temporarily blinded from its brilliance. The Host seemed to be made of white fire. In the center of the dazzling Host was a small opening of sorts. I cannot describe it any better. Suddenly, the Host splintered, it seemed to burst open. A figure emerged. His appearance was so sublime, such depth of power emanated from him and he possessed such majesty that fear gripped me. I dared not look upon him. While I contemplated this unique Being, the thought kept recurring in my mind, "And yet there are two." But when I looked, I saw only one. Still my mind kept repeating, "And yet there are two."

And suddenly, from the center of the two there burst forth an indescribable light. In the light, I saw a Dove emerge out from the center. It shot faster than the speed of lightning down towards the globe, radiating such immense, dazzling light that I feared for my eyes. What sublime splendor! What magnificent glory! The soaring Being, majestic, powerful, regal: and the world now all bathed in light from the radiant Dove! A voice rang out, "He who eats me and drinks me, takes eternal life and receives the True Spirit."

All this lasted for a time. Then the Lady appeared again, exactly as she had appeared at the beginning. Now I saw, I knew the difference between her splendor and glory, and the grandeur and majesty of the soaring Being.

Total joy seemed to envelop the Lady and I heard her say very softly in the distance, "Adieu!"

The visionary speaks of these times as "the Times of the Holy Spirit." The Lady of All Nations disclosed:

"The struggle is intense, it is hard, but on the condition that you all collaborate, the true Spirit will triumph. . . .

Remember the first and principal commandment: Love. It contains all else."

At Amsterdam, the Lord God chose to bring to humanity a new era. He sends Myriam, Mary, as the Mother of All Peoples, the Lady of All Nations, to carry spiritual unity to His people of this world. As theologians study the important messages from Amsterdam, the Church continues to investigate the apparitions.[6]

Philippines: 1948 and 1986

The ash was slippery on the streets and it was raining gravel and sand. The earth was still trembling underfoot from the eruption of Mount Pinatubo. As we drove through the darkened streets of Manila, our hosts said much of the Philippines now resembled purgatory as described by Vicka of Medjugorje. Countless multitudes of pilgrims from around the world have heard Vicka speak of her journey with the Blessed Mother to Heaven, Hell, and Purgatory. Vicka said of Purgatory:

We could see people in Purgatory, just like a misty, gray fog. It looked like ashes. We could sense persons weeping, moaning, trembling, in what seemed like terrible suffering. The Blessed Mother said:

"These people need your prayers, especially the ones who have no one to pray for them."[7]

Experts in the Philippines say that Pinatubo is the most devastating volcanic eruption of the twentieth century because it will form a permanent layer, a type of ring around the earth, consisting of ashes spewed from the volcano which will alter the climatic temperatures of the entire planet.

In the summer of 1991, my husband and I saw and experienced much goodness, kindness, and graciousness among the people of the Philippines. The climate there is gentle. The vegetation in the countryside is lush. The palm trees are gorgeous. The flowers and the shrubbery are beautiful. Melons and coconuts grow in profusion; people pick them as fast as they can. Everything seems to grow in the soil though much of the land is not tilled. Many do not have the strength to do the backbreaking work that the fertile land demands from sunup to sundown. What a difference a truck would make here, or even a wheelbarrow!

Filipinos are in the process of bringing modern agricultural methods to the Philippines. They supervise coconut orchards, citrus orchards, all different kinds of native fruit trees and their imported counterparts. In the Philippines, nature can be harsh. It is tropical and lush there, but because of the winds and the rains, people must continually sweep the debris, gather the fallen coconuts and the tree limbs and branches. The physical work never abates. It requires many hands to keep up with nature, and big families are valued.

The Philippine Islands have been plagued with earthquakes and typhoons, which have broken down much of the infrastucture in the northern provinces. Some of the concrete highways caved in, the bridges collapsed. Even the buildings that foreign engineers said were structurally sound collapsed like dominoes. Many people lost their homes and their livelihood. Rebuilding continues constantly.

Many Filipinos were living in the most rudimentary huts. Some were so poor they would use anything they could obtain to fashion a roof over their heads. Some of the women in such circumstances looked overworked, and the men looked hopeless. Even the cows looked weary. Two- and three-year-old children were clearing away tree limbs that were knocked down by the storms that followed the eruption of Mount Pinatubo. Though the situation looked dire for the people because of the damage from the volcano, there was a joy and a contentment in the people's demeanor as they clung to one another. There was contentment in the provinces that transcended materialism. The children smiled. The parents beamed as they looked at their children. There seemed to be families everywhere.

In Manila, within a short bicycle ride of the United States Embassy, was some of the most beautiful waterfront property in the world. There, young economists, technocrats, and various leaders of the country shared some of the dramatic political, economic, and spiritual episodes that they and the nation had recently experienced.

Author and television personality June Keithley described a few of the events that took place during the extraordinary days preceding the resignation of President Marcos. The People Power revolt of 1986 drew vast throngs of Filipinos who were chanting in the streets for redress. Their chants, however, were sounds of the recitation of the Rosary, of hymns. Throughout this period, people were also praying and fasting for political reforms in the churches, convents, and homes. Government troops were ordered to disperse the people.

Mrs. Keithley told us that she was dressed in army fatigues as she broadcast news of the extraordinary, peaceful uprising on live television. The masses of people in the streets continued to pray the Rosary endlessly. Many carried statues of the Blessed Mother, whom they fondly referred to as "Mama Mary." Some offered garlands of flowers to the soldiers who stood guard. Some brave nuns climbed up on the tanks that were approaching. Other people lay down on the ground, stopping the oncoming tanks.

No one seemed to be afraid. Everyone shared their food. People who remained at home sent supplies of food and drinks to the streets for those who were demonstrating. Sandwiches were even passed to the soldiers inside the Presidential bunkers, and to Marcos's special officers. A bond of love held the Filipinos close. The Rosary was recited continuously. The melody of the *Ave* sounded after each decade.

Suddenly a "Beautiful Woman, encased in immense bright light and dressed as a nun," was clearly visible. The light was dazzling as the crowds of Philippine people saw her standing in front of the tanks sent to disperse them at any cost to life or property. Mrs. Keithley said she was "stunned" at the beauty of the woman: "She extended her arms outward and spoke in a voice that was clearly audible to everyone:

"Do not kill my people!"

The soldiers in the tanks obviously saw and heard the Beautiful Woman, for they immediately disarmed, refusing to fire on their fellow citizens. Mrs. Keithley broadcast this extraordinary event on live television, and untold thousands of exuberant Filipinos took to the streets. Mama Mary was with them. She herself had come to save them! That night President Marcos left for Hawaii. Many Filipinos told me they know it was the Blessed Mother who was there with them.[8] Expect great things of the Philippines, for it is Mary's garden and the Filipinos are her children. Wherever Mary is, there also is her Son.

People in the Philippines have great devotion to the Mother of God; she is a deeply ingrained part of their culture and heritage. Many of the leaders spoke of the extraordinary graces that the Blessed Mother has brought to the people of the Philippines. Prayer groups have sprung up throughout the islands. People fast voluntarily on Wednesdays and Fridays. Families are trying to live Mama Mary's messages together. A special devotion to Our Mother of Perpetual Help sees almost all the churches filled as people make the novena each Wednesday. Traffic jams caused by the novena-goers do not stifle the enthusiasm of Mama Mary's children.

Philippine leaders observed that people all over the world who revere the Blessed Mother feel networked. The children of Mary experience a mysterious familiar desire for global, national, and local sharing.

The Mother of God gives a powerful message:

"Dear children, prayer and fasting will stop war. It will change the natural law."

Though the Filipinos suffered much themselves from the volcano, they have responded to their brothers and sisters in Bosnia with love, sending food, blankets, medical supplies, money. That attitude on the part of others toward the people of the Philippines could supply farm and building equipment, seed, fertilizer, farm animals, educational scholarships. Human generosity can make the Philippines and the entire world a glorious land of bounty, peace, and contentment.

The Philippine leaders seemed to agree that there are urgent divine revelations coming from the four corners of the earth in these times. They also spoke of miracles that are reported on the five continents as signs of the seriousness of the apparitions. The Philippines has its own special spiritual gift.

We traveled to Lipa where, our hosts said, showers of rose petals were falling from an unknown source.

In 1948, a young novice, Teresita Castillo, was in training to become a Carmelite nun at the Carmelite Convent in Lipa. Sister Teresita had the privilege of several apparitions of the Blessed Mother, who identified herself as Mediatrix of All Grace. The Blessed Mother appeared to her, dressed in white, on at least fifteen occasions. Teresita says she was asked to inform people that the Mother of God would like to be honored on Saturdays under the various titles by which she has been manifested to God's children.

While Teresita was in residence at the convent, extraordinary showers of rose petals fell within the convent walls on several occasions. Many of these rose petals still exist nearly fifty years later and have not spoiled. In May 1949, hundreds of Filipinos reported that they all saw the Blessed Mother as Mary Mediatrix of All Grace appear briefly in the sky above Sampaloc Lake as they assembled to form a procession, carrying an exact replica of the image manifested in Teresita's apparition. There were reports that she was also seen in the San Agustan Cathedral of Cagayan de Oro City.

The rose petal showers continue into present times in various places, often indoors. Many people showed me their rose petals. Some were fresh: They still bore the sweet scent of the flower though it was said they were weeks old—or, in some cases, nearly a half-century old. Each petal was beautiful. Images imprinted upon the petals were of the Blessed Mother, the Lord Jesus, an angel, even Saint Joseph.

The people who showed me their petals believe that the Blessed Mother desires her children to spread the fragrance of the rose petals throughout the world by prayer, fasting, almsgiving, and other good works. Such behavior, they said, fills the heavens with the aroma of the petals.

The members of the Center for Peace in Asia say that every bead of the Rosary is a means to create a rose petal to give back to God. They believe that to say the name of Jesus (which is said at least 150 times during the recitation of the Rosary) with faith, hope, and love is to close the gates of hell for a second. They indicated that when the heavens are filled with rose petals made by God's children of the earth, Satan and his minions will no longer find any space on the earth.

Teresita's final message from the Blessed Mother at the Carmelite Convent on November 12, 1948, was:

"Pray. The people do not heed my words. There will be persecutions, unrest, and bloodshed in your country. The enemy of the church will try to destroy the faith which Je-

sus has established and died for. The Church will suffer much. Pray for the conversion of sinners throughout the world. Pray for those who have rejected me and for those who do not believe my message in the different parts of the world. Spread the meaning of the Rosary because this will be the instrument for peace throughout the world. The love of my Son will soften the hardest of hearts. My motherly love will be their strength."[9]

The apparitions continue to be investigated and it is said that the rose petals continue to fall. The Church has not yet approved the apparitions. Teresita, however, greets pilgrims who come to the Carmelite Convent of Lipa on Saturdays. She shows them the replica statue of Our Lady Mediatrix of All Grace on a side altar of the convent chapel. She speaks to the pilgrims about her messages from Mama Mary.

In the Philippines, the presumed presence of the Blessed Mother has brought spiritual showers of roses among the people everywhere. Countless are the faithful who are actively involved with prayer groups, daily Mass, recitation of the Rosary in homes, schools, hospitals, and businesses. Roses beget roses. Love begets love. Abundance begets abundance. Peace begets peace. Filipinos pray for the time to come when showers of roses fill the earth and the heavens.

PART THREE

Mother Most Faithful

Messages from Heaven flood the twentieth century with awareness of the divine horizon against which all human activity occurs. People of all faiths, all religions, and nations are hearing and seeing the Mother of God as never before in recorded history. Just as she manifested her Infant Son to Saint Joseph, the shepherds, and the wise men on the first Christmas, so now in this time of the new advent the Mother of Jesus Christ is manifesting her Divine Son to people all over the world. The Mother of Jesus Christ is forever His Mother Most Faithful, for she leads all those who respond to her global call to her Divine Son Jesus with the words:

"Do whatever He tells you."

The message of the Gospel is eternal. Jesus said:

"If you love me, you will keep my commandments. And I will ask the Father, and he will give you another Advocate

*to be with you always, the Spirit of truth, which
the world cannot accept, because it neither sees nor
knows it. But you know it, because it remains
with you, and will be in you. I will not leave you
orphans; I will come to you. In a little while the
world will no longer see me, but you will see me,
because I live and you will live. On that day you
will realize that I am in my Father and you are
in me and I in you. Whoever has my commandments and observes them is the one who loves me.
And whoever loves me will be loved by my Father,
and I will love him and reveal myself to him."*

JOHN 14:15–21

You shall see in Part III that, in a special way, the
Blessed Mother prepares human souls to comprehend the depths of the truths of the Gospel of her
Son when she appears on the earth. The Blessed
Virgin Mary has always been known as the Mediatrix of All Graces by the Universal Church. The
graces she mediates have their source in the divine
mercy of her Son.

Apparitions of the Blessed Mother during the
last fifteen years have preceded immense periods of
change that have swept away life as people understood it. Her appearances at Rwanda were followed
by brutal war that turned the area into a sea of
blood. Her ongoing appearances now in Medjugorje, Bosnia, present the entire world with the
opportunity to respond to her global call for peace.

Apparitions of the Blessed Mother at Medjugorje are of a number and duration unlike any others in the recorded history of Christianity. The Blessed Mother speaks at Medjugorje of her final apparition on earth. Six visionaries there speak of ten secrets that involve the final chapter in the history of the earth. At Medjugorje, the Blessed Mother told the visionaries that she would appear in every home on earth, if necessary, in these times. "Everyone will be warned!" state the visionaries.

Throughout history humans have always intuited a divine horizon against which all human activities occur. From the beginning, they have perceived that they are accountable to the divine for their behavior, and they have responded in diverse ways.

People's values and perceptions of personal worth are deeply rooted in specific family and cultural traditions. As the twentieth century ends, telecommunications has created a global village. Intercultural exchanges happen now in the privacy of one's home.

A crisis of values now challenges everyone. Values are dangerous when they are not rooted in truth. Secular morality has failed. The people of the world cry. There is a universal longing to be anchored in the divine reality that exists beyond the mind, yet summons all those who think and reason.

A global hunger for truth sends peoples of all races, cultures, and faiths to the mountains of Fatima, Portugal, in search of God, to the Bosnian village of Medjugorje, to the heights of the Andes in the teeming rain of Ecuador, to the ancient shrines in the Holy Land, in Kiev, in Constantinople, Peking, and Rome.

Thinking, feeling, caring people today search for tools of their own bright renaissance. Enlightened people recognize that the twenty-first century demands a new rationality that encompasses our whole human personality and does not simply pay homage to reason alone.

No one scoffs at the possibility that our high-tech towers of babel could crumble before our eyes in the wake of natural disaster or nuclear holocaust. Tools to prevent war and natural disaster are a gift of the apparitions of the Blessed Mother in the twentieth century. At Medjugorje, the tools are emphasized repeatedly. The simplicity of the messages belies their profundity. The miracle of the sun that first awakened the world at Fatima occurs at Medjugorje, and around the world for those who respond to the messages of Medjugorje.

The many other apparitions of the twentieth century, several of which will be presented in the following pages, have told the Gospel message of Jesus Christ throughout the world in the voice of a tender mother who loves each person on earth with total and unconditional love. She speaks the simple message of her Son Jesus:

"The Lord our God is Lord alone. You shall love the Lord your God with all your heart, with all your soul, with all your mind, and

with all your strength. . . . You shall love
your neighbor as yourself."

Apparitions of the Blessed Mother teach all people
how to do that.

The Blessed Mother asks people to share their
homes, their goods, their talents. She asks people to
help one another. She pleads with people to forgive
one another.

It is virtuous to share. Those who do not share
their expertise, their goods and services to help the
extremely poor create the conditions for their own
destruction. From earliest times virtue has proved
to be its own reward. Goodness begets goodness.

Those who share demonstrate that they comprehend the divine hand of the Gift-giver. They
drink deep of the wellspring of life. Those who do
not share, who live at the beck and call of their sensual appetites, only consume and die. Those who
recognize truth rise above the mountain of human
concerns to the empyrean heights of love.

Apparitions of the Blessed Virgin Mary and
her Divine Son Jesus bring glorious opportunities
and gifts to those with the courage to look and to
respond. Love begets love.

CHAPTER NINE

Queen of Peace

"Much will be required of the person entrusted with much,
and still more will be demanded of the person entrusted
with more."

LUKE 12:48

Medjugorje, Bosnia: since 1981

The Bible indicates that the prophet Elijah did not die.
Rather he traveled by chariot to an unknown place. His return is expected in the end times (Matthew 17:11). Local
villagers in Medjugorje claim that they began seeing the
prophet Elijah riding his chariot in the sky during the
month of May 1981, one month before the reported apparitions of the Blessed Mother began there on the feast of
John the Baptist.[1]

An ecumenical apparition that has attained extraordinary international significance occurs in the former
Republic of Yugoslavia, in a tiny farm village known as
Medjugorje, located in the heart of war-ravaged Bosnia. Between fifteen and twenty million people of all faiths, races,
and nations have traveled to this remote hamlet since 1981,
though the apparition remains under investigation by the

Church and is yet to be approved. The local bishop, however, has arranged pastoral support for the unprecedented numbers of pilgrims who continue to swarm to this humble village paradoxically known as the "oasis of peace."

The East and the West touch at Medjugorje. Catholics, Muslims, Croats, and Serbs live side by side. Each group, separately and collectively, reveres and venerates the Blessed Virgin Mary with personal traditions and devotions.

There, on June 24, 1981, a brilliant light hovered over a small mountain known as Podbrdo. In that mysterious light, sixteen-year-old Mirjana Dragicevic from Sarajevo, and her fifteen-year-old friend from Mostar, Ivanka Ivankovic, both saw a Beautiful Woman standing on Podbrdo, holding a baby. According to the girls, she was surrounded by exquisite rays of light and they could see her quite clearly even though she was at a distance of more than three soccer fields. The girls were quite frightened and fled to the nearby relatives' houses where they were spending the summer. Later that evening, Mirjana, Ivanka, and a few other teenagers went back to the mountain, where they once again saw the woman of extraordinary beauty.[2]

Jacov Çolo was nine years old when the apparitions began. He and his mother, who was ill with alcoholism, lived in a small house located near the home of Mirjana's relatives. Jacov was a small, frail child whose father had abandoned him when he was very young. He was quite fond of Mirjana and often followed her around the village. Mirjana, a deeply sensitive person, always felt kindly towards Jacov.[3]

On the first night of the apparition, Jacov heard the

girls in the neighborhood speak excitedly about the vision that Ivanka and Mirjana had seen earlier. He was intrigued by the possibility that the baby they spoke of seeing might be the Lord Jesus. Jacov had always taken delight in the large manger scene on display in the parish church of Saint James during the Christmas season. He disclosed later that he has always had a special fondness for the Infant Jesus.[4]

When a few teenagers decided to return to Podbrdo on the next evening, June 25, to see if the vision they had seen the previous evening would happen again, Jacov asked Mirjana to take him along. Mirjana could not refuse him, because his eyes were "shining with love." As the group ran to the mountain on that warm, humid evening, Jacov tugged at Mirjana's arm, saying, "Will you ask her [the Blessed Mother] if I can see her Baby too?"[5]

Others who were running to the mountain with Mirjana and Jacov were Ivanka, who was leading the way; her friend Vicka Ivankovic; Vicka's neighbor, Marija Pavlovic, whose sister Milka had been in the group the night before; and sixteen-year-old Ivan Dragicevic. Several villagers followed the children at a distance. Suddenly the children stopped; then, as though they had wings, they ran towards an invisible being, totally unaware of the jagged rocks and dense vegetation that seemed no barrier under their flying feet.

The adults were frightened when they saw the way the children ascended to a higher place on the mountain. Then they saw the children fall to their knees in ecstasy. Scrambling over the rocks to approach the children, they began to shout: "Is it the Blessed Mother?" "Ask her about . . . [The villagers began to inquire about their family members who were dead. They wanted to know if their relatives were in Heaven. They also asked for cures for their sick and injured].*"

The six visionaries each saw the Blessed Mother quite clearly. She was surrounded by a light so intense as she stood on the mountain that the children experienced her clothed with the sun itself. She wore a crown of twelve stars. Her veil was of luminescent white and she wore a pearl-gray dress. She held a baby in her arms. Slowly she covered the Infant; then she was seen to uncover Him to show Him to the children.[6]

As the apparition ended, the Blessed Mother told the children that she would come the next day to the place lower down on the mountain where she had appeared to them the first day. Then she said:

"Go in the peace of God."

Mirjana and Ivanka were swooning. The other children were silent. The visionaries began to walk slowly down the mountain. Crowds followed behind.

Suddenly Marija bolted to the left and ran down a small path. Others went behind her to see what had excited her. They found her kneeling in ecstasy. Marija later explained that she saw a shining cross radiating all the colors of the rainbow. The Blessed Mother was standing in front of the empty cross weeping copiously as she said:

"Peace. Only peace! You must seek peace. There must be peace on earth! You must be reconciled with God and with each other! Peace! Only peace!"

Marija knelt there in the light of the shining cross and entrusted her entire life to the beautiful Blessed Mother of Medjugorje. At that moment, she realized that the Blessed Mother of the Lord Jesus Christ had come to Medjugorje to inspire the entire world to peace: "Peace in our own hearts, peace in our families, then peace in the world."[7]

Communist officials suspected that the six visionaries were part of a nationalist plot, so they persecuted the children, their families, and the pastor, Father Jozo Zovko. Father Jozo was thrown into prison and held for several years on charges of sedition. (A movie of his trials and the surrounding apparitions, entitled *Gospa*, opened in American theaters in the spring of 1995.) Each day the children continued to have their daily apparitions. The visionaries seemed immature, even superficial, to the officials, who sometimes forbade them from going to the mountain for their apparitions.

A real problem the officials recognized was that few in the village were doing any work. The people were following the visionaries. Everyone wanted the glimpse of Heaven that they hoped the Virgin could bring to their harsh lives. In response to her apparitions, confirmed for them by the great rays of light seen while the visionaries were in ecstasy, the Catholics flocked to Saint James Church to attend Mass, to recite the Rosary, to return to sacramental confession after many years, to receive the Holy Eucharist. The Muslims and the Orthodox in the village also dramatically increased their prayer life in response to the apparitions.[8]

Gradually people from all over the world found out about the daily apparitions and came to Medjugorje to experience such blessings themselves. Dramatic miraculous physical healings have increased the worldwide popularity of Medjugorje. Yet Church officials deny that Medjugorje is a place of physical healings. They stress that "Medjugorje" is no longer just a location in Bosnia, but rather is "a condition of the heart" that is meant for everyone on earth and the souls in purgatory.[9]

Medjugorje, the visionaries say, is about conversion of each human heart. The Blessed Mother has disclosed that all people on earth are seeking that gift, for at the deepest level the human heart longs and pines for union with God.

Millions have witnessed and are witnessing at Medjugorje and throughout the world now the cosmic miracle of the sun that first manifested at Fatima on October 13, 1917. Millions around the world who have responded to the requests of the Blessed Mother at Medjugorje have been shocked to witness the chain of their own rosary beads turn to gold. Vicka says that the Blessed Mother smiled as she saw the delight of the many pilgrims whose rosaries turned gold during the recitation of the Rosary on a cold winter evening of her apparition in mid-January 1982. Vicka says the Blessed Mother told her that golden rosaries are meant to be a sign that prayer changes human hearts, human circumstances, human endeavors:

"Prayer changes all life on earth and hereafter."[10]

All religions are represented among the pilgrims who have flocked to the village of peace in the heart of Bosnia. The Beautiful Lady announced from Apparition Hill:

"Do not be afraid, dear angels. I am the Mother of God. I am the Queen of Peace. I am the Mother of all people."

Mirjana and Ivanka report that they have received ten secrets from the Blessed Mother that contain the final chapters in the history of the world. Further, the two say that the Blessed Mother desires them to advise everyone in the world that after the secrets are fulfilled she will have no need to appear on earth again.

Mirjana and Ivanka each now experience a public apparition of the Blessed Mother once a year. The purpose of the yearly apparitions is to strengthen the visionaries regarding the secrets they carry, all of which shall unfold during their lifetime. Mirjana and Ivanka each deliver a public message at the conclusion of their annual apparitions to strengthen the interested people of the world as they prepare themselves for what lies ahead. The other four visionaries continue to see the Mother of Jesus Christ daily.

A paradox of the messages of Medjugorje, which many experience in futuristic terms as they ponder what the ten secrets might be, is the power of the messages in the present moment. Each message holds enough wisdom to lead people deep into the beauty, dignity, holiness, and opportunity of the here and now. Today well-lived makes tomorrow a happy vision and yesterday a joyful memory.

In the heart of Bosnia, the Mother of Jesus Christ continues to warn people through the six visionaries that peace in the world is fragile. She says that God has sent her to these times to help everyone on earth seek immediate conversion of heart through intense prayer. In the spring of 1982, the Blessed Mother promised the visionaries:

"If it is necessary, I will appear in each home."

On April 4, 1985, the Blessed Mother told the world, through the six visionaries:

"I wish to continue giving you messages as never before in history since the beginning of time."

On August 25, 1987, the Blessed Mother announced from Medjugorje:

"Dear children, . . . God has permitted me . . . to speak to you and to spur you on to holiness."

People all over the world claim that they hear the voice of the Blessed Mother in these times. Theologians admit that there has never been a global outpouring of divine manifestations of this magnitude in the known history of the world.[11]

The visionaries of Medjugorje have each said that no one in the world will be excluded from the messages delivered by the Blessed Mother. People everywhere are becoming aware of the seriousness of the times and the opportunities entrusted to humanity. The Queen of Peace calls personally to everyone in the world from the mountains of Bosnia:

"Comprehend the greatness of this message I am giving you" (October 25, 1988).

She announces:

"I intercede for you before God that He will give you the gift of conversion of heart. I call you and exhort you to a deep spiritual life and to simplicity" (December 25, 1989).

The original six children are by now among the most famous visionaries in the world. The Blessed Mother told them that no other visionaries in history have received the graces they have been given, nor will any others be called to their graces. The visionaries of Medjugorje are therefore highly chosen souls. They did not earn the gifts they have. They possess the freedom to respond to these graces as they choose.

The Blessed Mother is said to have told the six visionaries that God permitted her to choose any children on earth for the gifts she has brought to the visionaries at Medjugorje. When they tearfully asked her why she chose them, the Blessed Mother smiled with pure love as she advised them:

"I do not always choose the best!"

The Blessed Mother disclosed a love-filled fact:

"You shall find me in many places that are not pleasant."

Mirjana and Ivanka, the first to see the Blessed Mother, continue to guard their ten ominous secrets, which, they say, include chastisements for the wickedness of the times and involve the final chapters in the history of the world. The two specify that after the events foretold to them by the Blessed Mother occur, during their lifetime, those who are still alive will have little time to convert. The visionaries report that after the secrets of Medjugorje are realized, the Blessed Mother will no longer need to appear on the earth. Since Marian apparitions are deeply rooted in human history, such information is a mystery.

During the winter of 1993, as the Bosnian war raged, a small group of young men went into Sarajevo and rescued a busload of residents who were trapped in the besieged city. Among those rescued were Mirjana's father and younger brother. While the father and brother were trapped, Mirjana and other family members took seriously the Blessed Mother's message:

> *"My children, you have forgotten. Prayer and fasting can put off wars. It can alter the laws of nature"* (July 21, 1982).

Committing herself to intense prayer and fasting on behalf of her loved ones, Mirjana lost in excess of twenty pounds.

The Blessed Mother told the visionaries on June 26, 1982:

> *"I desire to be with you in order that the entire world may be converted and reconciled."*

On many levels, the apparitions are a macabre paradox. Bullets fly, bombs explode, UN troops are held hostage, and casualties escalate in Bosnia, yet the daily apparitions of the Queen of Peace continue in Medjugorje.

By June 1995, no war casualties were reported in

Medjugorje, where the six visionaries continued to dwell, though they could, if they chose, live anywhere in the world. The heavenly promise of conversion and reconciliation of the entire world remains a profound mystery as war continues daily in Bosnia.

The Messages of Medjugorje

Faith: Strong faith in the presence, love, and providence of God.

Prayer: Especially the Rosary. The Blessed Mother continues at Medjugorje to ask all people on earth, of all religions and beliefs, to meditate on the life of her Divine Son Jesus each day by praying all fifteen decades of the Rosary. The fruit of such prayer, she reminds people, is *enlightenment*, which brings *peace* in the heart, *peace* in families, *peace* in cities, *peace* in nations, and *peace* in the world. The history of nations where the Rosary is prayed by the population demonstrates that peace and prosperity are fruits of the Rosary.[12]

Prayer Groups have been requested by the Blessed Mother. She asks that all people on earth form prayer groups as a personal spiritual support system in these times. The Blessed Mother has even given the rules for the prayer groups.[13]

The Bible: The only international language that binds people together in peace and abundance is the sacred Word and will of God. The Blessed Mother at Medjugorje asks all people on earth to read the sacred books daily and allow their meaning to be realized in the behavior of daily living.

Fasting: The Blessed Mother has requested all people on earth, of all religions and beliefs, for voluntary fasting on Wednesdays and Fridays for world peace. People of all beliefs, from all over the world, fasting from nonnecessities themselves, have sent money, food, clothes, blankets, and medical supplies to Bosnia to share with the less fortunate caught in the war. If people learn to fast for the love of God and one another, no one on earth will do without. All will have enough.

Reconciliation: The Blessed Mother warns all people of all nations: *"Hurry and be reconciled."* The Blessed Mother asks people to quickly make peace with one another and with God. A sacramental way for those who are able is sacramental confession, a means of starting life over again with a clean slate. The Blessed Mother tells the world at Medjugorje that the giving and receiving of forgiveness is the only path to peace.

Mirjana

The weather was miserably hot in Medjugorje, Yugoslavia. Few houses in the small village that swarmed with pilgrims from all over the world had adequate running water. Food supplies were meager, though the huge black grapes that hung in profusion on the arbor of each tiny stucco house provided a welcome supplement. Cows and chickens languished in the humidity. There was no hint of a breeze as our small group assembled at the home of university student Mirjana Dragicevic, from the nearby city of Sarajevo. The date was August 15, 1988.

Mirjana was most hospitable. She graciously welcomed my family and some friends who were with us and invited us to sit in the cool dining room of her uncle's home. There she answered questions about her apparitions and the ten secrets she carries.

The Blessed Mother disclosed the ten secrets about the future of the world during daily apparitions to Mirjana in 1981 and 1982. According to the visionary, these ten secrets, which involve the whole world, have been written by a divine source on a parchment that only Mirjana can read. She asserts, however, that she herself has no need to refer to the parchment, for the secrets she carries are of such a cataclysmic nature that Mirjana can never forget the day or the date on which each event will occur.

Ten days before the event described in each secret occurs, Mirjana will be permitted to reveal the event to Father Petar Ljubicic, a local Franciscan friar. He has agreed to fast and pray for seven days after he receives the secret. There is some question whether Father Ljubicic must communicate the secret to the world, as Medjugorje centers around the world await, or whether he is to inform only Church officials and their diplomatic contacts. The major news bureaus of the significant broadcasting media have been to Medjugorje, and their experts have questioned the visionaries and the villagers. They are prepared.

During that memorable visit in Medjugorje on August 15, 1988, Mirjana's graciousness belied the gravity of the stories she shared. She said that during one unforgettable apparition the Blessed Mother was quite sorrowful and was in fact weeping. Mirjana said she was deeply distressed to see the tears of the Blessed Mother, who by that time had become even closer to her than her own mother. "Why are you so sad, dear Blessed Mother?" she asked, trying to console the Mother of Jesus. Mirjana said that the angels surrounding the Blessed Mother seemed to bear her sorrow as she confided:

> *"Many of God's children have fallen into error in these times. They have responded to the test that the angels once endured with similar rebellion. They bring much suffering upon themselves and their children because they do not recognize truth."*

Mirjana explained that the first secret will break the power of Satan. The Blessed Mother told her of this twentieth century, in which Satan and his followers have tremendous powers never available to them before. After the first secret is realized, these powers will never be given to them again. The people of these times live in a period of immense trials and tribulations as they continuously battle the power of evil.

Mirjana quietly, but with a gentle firmness, confided that the Blessed Mother is appearing in these times by a special mercy of God to warn all people of the ubiquitous power of Satan and to lead God's children from his snares. Demonic power will be broken as the first secret entrusted to Mirjana unfolds. Only the visionary knows the second secret.

The Third Secret of Medjugorje

The third secret has been described by all six visionaries of Medjugorje as a permanent, indestructible, and beautiful sign on Apparition Hill at the site of the first apparition of the Blessed Mother. There is some conjecture that the permanent sign at Medjugorje will be the great column of light, the Shechinah that the Jews followed out of the desert to the Promised Land. If indeed such is the permanent sign, the faithful Jews will be the first to recognize its divine significance.

The time preceding the permanent sign is described by the visionaries as a period of grace for the deepening of the faith of all people; the result will be conversion and reconciliation among people throughout the entire world. The visionaries of Medjugorje all firmly announce that the permanent sign will occur during their lifetime.

The visionaries say that no one will be able to touch the permanent sign. It will, however, be possible to see it and to photograph it.

Jacov Çolo has shared his understanding that world leaders will be the first ones to see the permanent sign on Apparition Hill. He said that those who know how to pray develop eyes to see truth. They comprehend that peace flows from the river of love. The river of love flows from the heart of God. He explained that it is urgent for all those who want to live to follow the messages of the Blessed Mother and learn to pray with the heart now. (See Vicka section herein.)

Mirjana says that by the time the third secret occurs those who are still alive will have little time to convert.[14]

Her apocalyptic statement is shocking. Will much of the world's population die before the permanent sign comes? Mirjana's face filled with compassion as she pondered the question. Though she responded in the affirmative, she said that for believers death is a gentle passing from one place of existence to another. "Believers are happy on earth and in Heaven too," she said. "The only importance is to always do God's will faithfully. Those who know and obey God's will have Heaven on earth!"

In 1981, when the apparitions began, no one had ever heard of the HIV virus. People believed that, with antibiotics, microbial infection as a death sentence was finally eliminated. The world also trusted that concentration and rape camps in Europe were a nightmare of the past. The conflicts in Bosnia and Rwanda have awakened the entire world to the insufficiency of human reason in the face of insanity.

People all over the world address the questions: Do the apparitions at Medjugorje and on all the continents signal to the world that humanity has entered the final stages of the end times referred to in the New Testament? Do Mirjana's apparitions concern the Apocalypse or the Second Coming of Christ as prophesied in Scripture? She herself has answered.[15] As urgent as the messages of Medjugorje are, they present nothing that is not already contained in the Gospel.

Mirjana frequently quotes the Blessed Mother:

"Those who pray come to know God. Those who know God have only peace."

Marija

The Blessed Mother began giving monthly messages from Medjugorje to the world through Marija Pavlovic on March 1, 1984. Marija is tall, with dark hair and dark brown eyes. She was born on April 1, 1965. It is said that she suffered from malnutrition as a child, though Marija has spoken only with love of her family life. When her apparitions began, Marija was astounded to learn that other people had experienced apparitions of the Blessed Virgin Mary. She admits that she had never heard of any others, not even those of Lourdes or Fatima.

Marija's day was not unlike that of others her age in the village of Medjugorje, though she may have had more personal hardship than others. She tended sheep, washed the family clothes by hand, and hung them out to dry in her hilly backyard that abuts Mount Podbrdo. She cooked meals, washed dishes, and spent time with her friends. One thing, however, had changed forever: Marija's heart. She had given it with no strings attached to the Mother of Jesus at the shining cross on the first day of her apparitions. Marija even found a little time to pray.

The Blessed Mother always prays with the visionaries during their apparitions. In the first days when the Blessed Mother asked for recitation of the Rosary, Marija lamented: "Oh Blessed Mother, I don't have time!" The Blessed Mother asked Marija, and all the visionaries, to pray a minimum of seven Our Fathers, seven Hail Marys, and seven Glory Be to the Fathers every day for peace.

Marija's priorities began to change ever so slowly. She found time, not only for one, but for three Rosaries for peace every day. She found her way to daily Mass at Saint James Church. Marija helped the sacristan, helped the sisters in charge of cleaning the church, spoke to pilgrims in good weather and bad, and tried always to honor faithfully all the requests of the Blessed Mother.

The visionaries were asked by the Blessed Mother to fast on bread and water only on Wednesdays and Fridays. Thinking people began to fear ominous events on the horizon when they heard the requests for fasts coupled with intense prayer that were coming from the mountains of Medjugorje. The requests for prayer and fasting were extended by the Blessed Mother to the entire world for people of all religions, races, ethnic groups, and nations.

In 1988, Marija traveled to Birmingham, Alabama, where she donated one of her kidneys to her brother Andrew, who was mortally ill with kidney disease. Many Americans became quite close to Marija at that time. They admired her humility and her heroic generosity to her brother. Americans also began to notice Marija's wonderful smile, her quick wit, and her humor. Her love for family life was obvious to all who encountered her, for Marija gravitated to babies and small children.

Daily apparitions to Marija continued in the United States while she underwent surgery at the University of Alabama Medical Center and then recuperated. During that time, the Blessed Mother gave special blessings of peace, of conversion, and of love through Marija and asked that they be shared with all people everywhere. The Blessed Mother also gave special blessings for the United States.

On a few occasions during that time, the Blessed

Mother spoke to Marija in Hebrew. Marija was given the grace to understand the language. She already had the divinely infused gift of speaking, understanding, reading, and writing the Italian language.

Marija is one of the founders of a prayer community in Italy where those who are mortally ill with AIDS receive care and hope. Marija explained in 1988 that some have been miraculously healed from the AIDS virus. "There will be many more healings," she has promised.

Marija is now married to a man from Italy and they have a small son. She receives daily apparitions at her home in Italy, and in Medjugorje, where she continues to visit. Marija has received nine secrets from the Blessed Mother. She communicates a monthly message to the world from the Blessed Mother.[16]

On February 25, 1995, the Blessed Mother's message from Medjugorje extended God's invitation to everyone in the world once more:

"Dear children, today I invite you to become missionaries of my messages, which I am giving here through this place that is dear to me. God has allowed me to stay this long with you, and therefore, little children, I invite you to live with love the messages I give and to transmit them to the whole world, so that a river of love flows to people who are full of hatred and without peace. I invite you, little children, to become peace where there is no peace, and light where there is darkness, so that each heart accepts the light and the way to salvation. Thank you for responding to my call."

Vicka

Vicka Ivankovic was born on July 3, 1964. She was not known for her intellectual capabilities when the apparitions began. During the summer of 1981, she was attending summer school in Mostar because she had failed her first-year textile school examinations in mathematics. However, Vicka has matured into a strong, self-sacrificing young woman who is revered throughout the world for her kindness and her wise understanding of the mysteries of the Gospel, which she explains she has learned from the Mother of Jesus.

Those who know Vicka well are constantly surprised by her energy and her joy. She has a profound love for the sick and for those who are burdened with addictions. Vicka works in a rehabilitation center that she helped to found at Medjugorje. People with severe addictions have come to this center from all over the world. It is said that those who remain in the center for the requested three-year commitment leave with no addiction whatsoever and have undergone deep inner healing of the spirit as well.

Vicka and Jacov visited Heaven, hell, and purgatory with the Blessed Mother. Vicka said she saw people in all these places. Vicka says the Blessed Mother constantly urges everyone to pray that their beloved dead may rest in peace.

Vicka has a profound veneration for the Blessed Mother and a tender love for the Infant Jesus, whom she has seen on several occasions. The Blessed Mother has shared some of the details of her life in the Holy Family with Vicka, enough to fill three notebooks, which she says will be published "only when the Blessed Mother tells me to do so."

Vicka said to a pilgrim, "The Blessed Mother wants me to teach you to pray so that you can teach others." By the next morning, word had spread among the pilgrims, and several people, especially the sick who were seeking physical healing, gathered at Vicka's house. Certain sick people were carried up the steep stairs to the room where Vicka sees the Blessed Mother every day at 6:40 P.M. The small, simple room was comfortably appointed with a single bed, some chairs, and a chest the top of which Vicka used as a prayer altar. A crucifix and a statue of the Blessed Mother surrounded by what looked like thousands of requests from people all over the world to the Blessed Mother were neatly placed on the prayer altar. There were also many photographs of people who were seeking the intercession of the Blessed Mother.

Vicka spoke about God. She also spoke about prayer. Some of the people who had come were quite ill. Everyone wanted at least one miracle.

Vicka noticed, and volunteered, "The Blessed Mother promises that when the permanent sign comes, there will be healings all over the world. Some are happening now too, especially for the ones who pray the hardest!" As the Blessed Mother told the visionaries at Pontmain in 1871:

"My Son allows Himself to be persuaded by prayer."

Though Vicka had never heard of the apparitions at Pontmain, her knowledge of intercessory prayer is profound. Her eyes glistened as she radiantly told us how the Blessed Mother taught her to pray.

When the Blessed Mother took Vicka to visit purgatory, she asked the young woman if she would be willing to sacrifice her daily apparitions for forty days as an offering for the poor souls in purgatory. Vicka accepted the invitation and agreed to forgo her daily apparitions of the Blessed Mother. She also accepted a physical suffering for the forty days.

Vicka had no difficulty with her prayer life for about three days. By the fourth day, however, she was becoming aware of how "addicted" she was to the daily presence of the Blessed Mother, who has warned the visionaries that no person, no thing may come between them and God. She calls all people to pray for a pure heart: one that beats for God alone. Not even the Blessed Mother may occupy the human heart. That is a sacred place where God alone desires to dwell with His child.

By the hour of her usual daily apparition on that fourth day, Vicka was desolate. She could not pray, she could experience no peace, she was highly agitated. A form of mental and spiritual pain that Vicka had never before experienced gripped her like an invisible snake that was choking life out of her.

In the midst of her terror, Vicka heard the voice of the Blessed Mother:

"Fall on your knees in your imagination before Jesus our Father on the cross. Call to Him, 'Father, do You exist? Father, do You know me? Father, do You care about me? Father, do You love me?' Continue to call to Him day

*and night until you have ears to hear Him in the world, eyes
to see Him in the world, and a heart that beats for Him
alone."*

People in that upstairs room were spellbound by the
beauty of Vicka's face as she spoke of finding God for the first
time. Then she said, "Where do you think God is?" Someone
responded, "God is in Heaven." Vicka countered, "Where do
you think Heaven is?" A child reminded her, "Vicka, you
know where Heaven is. You have been there. Exactly where
is Heaven?" "Right here!" she announced elatedly.

"Right here? Can you see Heaven right now?" someone asked incredulously. Vicka paused for a long time. She
said, "Do you know where God is?"

Though Vicka's face was filled with joy, she seemed to
be listening intently in the silence that filled the room. Suddenly she exclaimed, "God is right here now! He is looking
at you this close!" Vicka held her hand up so that it was no
more than one inch from her eyes as she continued: "God is
this close to everyone on earth. He sees everything. He hears
everything. He knows everything. Only if you pray with
your heart will you see God, who is looking at you this
close!" Her hand was now a half inch from her eyes!

Everyone in the room tried to comprehend the close-
ness of Almighty God. Then, with the gentleness of a lullaby, like the sound of a lone bird at dawn or the melody of
springtime winds that blow away the darkness of winter,
came the same words Vicka had heard:

*"Fall on your knees in your imagination before Jesus
our Father on the cross. Call to Him, 'Father, do You*

exist? Father, do You know me? Father, do You care about me? Father, do You love me?' Continue to call to Him day and night until you have ears to hear Him in the world, eyes to see Him in the world, and a heart that beats for Him alone."

That afternoon, at the summit of Cross Mountain, the blind lawyer who had sat beside Vicka during the morning visit discovered that she could see once again.

Ivan

Ivan Dragicevic, the eldest of three sons, was sixteen when his daily apparitions of the Blessed Mother as Queen of Peace began on June 25, 1981. He was invited by the Blessed Mother to form a weekly prayer group that meets at night on Cross Mountain. Youths from around the world have participated, for varying lengths of time, at Ivan's prayer group. There are many stories of luminary phenomena that accompany the apparition. People claim to see the cross on Cross Mountain become a neon cross against the dark sky; they claim to see pulsating light during the apparition, or shooting stars.

When Ivan visits the United States, people often join him for prayer during his daily apparition. In November 1990, Ivan prayed at the Shrine of Our Lady of Lourdes in Emmitsburg, Maryland. During his apparition of approximately seven minutes, a gentle, warm rain fell. Amazingly, after the apparition ended, no one was wet; nor was the ground wet. Yet some who were standing or kneeling nearby did not experience the rain.

In the fall of 1994, Ivan was married in the United States to a Boston native who is renowned for her beauty. He has traveled the world as a tireless evangelist for the Blessed Mother. Ivan tells people everywhere that prayer and fasting can change the world. He acknowledges that few people trust anyone in these times. Most people, Ivan observes, are quite cynical.

Ivan Dragicevic says that he sees the Blessed Mother of Jesus Christ every day. He prays with her. He has learned to live in prayer and fasting as a result of her apparitions to him. Ivan says that without prayer he has no joy, no peace, no life. Because of his heavy travel schedule, Ivan has trained himself to rise at 5:00 A.M. in order to stay faithful to his two-hour daily prayer commitment.

Ivan says he recognizes that people believe it is easy for him to have such an optimistic attitude about the future because the Blessed Mother has shown him many scenes about the rest of his life. He states, however, that people misunderstand what that gift means. Ivan says that the Blessed Mother has instructed him how to read Scripture, the sacred Word of God. She has taught him that the solutions to the problems of the world, and to each life, are contained in the path Jesus brought us during His life on earth.

Ivan maintains we make or break our life on earth by our own choices. But he quickly adds: "Prayer can change things. Prayer can change everything for the better. God has solutions for even the most hopeless situations. To obtain those solutions, the Blessed Mother tells us we must pray, fast, and trust God's mercy."

"How can you keep the peace if there is no peace to be kept?" Ivan has often asked interested pilgrims who congregate at his doorstep in Medjugorje. "Peace comes from God." Ivan quietly continues: "Do we ask Him for peace? Do we keep His commandments? Do we forgive one another? The only road to peace is prayer and fasting, obedience to the commandments, reading the Bible, and always forgiving each other."

One man from South America was heard to mumble, "It sounds so simple. Try doing it!" Others encouraged the sad man: "Ask him how he is able to do all that!"

Ivan, who is a veteran of the compulsory military service that Yugoslavia imposed upon all eighteen-year-old male citizens, seemed to intuit the question. Though he was intellectually incapable of learning Latin and other complex subjects that were required for seminary training, Ivan overcame the experience of failure and shame he suffered when he was asked to leave the seminary. Ivan greets pilgrims like a man with a world mission. He epitomizes self-respect and personal dignity. Looking at Ivan with new eyes, the sad man understood.

Ivan shared:

The Blessed Mother has come as the Queen of Peace. She knows the value to God of each person on this earth. Unless we pray and fast, unless we respond wholeheartedly to the messages of the Queen of Peace, we suffer needlessly. Many people all over the world have heard these messages. In 1981, the Blessed Mother showed me that millions of people would come to Medjugorje. She said everyone would hear her messages. She said each person on earth has a role to play in God's great plan for His people that is being manifested here in Medjugorje.

The Blessed Mother tells us:

"Dear children, today I invite you to pray. God is granting special graces to you in prayer. Dear children, seek God by praying that you may be able to understand all that I am giving you here in Medjugorje. I am calling you to pray with your hearts. Without prayer you cannot comprehend God's Plan for you. Please pray! I desire that God's Plan for each of you may be realized, and that all the gifts He has placed in your hearts may multiply. Pray always that God's blessing may protect every one of you from the evil that is threatening you. I bless you, dear children."

Ivan shared that in prayer he has come to realize what a great gift his own life and the lives of every person on earth truly are. Ivan is now a young father. The world has much to observe and to learn from Ivan. He confided, "The Blessed Mother says the world is on the path of peace."

An Interview with Jacov Çolo

Q. Jacov, what significance do you believe the apparitions you have experienced every day since you were nine years old hold for the world?

A. God never loses.

Q. What does that mean?

A. The Blessed Mother has come to the earth in apparitions for the last time.

Q. Why is she here for the last time, Jacov?

A. The Blessed Mother has come here for the conversion and reconciliation of the entire world.

Q. Will that happen in your lifetime?

A. Yes.

Q. Jacov, what is conversion?

A. Conversion is the conscious awareness of God in all that lives.

Q. Is that why there will not need to be more apparitions?

A. After the secrets are realized, those who are still alive will walk with God. Love and innocence and purity will reign in God's holy house of prayer.

Q. Is that time what has been called the Triumph of the Immaculate Heart?

A. The Triumph of the Immaculate Heart occurs every time a person loves God and obeys His divine will.

Ivanka

Ivanka Ivankovic Elez is the first visionary who saw the Blessed Mother with the Infant Jesus on June 24, 1981. She was in deep mourning at the time because of the sudden death of her mother two months earlier. The first question she asked of the Queen of Peace was, "Where is my mother?" She was told:

"Your mother is with me. She is your angel in heaven."

The Blessed Mother later brought Ivanka's mother to her on four separate occasions. Ivanka said her mother looked "exactly the same." She hugged her mother and spoke with her. Her mother told her, "Ivanka, I am so proud of you that you have served the Blessed Mother so faithfully."[17]

Ivanka is married to Raico Elez of Medjugorje, who comes from a family of six sons. Raico and Ivanka have three young children and live an ordinary life with ordinary responsibilities even with the obligations of daily duty.

Ivanka is beautiful. She is quite tall, with long, dark hair, a wonderful smile, and a gentle spirit that permeates all her actions. Ivanka serves as wife, mother, daughter, daughter-in-law, and sister. At the same time, she is a world-famous visionary who carries ten secrets that she says involve the future of life on the earth. She is the most hidden of all the visionaries.

Ivanka has a prayer life that few understand, few penetrate, and few are even aware of. Ivanka's children are steeped in peace. They cling to their mother with obvious love and joy. They are caring children who have the same graciousness their mother demonstrates to all those she encounters.

Ivanka and her husband are no strangers to suffering. They reside near Medjugorje and have been traumatized by the war in Bosnia, as have all the visionaries and their families.

For Ivanka, however, one difference is that she, along with Mirjana, knows all ten secrets. She admits that without great prayer, her burden would be too great to carry. The other four visionaries have only received nine secrets. Ivanka spoke about the war. She encourages people everywhere to take the Blessed Mother's messages seriously and respond generously.

Ivanka now sees the Blessed Mother only once each year, on the anniversary of the apparition. During her yearly apparition, Ivanka receives additional instructions regarding the ten secrets of Medjugorje that have been entrusted to her by the Blessed Mother. She rarely speaks of the secrets.

Ivanka travels the least of any of the visionaries. She sees few pilgrims. She serves those who do visit her with generous hospitality and much kindness. Her voice is quiet and her mannerisms are refined. Ivanka knows the angels well.[18] She has a glorious prayer life that she learned as she prayed daily with the Mother of God.

Ivanka says that the Our Father, taught to us by Jesus, is a journey into the heart of God if we pray it with sincerity. She speaks of God our Father's immense, unfathomable love for every person He has ever created. She says the Blessed Mother asks us to love each other as Jesus taught us, for the love of God. In that way, Ivanka says, love is a joy, love is a gift, love is how we show our love for God who gives us everything. Ivanka says the Blessed Mother has asked us all to pray for a grateful heart because a grateful heart recognizes God's glorious plan for the salvation of His people.

A grateful heart knows peace. Ivanka said a grateful heart is peace: it is a fruit of prayer.

Ivanka does not single out any particular message of the Blessed Mother that she stresses in the dark times of war. Rather, Ivanka advises, "All the messages of the Blessed Mother here are urgent for everyone. The Blessed Mother prays and intercedes for everyone on earth by name. She has chosen to make a prototype of this parish for the world. The Blessed Mother says:

"No pain, no suffering is too great in order for my messages to reach each one of you. I pray to my Son not to punish the world. I beseech you, be converted. You cannot imagine what is going to happen, nor what the Eternal Father will send to the earth. That is why you must be converted! Renounce everything. Sacrifice yourselves for those who need your help. Express my gratitude to all those who pray and fast. I carry all these gifts to my Divine Son in order to obtain an alleviation of His justice against the sins of humanity. Persevere and help me that the world may be converted."

The Blessed Mother has come to Medjugorje as the Queen of Peace. People all over the world are learning of her role in God's plan for them. Peace is a divine gift. It is God who bestows peace upon the earth and its people.

The Eternal Father has a plan for His faithful children who keep His commandments. Their hearts are being prepared for the reign of God. All over the world, those who pray are developing eyes to see God and ears to hear His voice. These are dangerous times for those who do not recognize God's voice in the quiet of their hearts.

The apparitions in Medjugorje have yet to be approved by the Church. They continue, however, to be under ecclesiastic investigation, in spite of the war in Bosnia. Pope John Paul II encouraged pilgrims to go to Medjugorje before the outbreak of hostilities in the region. Pilgrims continue to make the journey.

On September 16, 1983, the Blessed Mother presented this message for everyone, and to the Holy Father in particular:

"I ask everyone, the Holy Father in particular, to spread the messages I have received from my Son to deliver to each of you here in Medjugorje. I wish to entrust to the Pope the word with which I come here: 'MIR' {peace} which he must spread everywhere. Here is a message which is especially for him:

"Bring together the Christian people through your words and your preaching. Spread particularly among the youth of the world the messages which you have received from God the Father through inspiration in prayer."[19]

CHAPTER TEN

Mother of the Word

Rwanda, Africa: 1981 to 1988

The Blessed Mother's presence brought an ecumenical message with apocalyptic dimensions to the world at Kibeho, Rwanda, beginning November 28, 1981, and ending November 28, 1988.[1]

Three of the visionaries who saw the Blessed Mother were boarding students at a school run by sisters in a poor area known as Kibeho. The other young visionaries lived in the bush. All the visionaries were thoroughly scrutinized by secular and ecclesiastic experts and pronounced normal.

One young teenage boy and six girls each began to see the Blessed Mother daily in Rwanda beginning in 1981. The visionaries are, in the chronological order of their apparitions:

Alphonsine Mumureka, born in 1965: apparitions of the Blessed Mother from November 28, 1981, to November 28, 1988.

Anthalie Mukamazimpaka, born in 1965: apparitions of the Lord Jesus and the Blessed Mother from January 12, 1982, to December 3, 1983.

Marie-Clare Mukangango, born in 1961: fifteen apparitions of the Blessed Mother from March 2, 1982, to December 15, 1982.

Stephanie Mukamurenzi, born in 1968: apparitions of the Blessed Mother from May 25, 1982, to December 15, 1982.

Emmanuel Segatashya, born in 1967: apparitions of the Lord Jesus and the Blessed Mother from July 2, 1982, to July 3, 1983.

Agnes Kamagaju, born in 1960: apparitions of the Lord Jesus and the Blessed Mother from August 4, 1982, to September 25, 1983.

Vestine Salina, born in 1958: apparitions of the Blessed Mother from December 15, 1982, to December 24, 1983.

Vestine had Muslim parents. The other five girls were from Catholic families. Emmanuel had no religious training at all. In fact, he had never heard the name Jesus Christ. The Blessed Mother never asked that the Muslim and Protestant people of Africa convert to Catholicism.

Rather, she spoke about all the people as her own dear children.

Alphonsine

Alphonsine, the first of these African visionaries, responded to a voice from the corridor calling to her, "My daughter," as she was serving the table at the Sisters' School in Kibeho on November 28, 1981. Alphonsine went to the corridor and there she beheld the Beautiful Lady from Heaven. She fell to her knees as she asked: "Who are you?" The Beautiful Lady responded:

> "*Ndi Nyina wa Jambo* [Swahili for I am Mother of the Word]. *I have heard your prayers. I would like you and your companions to have more faith. Some do not believe enough.*"

Alphonsine continued to have apparitions, many of which were public, at her school. She experienced some criticism and even persecution by those who did not believe that she was worthy of such a blessing.

Help came from Heaven, for the following year, on January 12, 1982, a school companion, Anthalie, had her first apparition of the Blessed Mother. Two months later, on March 2, their schoolmate Marie-Clare experienced her first apparition. By March 20, 1982, the bishop of Butari established a medical commission to scrutinize the apparitions at the Sisters' School. On May 14, 1982, he set up a theological commission to investigate the apparitions. Then Stephanie reported her first apparition of the Blessed Mother on May 25, 1982.

Large crowds of Africans gathered for the scheduled apparitions of Alphonsine from 1981 to 1988. People of neighboring Kivu, Burundi, and Uganda were also present. Some walked as far as 120 miles to be there for the apparitions. There were microphones so that the crowds could hear what she said to the Blessed Virgin, though only Alphonsine heard and saw the Blessed Mother. Alphonsine was frequently heard to address the Blessed Mother as *disi we Mabyyeryi*, which translates as "Darling Mother."

Emmanuel

An extraordinary event of immense global importance occurred in the bush in Rwanda on July 2, 1982. Emmanuel Segatashya was an illiterate fourteen-year-old. As he was picking beans, he heard a voice call to him: "Child, if you receive a mission, will you choose to accomplish it?" Emmanuel responded in his mind: "Yes, of course." The voice then said: "Go to those people who are nearby. Tell them to purify their hearts because the time is near." Emmanuel was quite curious by now and inquired: "What is your name?" The voice responded: "If I tell you My name, no one will believe you." Emmanuel felt the power of the message he had been asked to convey, so he asked: "What proof can I give the people that what you ask me to tell them is the truth?" The voice answered: "I am Jesus. Go and bring the message to the people."

Emmanuel approached a nearby group of people who were working in the field. He said, "Purify your hearts because the time is near." They laughed at him. "Says who?"

someone asked. Emmanuel responded, "His name is Jesus." Then the people rushed at him and tore his clothes. He heard the voice: "Tell them that the Son of Man came on this earth and they stripped Him of His garments. This has happened to you as a symbol of what they do to Me. Open your eyes and you can see Me."

Emmanuel ran away, confused and frightened. A great flash of light astounded him. Afraid, he turned to run from the light when he heard, again in his own dialect:

"My Son, come to Me."

In the immense light, Emmanuel saw a black man attired in the style of a typical Rwandan. Stunned, overwhelmed by the divine love that flowed from the presence of the man, Emmanuel had no words to speak. Emmanuel heard the man speak these words:

"I am Jesus before whom all humanity stands."

Many people, including Emmanuel's parents, thought he was unbalanced. Some said he was crazy.

Emmanuel began to experience apparitions of the Blessed Mother. She taught him to pray. Those who do not know God cannot make informed choices. She explained many of the effects of improper choices on the human body, the human soul, the human family, the animals, the earth, and the planets. She taught him about the Church of her Divine Son, where he could access the Word of God. He was baptized and confirmed in less than one year.

Emmanuel continued to receive profound messages

from Jesus about His Church on earth, especially about the necessity for a sacramental life. Jesus told Emmanuel that the sacrament of penance is the preparation people should make for His imminent Second Coming. The Lord Jesus told him to warn all people:

"All that is not seen will be seen."

The message Jesus gave to Emmanuel is:

"This world will come to an end. Prepare while there is still time. When I return on earth, the soul will find the body it had before, and then man will bring his own dossier. Do not lose time in doing good. There is not much time left."

While in the physical presence of Jesus, whom he saw as a living human being, as distinct from a distant vision, Emmanuel Segatashya's intellect was mysteriously opened and he was able to perceive the reality of the Gospel message. Segatashya, all on fire with zeal, became a tireless evangelist.

Jesus gave Emmanuel messages for the priests. Not everyone believed the messages. Some of the messages include the following:

"The priests and religious do not take enough care of those who are ill physically and morally. If they have freely promised the vow of chastity, they must observe it faithfully. They must reflect before taking such a serious commitment. Only God pardons sins, but He wants to use men

for this mission. Beware of the sins of hypocrisy, slander, calumny. These sins are fornication of the tongue. When I lived on earth I embraced voluntary poverty. True wealth resides in the heart."

Emmanuel was expelled from Burundi by unbelievers who found the Gospel of Jesus too difficult a challenge. He met with some success in Zaire. Emmanuel, who has become a Catholic, continues to preach the Gospel to all those who will listen. It is reported that theologians are astounded at the soundness of his doctrine.[2]

Emmanuel Segatashya's last encounter with Jesus Christ occurred on July 3, 1983. He proclaims that Jesus commanded him to spread His Gospel to the world now. The following are excerpts from the messages he received from Jesus.

Concerning the Blessed Virgin Mary:

"How can someone say he loves Jesus, adores Him, and lives outside His Blessed Mother's Immaculate Heart? My Mother is the Mother of the world."

Concerning prayer:

"Men should pray together with fervor. Do not ask for miracles because you will not arrive in Heaven by miracles but by true prayer which comes from your heart. The Rosary is the strength of the Christian."

Concerning the Christian religions:

"Beware of the divisions among yourselves. Try to receive the Word of God in the same way and you will find yourselves around the same God."

Concerning the Second Coming of Jesus:

"Too many people treat their neighbor without love, without honesty, without compassion. . . . The world is full of hatred. You will know My Second Coming is at hand when you see the outbreak of religious, ethnic, or racial wars. Know then that I am on the way."[3]

Agnes

On August 4, 1982, Agnes had her first apparition of the Blessed Mother in her own home. Born in 1960 of Catholic parents, Agnes had attended only a few grades of elementary school. Subsequently she began to have public apparitions of the Lord Jesus or His Blessed Mother which were accompanied by extraordinary signs. The sun would spin dramatically. Sometimes there would appear to be two suns; at other times two lines would divide the sun into three equal parts. At times the cross of Jesus or His crown of thorns would appear on the right side of the sun as Agnes would announce in ecstasy: "God wants to show us that He holds the world in His hands and He can bring it to an end at His will. We must be prepared. Pray that we are always at the right hand of the Lord Jesus." Often Agnes would ask for a blessing from the Lord Jesus or His Blessed Mother. The crowds could hear her request over the loudspeaker during her public apparitions. Every time the request was made, a gentle, light rain would fall upon the crowds.

Jesus appeared to Agnes dressed in white with a white or red mantle. He was surrounded with such light, such sanctity, sacredness, Godliness, that she could not describe His Presence.

On May 2, 1983, Agnes had a long public dialogue with Jesus. During her ecstasy, she quoted Jesus:

"Tell the people: Stop taking many different roads. You must choose the only way: penance and detachment from the things of this world. Who thirsts for Me, I will satisfy his thirst. Who trusts in Me, he will never be in need of anything."

On August 18, 1983, Agnes received a message from the Lord Jesus for the youth of the world:

"The behavior of youth and their ideas are in contrast with what God expects of them. They must not use their bodies as an instrument of pleasure. They are using all means to love and to be loved. They forget that true love comes from God. Instead of being at the service of God, they are at the service of money. They must make of their body an instrument destined to the glory of God and not an object of pleasure at the service of men. Pray to My Mother Mary to show you the right way to God. You must follow one way. Stop walking on two roads. Some will be called to give themselves completely to God. Others will be called to form a family. No matter what your vocation is, you must be completely for God, since your body and soul depend on Him."

The apparitions of Jesus ended for Agnes on August 29, 1983. Her final apparition of the Blessed Mother occurred on September 25, 1983. Agnes spoke always with much concern about the end of the world.

Anthalie

Anthalie is the fourth of eight children from a Catholic family. Her apparitions were of Jesus and Mary and occurred from January 12, 1982, until December 3, 1983. She is a member of the Legion of Mary and also of the Charismatic Renewal in the Sisters' School. The sisters spoke of her as deeply mystical. Some of her apparitions occurred in front of thousands of people who had gathered for the event. She quoted the Blessed Mother: "Wake up. Stand up. Wash yourself and look up attentively. Dedicate yourselves to prayer. Develop in the virtues of charity, humility, and availability."

Marie-Clare

Though Marie-Clare was born into a Catholic family in 1961, the family was not pious and Marie-Clare was somewhat dubious of the supposed apparitions of the others until her own apparitions began. She then became a zealous Christian and was heard to speak of herself as an apostle of the last days. She also spoke frequently of God's great mercy to allow such manifestations, which she experienced from March 2 until September 15, 1982. The message she announced for the entire world is: "We must meditate on the Passion of Christ and the deep sorrow of His Mother. We must recite the Rosary, and the beads of the Seven Sorrows of the Blessed Mother to obtain the grace of repentance."

Stephanie

Stephanie, the youngest of the African visionaries, was born in 1968. Her fifteen apparitions occurred between May 25, 1982, and December 15, 1982. She announced this message from the Blessed Mother for the world: "Be converted. Pray and mortify yourselves. Satan is real. He tries always to ruin you. God desires that we pray from our hearts."

Vestine

Vestine is the daughter of a woman who was raised Catholic but converted to the faith of Vestine's Muslim father when she married him. Since Vestine's apparitions, her entire family has converted to Catholicism and been baptized.

She claims to have had private apparitions since 1980. Her public apparitions occurred between December 15, 1982, and December 24, 1983. She announced that the Blessed Mother has chosen her to help shepherd the world to Jesus. Many people listened to her words. She has led large numbers of Africans to Christianity. She carries a walking stick as a sign of the staff of Jesus, the Good Shepherd. She frequently quotes the Blessed Mother:

"The walk to Heaven is through a narrow road. It is not easy. The road of Satan is wide and easy because there are no obstacles. Therefore, with Satan you run. You go fast."

Vestine experienced mystical voyages with the Blessed Mother that sometimes lasted up to forty hours. During that time, her body appeared to be in a coma as the eyewitnesses watched. The apparition was medically observed. The other African visionaries also had similar experiences.

Vestine was observed in her coma-like apparition trance from Good Friday to Easter Sunday, April 1 to April 3, 1983. She later explained that she traveled with the Blessed Mother during that time to places not on the earth. She said that she was in a vast universe quite different from ours, from any that we know about or can even imagine. She visited a place of immense fire. The Blessed Mother, however, told her that hell is not fire but a place where the suffering is from the privation of seeing God. She also visited a place where many children were praying and singing. Though they seemed happy, they were suffering. The Blessed Mother told her that purgatory is a place of reconciliation before reaching God.

Vestine spoke forcefully about the need for detachment from the world's goods and a continuous searching for God. She was very much aware that everyone on the earth is a mere traveler, a pilgrim destined for Heaven. She spoke always about the imminent return of Jesus and pleaded with people to prepare for that event. She stressed the need for everyone on earth to find sacramental confession now: to obtain pardon for all the sins of humanity in the sacrament of reconciliation.

Father René Laurentin has emphasized that the messages of Rwanda include the following: The Blessed Mother is calling all people in the world, of all faiths or even those with no perceived religious affiliation, to an intimate relationship with God. She is asking us to abandon all behavior, all thoughts, all relationships that are not centered in God's perfect will for us. The Blessed Mother asked the people of Africa and, through them, the entire world for conversion and for prayer to access the power of the angels in these difficult times.

The Blessed Mother appeared to the children at Rwanda with dark skin and long dark hair. She was of an exquisite classic beauty, glorious beyond description. She wore a long white dress with no seams and a long, flowing white veil. Some of the visionaries occasionally saw her wear a blue veil. She wore no shoes. Her hands were joined together and her fingers were pointing towards Heaven. The visionaries described her voice as sweet, like the sounds of the finest music. They said that the Blessed Mother was surrounded by such intense light that it seemed brighter than the sun, yet emitted no heat. They spoke of her as being wrapped in a luminescent brilliance that filled their world with joy. Each has referred to her as "pure love."[4]

The Blessed Mother told the children:

"Although I am the Mother of God, I am simple and humble. I always place myself where you are. I love you as

you are. I never reproach my little ones. When a child is without reproach in front of her mother, she will tell her everything that is in her heart. I am grateful when a child of mine is joyful with me. That joy is a most beautiful sign of trust and love. Few understand the mysteries of God's love. Let me as your Mother embrace all my children with love so that you can confide your deepest longings to me. Know that I give all your longings to my Son Jesus, your brother."[5]

The visionary Alphonsine confided: "The world is coming to an end. The eternal Jesus is here. The end of the world is not a punishment, but it has always been foretold. The Queen of Angels comes to advise us to prepare for the coming of her son. We have to suffer with Jesus, to pray and be apostles to prepare for His return."[6]

It is not clear whether Alphonsine refers to an objective "end of the world" that involves all people on earth, or the subjective "end of the world" as she knew it. In November 1994, Alphonsine was a refugee in Zaire. Her entire family had been slaughtered in the Rwandan war of summer, 1994. For her it is certain that the world she knew at the time of her apparitions passed away before her eyes in the holocaust of the bloody dispute in her native Rwanda.

Public devotions at Rwanda were approved on August 15, 1988, by the Roman Catholic bishop, Monsignor Jean Baptiste Gahamanyi, of the diocese of Butare in Rwanda. By signaling his approval, Monsignor Gahamanyi encouraged spiritual devotions at the site of the apparitions.[7] The brutal war that subsequently erupted has precluded pilgrimages to the site.

The final apparition, on November 28, 1988, was videotaped. The demeanor of Alphonsine during her ecstasy allows viewers to witness the apparition phenomenon from the heart of Africa, preserved as a gift of twentieth-century technology.[8]

By the spring of 1995 it was known that Marie-Clare, the visionary whom the Blessed Mother asked to spread devotion to the Rosary of the Seven Sorrows of Mary, had been killed together with her husband during the 1994 summer of violence in Rwanda. One other visionary is reported to have been killed. As far as is known, the other four visionaries are still alive, though they may be dwelling in a refugee camp somewhere in Africa.

Damascus, Syria: since 1982

Maria Al Akharas, known as Myrna, was eighteen years old when she married Nicholas Nazzour in May 1982. She is a member of the Melkite Byzantine Rite and her husband is Greek Orthodox. They live in the old city of Damascus, within walking distance of the home of the biblical Ananias. Pilgrims still visit the site because Saint Paul came to Ananias and stayed in his house for a time after being struck blind by the presence of the Lord Jesus on the road to Damascus. Neither Myrna nor Nicholas thought much about religion. They enjoyed dancing. They also enjoyed going out in the old city with friends.

Layla, Nicholas's sister, suddenly became quite ill in November. Everyone was concerned for her life. Myrna began to pray fervently for her. On November 22, 1982, an extraordinary phenomenon began for Myrna as she, an Orthodox Christian, and a Muslim prayed over Layla. With no warning, Myrna's hands suddenly began to exude oil. She was confused. The other two women excitedly commanded her: "Quick! Put your hands on Layla!" Myrna did, and Layla was instantly healed. Several days later, on November 27, a three-inch-tall image of the Virgin with the Christ Child, in Myrna and Nicholas's bedroom, also began to ooze oil, enough to fill a saucer.[9]

Myrna's husband did not understand what was happening in his home. He summoned his relatives. The family decided to pray together. To their astonishment, four dishes of oil came from the small icon within an hour. Though the family did not understand the significance of the oozing oil, they continued to pray out loud. Suddenly, Myrna could hear nothing. Her auditory sense was mysteriously blocked from the sounds around her in the room. In a moment she heard the incredibly beautiful words: "Mary [Myrna means Mary], do not be frightened. I am with you. Open the doors and do not deprive anyone from seeing me. . . . Light a candle for me."[10] Then Myrna could hear normal sounds in the room once again. The icon continued to pour oil for four days.

Nicholas sought advice from the clergy. The first instinct of each priest or minister was to search for fraud. An intense investigation of Myrna, Nicholas, their home, their icon, and their family began.

Then the civil authorities began to investigate for chicanery. They discovered that the oil was coming from the icon itself and not from the frame. The source of the oil remains totally unexplainable. Experts demanded that Myrna wash and rewash her hands in their presence. She complied. Then they asked her to pray in their presence. She did so and the oil began to exude from her palms.

Clergy became intensely interested in the state of Myrna's soul. They interrogated her, only to discover that her prayer life was, at the time of the first miracle, limited to the daily recitation of one Our Father and one Hail Mary. They admitted they were surprised. She only attended church on Wednesdays, when she accompanied her mother-in-law to the Church of the Holy Cross. She and her husband of seven months continued to dance, swim, and laugh.

One day a priest was kneeling near Myrna while she was praying. He heard her say, "Father, I feel like the Virgin has entered into me!" The priest then saw "a brilliant liquid flowing abundantly from her palms."[11] A bishop who was in the room noted that the oil had the scent of myron, or holy oil.

Medical doctors and other scientists assembled to decipher the human origin of the healing oil that continued to exude from Myrna's hands when she prayed. Thousands of people began to visit the icon in Myrna's home. The sick began to come to the courtyard of Myrna's house, asking to be anointed with the oil from Myrna's hands. Phenomenal cures resulted for many. Word spread and the crowds became more frequent, more numerous, and more demanding.

On December 15, 1982, at 11:37 P.M., while a huge group of people were praying in front of Myrna's icon, she felt an invisible being tug at her arm and firmly escort her to the roof garden. Myrna was afraid. She knelt on the tile floor. Myrna describes the experience: "When I raised up my head, I saw the Virgin Mary in front of me. She shined as if she were covered with diamonds. I was afraid, and I ran away screaming."

Nicholas was overwrought. The whole family was in a state of confusion. A clergyman who had training in mysticism comforted them by explaining that the Blessed Virgin obviously had a mission for the family and that she would return if the apparition was from God. He taught Myrna to pray:

"O Virgin, prepare me to receive you well, to understand better what you want to tell me, Amen."[12]

On December 18, 1982, Myrna was once again mysteriously escorted by an invisible being to the roof garden of her house. This time, her husband and nine others followed her. Myrna saw across the street, in the upper part of a large tree,

> a large, luminous, white globe like a large diamond ball sitting on a tree limb. . . . [T]he ball opened, splitting from the top and dividing into two half-moons. As the halves opened, a bow of light appeared over the top, and inside was the same Beautiful Lady. As the ball disappeared, the Lady seemed to be standing on the branch of the tree. She had a white veil that covered her hair. The veil was a part of her dress. Over her right shoulder was a sky-blue cape that wrapped around her back and over her left side. The white dress

covered her feet, and only her hands could be seen. The dress and cape seemed to be made of white and blue light. From her right hand, between the second and third fingers, hung a long Rosary.[13]

The vision floated toward Myrna along a stream of pure light that formed a road in the sky. Passing right through the railing of the terrace, the Beautiful Lady stopped two feet from where Myrna knelt. Speaking in classical Arabic, the Blessed Mother said:

"My children, be mindful of God because God is with us. You know much, but you really know nothing. Your knowledge is incomplete. One day you will know everything as God knows me. Do good to evildoers. Do not mistreat anyone. I have given you oil, more than you have asked. I give you something stronger than oil. Repent and believe! Be mindful of me in your joy. Announce my Son Emmanuel. He who announces Him is saved. He who does not . . . his faith is in vain. Love one another.

"I do not ask you to give money to churches. I ask you to love. Those who give money to the poor and to the churches and yet have not love have lives of no value. I will visit the homes of my children more frequently, because those who go to church do not always go there to pray.

"I do not ask you to build a church for me but a shrine. Give. Do not deprive anyone who asks for help.

"Be humble, my children. Do not insult the proud. Forgive them. Then you will be forgiven."

After this message was concluded, the Beautiful Lady from Heaven raised her right hand, in which she held a rosary. The brightness enfolded her as she disappeared into the dazzling light.[14]

The Blessed Mother gave the world this prayer at Damascus:

"God saves me. Jesus enlightens me. The Holy Spirit is my life. Therefore I fear nothing."

The Blessed Mother continued to appear to Myrna. She spoke frequently about church unity during her visits at Damascus:

"The church is the Kingdom of Heaven on earth. Those who divided it have sinned. Those who rejoice in the division commit sin. Jesus founded the church on small beginnings. As it grew divisions also grew. Those responsible for these divisions do not have love. Come together. Pray. Pray. Pray.

"How beautiful my children are when they are humbly on their knees. Do not be afraid. I am with you. Do not be divided. Teach these words to all generations: UNITY. LOVE. FAITH."

On December 19, 1982, a man carried his paralyzed nine-year-old son into the bedroom where the icon was kept. Oil poured from Myrna's hands while she and the boy's father prayed over him. As Myrna anointed the boy's legs, the twisted limbs straightened out and the boy indicated that he could feel his legs for the first time in his life.

The father raced to the courtyard, screaming: "My son can walk! My son can walk!" His tears fell to the ground. The boy ran to his father, jumping and dancing. "I can walk, Dad! See! I can walk!" he excitedly exclaimed.[15]

Finally, on December 30, 1982, His Beatitude Patriarch Ignatius IV Hazim, who had studied the phenomena surrounding Myrna, interviewed the couple. The next day, an official declaration giving recognition to the supernatural events in Myrna's life was read to all the Greek Orthodox churches in Damascus. On January 5, 1983, a Muslim woman who was completely blind recovered her sight.[16]

The oil that continues to exude from Myrna's hands is used for healing. Claims are made that over 100,000 people have seen the various miracles with their own eyes and over one million persons have seen films of them.[17] Certainly the healings lend credibility to the powerful messages of unity that Myrna quotes from the Blessed Mother.

A small group, calling themselves "The Messengers of Unity," has formed to spread the messages of Damascus. A large, bold-lettered sign posted at Myrna's house in the early days of the apparitions announced: "Myrna and the Messengers of Unity have permission from the Bishops of Damascus to announce the messages and the miracles of Soufanieh [area where Myrna resides]. We do not have permission to spread information about any other apparition. Please do not talk about or bring literature about any other reported miracle."

The Messengers of Unity made a commitment to remain totally obedient to the bishops of Damascus, who have approved the miraculous events that are occurring through Myrna. The Messengers of Unity have found that whenever non–Church-approved apparitions, or messages from such reputed events, are discussed or promulgated in Myrna's presence, no oil flows, no healings occur. They attribute the extraordinary nature of Myrna's gifts to the obedience that she and those associated with her bear to the Magisterium of the Church.[18]

The miraculous oil continues to flow. In 1988, Myrna and her husband, son, and daughter traveled to several destinations to speak of the apparitions of the Blessed Mother and the messages that Myrna was asked to convey. The oil from her palms continued to exude whenever and wherever she prayed. Healings continued to be wrought for many of those who were blessed by Myrna's hands.

On June 18, 1990, the Roman Catholic archbishop of Damascus attested that he himself was "more than one time, an eyewitness of the oil coming out of the hands and face of Mrs. Myrna and from copies of the Soufanieh Icon."[19]

In 1984 and 1987 the Orthodox and Catholic Christians celebrated Easter on the same day. That coincidence will once again occur in the year 2000. Those who enjoy signs that portend future events do ponder the unity issue for the year 2000. Myrna bore the stigmata on the Fridays preceding those joint Easter celebrations. The experience is somewhat grotesque to behold. A video of the event clearly demonstrates the bloody outline of an unseen crown of thorns on her forehead. Myrna's hands exhibit gaping wounds in each palm. She is seen to be writhing on a bed in obvious pain. Her husband, her mother, some clergy, and other family members are with her as she endures the wounds for three hours.[20]

Myrna began to long to hear and see the Lord Jesus Christ. Her spiritual director warned her that for such a gift she would pay a terrible price. That same day, May 31, 1984, at 3:00 P.M., oil began to exude from her forehead, face, neck, hands, and eyes. The pain in her eyes was excruciating. Then she fell into ecstasy and heard the voice of Jesus for the first time.

"My daughter, I am the beginning and the end."

His messages to her continue.

On October 15, 1986, Myrna received a message from Jesus Christ that is a consolation for the entire world:

"My daughter, how beautiful is the earth.
In this place I shall establish my Kingdom and My peace.
I shall give you My Heart in order to have yours.
Your sins are forgiven because you are looking for Me.
He who looks for Me, I shall imprint My image in him. . . .
Tell My children to come for Me, for
I am with them at all times."

Myrna has said that she has no idea why she has been given the mysterious oil and the assignment of receiving the apparitions of the Blessed Mother and communicating her messages. She also has said that she does not know why she was chosen to endure the pains of the stigmata. She rightfully treasures the spiritual gifts she has been given. She encourages all who approach her to take the times, the signs, and the messages from heaven seriously.

In the home of Nicholas and Myrna and their two children, Myriam and John Emmanuel, people, and even leaders of all the different Orthodox, Catholic, Jewish, and Muslim churches, pray together as one body. Myrna and Nicholas understand well that those who find the Blessed Mother receive Jesus Christ from her.

CHAPTER ELEVEN

Mother of Good Counsel

"I will give you a new heart and place a new spirit within you, taking from your bodies your stony hearts and giving you natural hearts. I will put my spirit within you and make you live by my statutes, careful to observe my decrees."

EZEKIEL 36:26–27

Naju, South Korea: since 1985

Julia Kim is a middle-aged housewife, mother of four, and a trained hairdresser. She lives in Naju, South Korea, a small city at the southwestern tip of the Korean peninsula, about a three-hour drive from Seoul.

In the early 1980s Julia was sick and depressed. A priest explained the Gospel message to Julia, who was a recent convert to Catholicism: "Bear your sufferings patiently with love. They are a bigger grace than getting well." Julia prayed for the grace to change her way of thinking about suffering. Shortly thereafter, Julia had a vision of Jesus on the cross, suffering and bleeding for the redemption of all people. When Julia witnessed the love of Jesus in His passion, she asked Him to allow her to suffer with Him. Within a short period of time, Julia began to suffer the pains of the stigmata. For a while, the wounds were visible. Though she sometimes experiences such pain now, the wounds are no longer visible.

Julia has received several other unexpected gifts and signs from Heaven, including personal meetings with the Mother of Jesus Christ and Saint Michael the Archangel. Messages for the entire world have been imparted to Julia.

Between June 30, 1985, and January 14, 1992, a small statue of the Blessed Mother owned by Julia shed tears and oozed blood from the eyes for 700 days. Samples of the blood from the eyes of the statue were tested at the medical laboratory of Seoul National University and were found to be human blood.

In Korea, only 4 percent of the population is Catholic. But word about the weeping statue spread, and great crowds assembled to see the phenomenon. There was much shock when people witnessed the statue weeping blood.

From November 24, 1992, until October 23, 1994, fragrant oil flowed from the head of Julia's statue of the Blessed Mother.

The Blessed Virgin Mary has brought seven miraculous Eucharistic signs through Julia to awaken the world to the true presence of her Divine Son Jesus in the Blessed Sacrament. The seventh one occurred on November 24, 1994, when the apostolic pro-nuncio in Korea and a Vatican archbishop made a surprise official visit to Julia's home as representatives of the Holy Father, Pope John Paul II. Though the visit had not been officially announced (which is standard for such investigations), seven priests and approximately seventy people were present in the chapel of Julia's home to celebrate the second anniversary of the flowing of oil from Julia's statue when the Vatican representatives arrived.

While the archbishop and the apostolic pro-nuncio were praying with the group in the chapel, Julia received a message from the Blessed Mother requesting her to obtain the archbishop's blessings upon her hands. Julia obeyed.

The Blessed Mother then summoned Saint Michael the Archangel. He arrived immediately. Only Julia could see the Blessed Mother and Saint Michael the Archangel. But everyone knew that something extraordinary was happening to Julia by looking at her.

Suddenly, the Holy Eucharist appeared in Julia's hands. Julia later explained that it was brought to her by Saint Michael the Archangel at the request of the Blessed Mother. It was a large Host like the ones that priests use at Mass, broken in half. The archangel placed one half in her right hand and one half in her left hand. Julia then became enveloped in dazzling light and fell to the floor in a swoon.

The apostolic pro-nuncio removed the Sacred Host from Julia's hands and broke the pieces into smaller pieces so that others, who were in total amazement and awe, could receive the Holy Eucharist too. Even though it was only one Host, everyone in the chapel received Holy Communion.

The apostolic pro-nuncio preserved a small portion of the Sacred Host in a pyx for later investigation. He asked Julia whether she knew the origin of the Host brought to her by Saint Michael the Archangel. Julia asked the Blessed Mother and was told that the Host was about to be consumed by a priest when Saint Michael (for a spiritual reason) removed it from his hands.[1] (There are videos available that present details of these phenomena.[2])

The Blessed Mother has taught Julia a new way to pray. She has shared many great spiritual truths with her.

The apparitions and messages are so profound that Julia resigned her job as manager of the local hairdresser salon to devote herself full time to spreading the messages of the Blessed Mother. Julia explains that she has learned from the Blessed Mother that the whole world suffers because of errors that plague Christendom.

Through the prayer life that she learned from the Blessed Mother, Julia began to experience the presence of Jesus by interior illumination. Jesus has expressed to her His sorrow at the abandonment He experiences in these times because of the coldness and indifference of His followers who disregard his actual presence in the Holy Eucharist. He calls to His people to approach him in the Blessed Sacrament the way the shepherds and the wise men did on that first Christmas.

Julia has received six other Eucharistic miracles at Naju. On six separate occasions, the Sacred Host that Julia received in Holy Communion during Mass turned into visible flesh and began bleeding in her mouth. This phenomenon was witnessed by hundreds of people and was photographed and videotaped. The locations and dates of these miracles as well as the celebrants of the Masses are: Holy Rosary Church in Naju, South Korea, on June 15, 1988 (a Korean priest); Holy Rosary Church in Naju on May 16, 1991 (Father Jerry Orbos and Father Ernie Santos of the Philippines); Mass in hotel in Rome, Italy, on June 1, 1992 (Father Jerry Orbos); Catholic church in Lanciano, Italy, on June 2, 1992 (Father Jerry Orbos); Holy Rosary Church in Naju on September 24, 1994 (Father Jerry Orbos); and St. Anthony's Church in Kailua, Hawaii, November 2, 1994 (Father Martin Lucia).

Julia speaks about a great sign from Heaven that will be given in Korea for all the world. Jesus, truly present in the Eucharist, is central to the messages and charisms of Julia Kim. Julia says the Blessed Mother has spoken in depth to her about her Son Jesus, who hides His glory and power behind the appearances of bread and wine in a validly consecrated Host. Julia imparts messages for the world's priests, whom she says the Blessed Mother refers to as the successors of His apostles.

The Blessed Mother, Julia says, warns that only those who pray with the heart as the shepherds and the wise men did are able to recognize Jesus in His Eucharistic Presence. She has reminded Julia that her Son taught: "Blessed are the poor in spirit for they shall see God." Julia Kim quotes the Blessed Mother: "Those who are poor in spirit are the ones who hear the Word of God and understand. Those who are poor in spirit today see Jesus who is God, the Second Person of the Blessed Trinity hidden in the Blessed Sacrament."

An Interview with Julia Kim

Q. Julia, will you disclose some of the details of your visit to Heaven with the Blessed Mother?

A. It is very beautiful in Heaven. It is a place of pure peace, harmony, tranquillity, knowledge, understanding, and total, incomprehensible love that has no limit. It is impossible to describe the glories of Heaven.

Q. Did you see human beings in Heaven?

A. I saw the arrival of one of the children of the Blessed Virgin Mary into the heavenly Kingdom of God.

Q. Do you remember the details, Julia?

A. *(Smiling with great radiance)* I saw Jesus sitting in a chair. His Mother called to Him. He looked up in the direction of her voice with eternal love in His eyes. She exclaimed: "Jesus My beloved, *(name withheld)* is arriving from the earth!"

Q. Did you see the person?

A. Yes. I saw the person clinging to the Blessed Mother. The Blessed Mother was taller. She had both her arms around the person. She was smiling, a triumphant smile. She called to Jesus again: "Oh Jesus, isn't————— beautiful!"

Q. What did the Lord Jesus do?

A. Jesus leaped from His chair. He ran towards His Mother who placed the person out in front of her. Jesus enthusiastically embraced the person with great love, great joy, great gratitude. He was filled with love. He was filled with gratitude. He kept hugging the person. Then He stopped, looked into the eyes of the person and said joyfully:

"I have prepared a place of great glory for you! Come! Our Father is waiting for you!"

Q. Julia, how amazing!

A. How beautiful!

Q. Did you see anything else?

A. I saw Jesus and His Blessed Mother escort the person to a place I could not see.

Q. Julia, is it possible for you to describe Heaven? Did you observe any trees, flowers?

A. *(Smiling longingly)* I saw magnificent flowers, trees, sloping lawns, and the lushest of vegetation in heaven. The profusion of colors and textures were of such exquisite variety that I began to ponder only one leaf of a heavenly flower, yet it has "eternal variations."

Q. Does that mean that you could spend eternity looking at only one leaf and yet there would be too much to see to ever comprehend God's glory in the leaf?

A. *(Tears beginning to flow)* Too much to see. Too much to comprehend. Too much to speak. Heaven is love. Only love. Love is everything good because God is love.[3]

The Blessed Mother has given many signs and messages to Julia Kim, including:

"Recite the Rosary with fervor for peace in the world, in families and for the conversion of sinners.

"Revive the holiness of the family. Love each other in a spirit of humility. Serve one another in a spirit of trust. Forgive one another and you will be forgiven. Do not judge others. God alone knows the hearts and motives of His children. God is love. Many are lost by falsely judging others."

On September 24, 1994, Julia attended Mass with friends and visitors from the United States and the Philippines. At the consecration of the Mass Julia said that she saw the "merciful and smiling Jesus in the Sacred Host." After Julia received Holy Communion she entered into rapture and experienced the following vision:

Numerous people were on board several large ships which were sailing in the ocean. I was in one of them. The ship I was in was simpler than the others, lacking the luxurious decorations that other ships had, but had a large image of a dove at the head of the ship and also two banners in the middle of the ship. The banner on the right had the image of the Eucharist and a Chalice and the other on the left had a large *M* on it. Between the two banners was Our Mother of Mercy, wearing a blue mantle. She was so beautiful and filled with love. She was guiding the ship.

Other ships, on the other hand, had an image of the red Dragon erected on board and were brightly and luxuriously decorated in different colors: red, green, yellow and so on. There were large crowds of people in them eating, drinking and noisily enjoying themselves. At that moment, several people in our ship looked at the people in other ships with envious eyes. Immediately, those in other ships helped them cross over to their side. The Blessed Mother implored them not to go, but they ignored her and left. The Blessed Mother was shedding tears silently and sadly.

Some time passed. All of a sudden, a big storm was approaching and the sky was turning black. Soon, fireballs were falling down from the sky. The Blessed Mother promptly stretched out her mantle and covered us. We were safe. But those in the other ships were burning and screaming. They fell into the ocean and drowned after some struggle. It was a terrible scene that one could not even look at with open eyes. The Blessed Mother was watching this, shedding tears, and with so much anxiety. She began rescuing several people in the water who were approaching our ship, calling the Lord and asking for the Blessed Mother's help. They were people who had been blind, and fallen into the devil's temptation, but repented and sought the Lord at the last moment. When the Blessed Mother finished rescuing them, the storm ended and the ocean became calm. The sky became clear and blue again and a bright light was shining upon us. There were sounds of the angels singing: "Ave, Ave, Ave Maria." . . . At that moment, the Blessed Mother began speaking to all of us with a kind and gentle voice. . . .

"My most beloved children! In these end times, I called you to be my apostles and placed you in the refuge of Mary's Ark of Salvation which I prepared for you, as a hen gathers her chicks under her wings. Keep this in mind and do not look back or get off the Ark. I clearly tell you that, in this age of purification, I love not only your soul but also your body and walk with you holding your hand on this perilous road. This place is the shortcut to heaven where you can fully participate in the glory of my Son Jesus. I guide you all with my love so that you may become my little spiritual children. In that way, my Son Jesus and I converse with you and dwell together as a family.

"If all my children in this world transcend national boundaries, racial barriers and factional differences, form a unity and harmony with each other, and display the power of love, the Church will be revitalized, a shining new Pentecost will be realized and this world will be saved through the Lord Who is present in the Eucharist. . . . Humans can make mistakes, but remember that the Lord can turn evil into good, and use even our mistakes. Therefore do not judge and criticize others in human ways. The smaller separated churches have not accepted me yet, but they will gradually accept me as Mother of the Church. My beloved little souls! As I was together with the Apostles in the cenacle in Jerusalem, I will be always with you. Spread my words of love not only to Catholics, but to all my precious children in this world.

"Keep your mind wide open all the time. . . . Meditate deeply . . . stay awake. Then instead of the terrifying chastisement of blood and fire which are coming to this world, the Lord's infinite mercy and blessings of salvation will be bestowed upon you."[4]

Seredne, Ukraine: 1954 and 1987

The Ukrainian people have a special devotion to the Mother of God, the Theotokos, that began with the missionary activities of Saint Andrew the Apostle.[5] From the Ukraine, Christianity spread north and east to the other Slavic peoples. In 1037, the ruler Yaroslav the Wise dedicated the Ukraine to the Most Holy Mother of God, and ever since, she has been revered as Queen of the Ukraine. In modern times there are over 155 miraculous Marian icons that are venerated for their supernatural powers.[6]

After World War II, the Ukraine was absorbed into the Union of Soviet Socialist Republics. Atheism was imposed upon the people as state-ordered thinking and behavior. Subsequently, a bipolar balance of terror gripped the world. Weapons became increasingly more deadly as technology increased the human capacity for violence and destruction. Though the postwar period saw great moral strides (the United States, for example, exported dollars and know-how to rebuild war-torn Europe), international pluralism has contributed to ethical dilemmas concerning human values and the proliferation of nuclear power.

In the remote Ukrainian village of Seredne, on the vigil of the feast of the Immaculate Conception, December 21, 1954, a young girl, Anna, saw the Mother of God in a small church as she prayed after Mass. Anna said that the Beautiful Lady was so beautiful that she began to weep with joy. The Beautiful Lady wore a glorious dress all of white like shining lights, and a blue sash. She wore a golden crown with twelve stars that twinkled with dazzling light.

Many waited outside the church to hear Anna's testimony, and she found herself repeating her story for each interested person who approached her. Anna repeated the message she received from the Blessed Mother:

"My daughter, you see that I hold so many graces for my children which I am unable to give them because they do

*not ask for them. Our Father in Heaven respects the free-
dom of His beloved sons and daughters. Only if you turn to
me and ask am I permitted to bless you with the graces my
Son has given to me for each of you."*[7]

As the group listened in the outside grotto, once again
Anna saw the Blessed Mother, who turned and gazed at
the valley below. Just then, a shrieking wind whipped
through the grotto, extinguishing the candles and covering the people assembled there with dust. Anna said the
Blessed Mother extended her hands over the little group as
she consoled them with the promise:

*"I greatly desire to help poor sinners. A catastrophe is immi-
nent just as in the time of Noah. Many will die, not from
flood but by fire, because certain of God's children have so seriously disobeyed Him. Their offense has consequences that will
harm many innocent people. Never in its history has humanity
fallen so low. This is the age of the kingdom of Satan."*[8]

At those words a sudden darkness descended upon the
hill though the valley below was bathed in sunshine. Anna
told the people that the Blessed Mother was weeping. She
repeated the Blessed Mother's words:

*"From this mountain I see the whole world and all its sin-
ners. How God loves you, dear little children. How He
longs to help you in your misery. From this spring of water
which flows here, I will give abundance to anyone who
comes in a spirit of faith with a repentant heart. Accept the
gift and live as children of God, my dear little children."*[9]

That evening the villagers saw the mountain ablaze in an orange flame. Some said they heard the voices of angels singing throughout the night.[10] From then on, pilgrims began to assemble on the hill to pray, to sing, and to drink or carry away the water from the brook. After the signs in the sky, few doubted that the Holy Virgin had in fact visited them in Seredne.

Anna saw the Blessed Mother on fifteen more occasions. Many of the apparitions were accompanied by phenomena such as a spinning sun, shooting stars, powerful winds, and unusual cloud formations that onlookers noticed and cherished. The Blessed Mother taught Anna to pray with her heart; she explained some of the profound tenets of the Gospel of her Divine Son Jesus Christ. Faith flourished among the people as they quietly integrated the messages as best they could.[11]

Shortly thereafter, on May 15, 1955, Saint Michael the Archangel appeared to the young girl in the grotto. She described him as "shining like the sun with a flaming sword which he brandished three times in a swooping gesture, leaving a trail of fire blazing through the heavens to eternity."[12]

As Anna gazed at the flaming heavens, she saw the Blessed Mother appear in the center of immense rays of brilliant light. As the pulsating rays spun and danced, Anna recognized that the Blessed Mother was attired in her traditional robes and tiara as Queen of the Ukraine. She was standing upon a black serpent. As it tried to move, the Blessed Mother, without seeming to notice, merely pressed down with the point of her shoe and the snake was powerless. The Blessed Mother spoke with concern and compassion:

"My daughter, look at my injured heart. You, my children, ask me to be merciful to sinners and yet none of you cooperate with me or are willing to make reparations for the sins and insults to my Son Jesus. Many who come here to this grotto do so out of curiosity. Their disbelief truly wounds my heart.

"Rome will be ruined and the Holy Father killed, but Rome will rise again and be renewed through my presence here on this mountain of Seredne. From this place, true faith will again spread throughout the world. There will be one church and one Pontiff and there will be peace on earth and mankind will marvel at my merciful heart."[13]

Anna had little understanding of the message she had heard. More sophisticated theologians, however, understood the "ruin of Rome and the killing of the Holy Father" to indicate an apostasy among bishops and priests who once faithfully preached the Gospel of Jesus. They who once accepted voluntary obedience to Rome now openly ridicule the teachings of the Holy Father.

When Anna least expected it, the Lord Jesus appeared to her during the Mass on the feast of Christ the King. He was seated on a throne from which He surveyed the world stretched out beneath His feet. A priest in golden vestments stood at the Lord's left side. He blessed the people in the church with a chalice. As he did so, a dark foreboding menace cast an ominous shadow over the priest.[14]

Some KGB and official atheist media scorned and mocked the beliefs of the people. The fame of Seredne was confined to the families of the few faithful who gathered to pray and hope. Fortunately, some had relatives abroad and the miracles, messages, and apparitions were preserved.[15]

Nuclear Warning

Since April 1987, as many as a half million people have claimed once again to see ongoing apparitions of the Blessed Mother with her holy angels in the Ukraine.[16] The visions began on the first anniversary of the explosion at the Lenin nuclear power plant in Chernobyl.[17] Following that nuclear disaster, radioactive materials were carried by the winds over Belorussia, Poland, and Eastern Europe and as far as Scandinavia and the United Kingdom.[18] More than two million people were affected by radiation. Untold numbers suffered and continue to suffer from severe burns, leukemia, and respiratory diseases.

Exactly one year later, hundreds of thousands of people began to see the Queen of the Ukraine in the sky in Hrushiv. The Blessed Mother spoke of the accident at Chernobyl as a warning to the world:

> *"Do not forget those who have died in the Chernobyl disaster. Chernobyl is a reminder and a sign for the whole world. . . ."[19]*

The site of the apparitions to the multitudes of Ukrainians was at one time a famous place of pilgrimage in the Carpathian Mountains. The Blessed Virgin Mary appeared there 350 years ago, and Ukrainians honored the heavenly visit with annual pilgrimages, processions, festivals, and hymns. The people of Hrushiv planted a weeping willow tree at the site and, after many years, a spring suddenly appeared beneath the tree. The people saw the spring as a divine manifestation. The sick and sorrowing came to the spring.

When the cholera epidemic attacked the village of Hrushiv in 1855, a local person dreamed that the Blessed Mother instructed the people to clear and reclaim the ancient spring, to have a Mass celebrated in honor of the Lord Jesus, promising that the epidemic would cease in the village. The people did as they were instructed. Not one cholera death was thereafter reported. By 1856, a small chapel was built in thanksgiving at the site of the reclaimed spring and named in honor of the Holy Trinity. In 1901, the chapel and spring were designated an official shrine.

On May 12, 1914, the Blessed Mother once again appeared in the Ukraine at the shrine of the Holy Trinity to twenty-two people who were working in the fields near the chapel. People gathered from the entire area to see the vision, which lasted into the next day. The message from the Blessed Mother of Hrushiv, as that event came to be named, was prophetic. There would be war. Russia would become a godless country and Ukraine would lose its sovereignty for eighty years, but would be free afterwards.[20]

The apparitions of 1987 were reported around the world. Atheists and believers alike saw the Blessed

Mother in the sky. Pilgrims from all over began pouring into the area. In Moscow, the *Literary Gazette* reported that as many as 45,000 people converged on the shrine daily.[21]

The KGB officer assigned to manage the crowds and disperse them at any cost, including life and property, was the father of only one small son. Suddenly the boy fell desperately ill with a mysterious illness. Doctors said he was dying and there was nothing they could do for him. An old woman assured the officer that if he refrained from bulldozing the chapel, as he had been ordered to do, she would ask the Lord Jesus to honor His Blessed Mother Mary with a total cure for the little boy.

As the boy neared death, his mother screamed at her husband: "Make the promise! Our son is dying!" The frightened officer got down on his knees and prayed to the Lord he thought did not exist: "Spare my son to honor your Mother and I shall never harm anyone or anything that belongs to you." That evening the boy was mysteriously restored to perfect health. Word spread and the numbers of people flocking to Hrushiv increased dramatically. The KGB officer kept his promise.[22]

Television cameras filmed the crowds gathered at the small shrine in prayer. The program showed an unusually bright light covering the crowd and the surrounding area.[23]

The message reported from the Blessed Mother follows in part:

"Forgive your enemies. Through you and the blood of the martyrs will come the conversion of Russia. Repent and love one another. The times are coming which have been

foretold as being those in the end times. See the desola-
tion which surrounds the world . . . the sins, the sloth, the
genocide. Pray for Russia. Oppression and wars continue to
occupy the minds and hearts of many people. Russia, de-
spite everything, continues to deny my Son. Russia rejects
real life and continues to live in darkness. . . . If there is
not a return of Christianity to Russia there will be a third
world war and the whole world faces ruin."[24]

In April 1988, once again reports of apparitions of the
Blessed Mother above the Holy Trinity chapel at the
shrine at Hrushiv began to draw crowds. By now officials
were indifferent to the crowds. Parts of the message that
was reported follow:

"Teach the children to pray. Teach them to live in truth
and live yourselves in truth. Say the Rosary. It is the
weapon against Satan. He fears the Rosary. Recite the
Rosary at any gathering of people.

"I have come to comfort you and to tell you that your
suffering will end soon. I shall protect you for the glory
and the future of God's kingdom on earth, which will last
for a thousand years. The Kingdom of Heaven and Earth
is close at hand. It will come only through penance and the
repentance of sin.

"This wicked world is feasting on depravity and im-
purity. Many lies are proclaimed against the Truth. The
innocent are condemned. Many come as false messiahs and
false prophets. Be diligent. Be on your guard.

"Happy are they whose lives are blameless and who
walk in fear of the Lord.

"My children, all of you are dear to me and please my heart. I make no distinction of race or religion. You here in Ukraine have received the knowledge of the One, True, Apostolic Church. You have been shown the road to Heaven. You must follow this path, even though it may be painful.

"The Eternal God is calling you. This is why I have been sent to you. You in the Ukraine were the first nation to be entrusted to me. Throughout your long persecution, you have not lost faith, hope or love. I always pray for you my dear children, wherever you are."[25]

Cuenca, Ecuador: 1990

Sixteen-year-old Patricia Talbot was beautiful. Her plan was to become a famous model, travel the world, and eventually marry and become a mother. For those goals, study and schooling were irrelevant. Or so Paci (pronounced *Pah-chee*), as she is familiarly known, thought. Though she attended a Catholic girls' high school, Paci was uninterested in spiritual matters and attended Sunday Mass only as an obligation. Then a great gift from Heaven arrived in Paci's life. The Blessed Mother began appearing to her on August 28, 1988.

Paci had a job as a model. In October 1988, her group of models participated in a fashion show in Mexico City. After the performance, the girls visited the sights. As Paci was kneeling in the grand Cathedral of Mexico City in Zocalo Square, she prayed fervently at the side altar of Our Lady of Guadalupe, "Why me, dear Blessed Mother? I am not good. I am not intelligent. I am not holy." No sooner did she finish her sorrowful questions than the Blessed Mother became visible. She showed Paci a vision of a field filled with children of all races. Their faces were pockmarked and quite scarred. The Blessed Mother disclosed to Paci that these children represented the people of all nations who live in these times. Everyone on earth is in need of great healing.

A few days later, Paci visited the famous Shrine of Our Lady of Guadalupe in Mexico City, where the original tilma of Juan Diego is enshrined. She may or may not have realized that the Mother of God herself appeared at that very spot in 1531. Once again the Blessed Mother appeared, this time to Paci, and communicated her messages for Paci to share with others. "Pray the Rosary. Go to daily Mass. Wear the brown scapular. Do works of mercy for others." The Blessed Mother then entrusted a secret message to Paci.

Paci soon decided to forgo modeling as a career. The Blessed Mother appeared to her and said that she had made a good decision that would bear much fruit. Paci began to pray more and more each day. She began to shift her focus gradually away from the passing delights of the material world to the eternal joys that God gives as surprises every day to those with eyes to see truth.

A group of young people gathered weekly with Paci to pray the Rosary. The Blessed Mother asked the group to gather clothing for the poorest in the town, and to provide a hot meal for the hungry poor. The young people responded with joy and enthusiasm. There is now a place where the poor can come six days a week to obtain clothing and a hot meal. Paci's Rosary prayer group staffs the center.

Paci has been led to pray for priests and religious. The Blessed Mother confided to her that Satan tempts them relentlessly and that confusion is their primary challenge.

The Blessed Mother asked Paci to locate a place where her children could come to her. She said that she desired to visit her children and to bless them. Just outside the city and high in the Andes Mountains, Paci found a lovely garden, El Cajas. The Blessed Mother appeared to Paci there and promised that she would come to the garden, especially on the first Saturday of the month.

On the first Saturday of February 1990, 100,000 people climbed the steep, tortuous, mud-filled path of the mountain in teeming rain. They spent the night on the mountain in the darkness, comforted only by their love for the Blessed Mother and her Divine Son.

When the Mother of God appeared in the morning, calling everyone present "My little children," every heart became more receptive.[26] The Blessed Mother consoled the people on the mountain, saying that hard times have already begun. Some grave warnings of future events have been entrusted to Paci. The Blessed Mother promised that at the end of all her apparitions in the world, she would leave a permanent sign in every place where she has appeared.

Though Paci's apparitions of the Blessed Mother ended in 1992, she continues to experience locutions from the Blessed Mother, the Lord Jesus, Saint Michael the

Archangel, and Saint Joseph. The Blessed Mother disclosed to Paci that just as Saint John the Baptist served as the precursor of the Lord Jesus, so the Blessed Mother is sent in these times before Jesus arrives as just judge. The messages of Paci stress prayer, fasting, reconciliation among people, penance, and works of mercy.[27]

PART FOUR

Mother of the Church

As the millennium draws to a close, the Blessed Mother is appearing all over the world with increasing frequency. In the final three chapters of this book you will read about her urgent messages to each one of us. Chapter 12 is devoted to apparitions of the Blessed Mother in the United States, where increasingly she is seen by both rich and poor. Chapter 13 will look at visions in Communist and formerly Communist nations, which show especially the fulfillment of the prophecies at Fatima. The apparitions in this book's final chapter reveal that each one of us can do his or her part, however small, to bring peace to this troubled world.

As you read this section, you will see that the Mother of the Church is mother to us all. Like all mothers, she wants her children to love each other, to put aside their grudges, and to forgive one another for the love of God. When we are able to do so, we will truly have peace on earth.

CHAPTER TWELVE

Queen of Angels[1]

"See, I am sending an angel before you, to guard you on the way and bring you to the place I have prepared. Be attentive to him and heed his voice. Do not rebel against him, for he will not forgive your sin. My authority resides in him. If you heed his voice and carry out all I tell you, I will be an enemy to your enemies and a foe to your foes."

EXODUS 23:20–22

Scottsdale, Arizona, and Emmitsburg, Maryland

Scottsdale is a suburb of Phoenix, Arizona. It is in a valley that nestles comfortably at the base of sharply jutting mountains against a usually cloudless sky. The desert lies beyond the mountains. Camelback Mountain actually looks like a resting camel against a blue backdrop. Tourists come, especially in winter, to play golf on the championship courses that sprawl below Camelback Mountain in Scottsdale.

Approximately half the population of Arizona is Catholic. Saint Maria Goretti parish is located in Paradise Valley, a suburb of Scottsdale that is jokingly referred to as the "millionaire's ghetto." Nine young people from the parish, who hardly knew one another, each approached the pastor, Father Jack Spaulding, with a strange story in late summer of 1988.

Two weeks earlier, on August 15, Father Jack, as he is generally known, was in Medjugorje for the feast of the Assumption of the Blessed Virgin Mary. He admits that he was somewhat appalled by the huge crowds in the village for the feast day, the humidity and intense heat, the general disorder that surrounds mobs of stimulated people. As he proceeded into the church of Saint James with nearly a hundred other priests and bishops from around the world, Father Jack spoke interiorly to the Blessed Mother, half in disgust and half in exhaustion. He never thought that she even heard him, let alone might answer him as he sighed, "You're not here, dear Blessed Mother. This place is like a carnival." To his shock and disbelief, he clearly heard a beautiful feminine voice say, "Oh yes I am here and I am coming home with you."

When Father Jack returned home to Scottsdale, several parishioners approached him to ask for a Medjugorje-type prayer group that would include recitation of the Rosary and the Chaplet of Divine Mercy, Benediction of the Most Blessed Sacrament, Mass, and a healing service in Saint Maria Goretti Church on Thursday evenings. Father Jack readily agreed, and the format of the nightly service in Medjugorje, during which the visionaries of Medjugorje experienced their evening apparitions, was adapted for Saint Maria Goretti. This format was being introduced in parishes throughout the world at the time.

Shortly after the prayer group began on Thursday evenings, Father Jack received a phone call from a thirty-year-old woman who had an unusual story to share with him. Gianna Talone was a pharmacologist who had visited Medjugorje in June 1988. While there, she told the pastor, the Blessed Mother had spoken to her. Father Jack was unprepared to comment, so he listened patiently, though with marked discomfort, as Gianna disclosed that both Jesus and Mary were now speaking to her. Father Jack suspected that this experience was a "me too" of the Medjugorje apparitions. (Such copycat experiences were reported throughout France after the apparitions of Saint Bernadette Soubirous were announced at Lourdes.) Father Jack advised Gianna to be prudent and to pray for guidance. He told her to tell no one of her experiences.

Within a short period of time, eight others—Annie Ross, Mary Cook, Jimmy Kupanoff, Steve and Wendy Nelson (brother and sister), Stephanie Staab, Susan Evans, and James Pauley—came to see Father Jack. Except for Steve and Wendy, none of them knew that anyone else was experiencing the same phenomenon.

"I think I am going crazy, Father!" was the typical comment. "A voice is speaking to me!" Father Jack strongly advised and requested each of them to tell no one of the experience. The young people ranged in age from nineteen to thirty-one. There were six women and three men.

Shortly after the last person made himself known to Father Jack, Gianna returned to see him. "Father, I had a vision of Our Lady. Seven of us were kneeling at Our Lady's feet. Two people were standing. The only person I recognized was Stephanie."

Father Jack began to pastor the group of nine. They began to meet together to pray. The voices, known as interior locutions, continued for the group. Certain ones also began to report experiencing apparitions. On December 19, 1989, Gianna claimed that the Blessed Mother appeared to her in her home. Nine days later, on December 28, 1989, the Blessed Mother appeared to Gianna and to Annie in Saint Maria Goretti Church during the Rosary at the Thursday night prayer group. Thereafter, each Thursday evening, during the Rosary, the Blessed Mother continued to appear to either Gianna or Annie, or both. Father Jack made a practice of reading the message the women recorded after their vision to the prayer group.[2]

News of "the Scottsdale apparition" spread throughout the United States and abroad among the Marian Medjugorje Centers. At the time, few people understood what the phenomenon meant. Spiritual directors and theologians were cautious but interested. Father Jack was extremely careful and always gracious to people from around the world who began to seek information. The bishop, a personal friend of the pastor, was sensitive and wise.

Gianna Talone Sullivan is a vivacious, small-boned woman with a doctorate in pharmacology from the University of Southern California. She is multi-talented, with a background that includes experience as a television personality. She performed in different television series, did commercials and fashion modeling. When she was nine years old, she and her older sister Claudia were special hostesses at the Convention Ball in Beverly Hills that honored Ronald Reagan as governor of California. As a youngster, Gianna lived in Beverly Hills and was involved in the glamour and excitement of Hollywood.

By now in her late thirties, Gianna says that Jesus has

identified Himself to her as "Jesus of Mercy" and has communicated messages to her for the world.[3] These messages have been compiled and are available for interested readers.[4] Gianna says the appearances of Jesus to her are a universal call to holiness, as His first message indicates:

> *"My child, I would like you to start being and living the holiness of Me . . . not only in your actions but also in your daily thoughts and feelings. Do not be holy only superficially, be holy within and throughout your entire body. BE ME!"*[5]

In 1993, Gianna and her husband, a physician and internist by specialty, felt called by the Blessed Mother to move to Emmitsburg, Maryland. In that place where Saint Elizabeth Ann Seton, the first canonized American saint, resided, Gianna and her husband are involved with the Mission of Mercy, an ambulatory medical care center for the rural poor. A medical team that sometimes includes Gianna, her husband, and others goes out daily by van, stocked with medical supplies, to sick shut-ins, or to sick persons with no medical insurance or funds who have no other access to medical care. The Mission of Mercy mobile unit brings free medical diagnosis, hands-on care, prescriptive drugs, and supplies. The stated goal of the Mission of Mercy is to bring medical care, compassion, and dignity to the poverty-stricken sick.

Since 1994, on Thursday evenings at 7:00 P.M., Gianna and her husband attend a Medjugorje-type prayer group cenacle that includes recitation of the Rosary, the Chaplet of Divine Mercy, Consecration to the Immaculate Heart of Mary, Benediction of the Most Blessed Sacrament, Mass, and a healing service in the historic Saint Joseph's Catholic Church in Emmitsburg, Maryland. During Eucharistic Adoration in front of the Blessed Sacrament, the Rosary is recited as a form of meditation on the scriptural passages of Jesus' life on earth. At the third mystery, Gianna is seen to fall into ecstasy. People wait in silence. After the ecstasy, Gianna writes whatever message she receives from the Blessed Mother for the prayer group. Gianna indicates that sometimes a special blessing from heaven is given to those who are present.

President Bill Clinton was playing golf on the course in front of Gianna's home in the summer of 1994. Gianna walked through the Secret Service agents to the president and handed him a copy of a letter she had recently written and forwarded to him; the letter contained information for him based on her visions and locutions concerning the United States. Gianna has also sent messages to the Holy Father, Pope John Paul II, and to other people as well. She says she is the recipient of several secrets from the Blessed Mother that involve the future of the United States and the world.

The pastor of Saint Joseph's Church, Father Alfred R. Pehrsson, reads Gianna's message from the pulpit each week. On February 2, 1995, Gianna said that the Blessed Mother appeared to her with the Christ Child in her left arm; the Blessed Mother was holding a golden scepter adorned with rubies in her right hand as a sign of her Son's kingship. The Blessed Mother was dressed all in white as was her Divine Infant, and both wore golden crowns.

A few minutes earlier, there was silence in the church as Gianna gazed into the vision that only she saw. The disabled in their wheelchairs stared at the blank space into which Gianna peered. Some of the sick were weeping. Gianna's ecstasy lasted nine minutes. Then she slowly put her head into her hands as people once again began to recite the Rosary. Shortly thereafter, Gianna recorded the following message in her notebook for the pastor to read:

"My dear little children, praise be Jesus! Little ones, fear is useless. What is needed is trust in God. Trust in Him at all times, in all instances, under all circumstances. Trust yourselves to Divine Providence. God is with you. God loves you. Little children, praise Him for allowing your eyes to gaze upon Him. If you are intimately united to His most Sacred Heart you will tap the source of repentant tears in admonishment of your sins. Seek to be cleansed of all your sins so that you will gain the joys of Heaven. . . . {B}e inspired by love of Jesus. Look to God and love all people. Consecrate all your affections and thoughts to God. Live in peace of conscience and joy of God's love for you. Do not reject anyone. Love and care for all people. I bless you, little ones, and take your petitions to my Son. Peace. Ad Deum."

On March 31, 1989, Annie Ross Fitch, one of the group of nine from Father Spaulding's parish, was attending a ceremony of dedication of the statue of Our Lady of Guadalupe in Saint Maria Goretti Church. She clearly heard a beautiful feminine voice speak to her:

"My child, you must make a decision. You must decide to give your life to me, or not. But you must make the decision now. There is no more time."

Annie decided immediately and walked up to the statue with her flowers. She placed them at the feet of the statue and interiorly gave her heart to the Blessed Mother forever.

That evening, when Annie returned to her apartment, she again heard the voice:

"My child, I desire for you to write my messages."

Since then, Annie has been receiving messages from the Blessed Mother. The Lord Jesus also began to speak to her. They have been helping Annie to let go of her former way of thinking, problem-solving, and living.

Annie confided many things about her conversations and visions. She said that the Blessed Mother explained to her:

"In your joy and in your enthusiasm, you are harming yourself and my other chosen ones. Silence, my dear one, is crucial. Silence is a gift. A grace. Silence is difficult and sometimes painful for the beginner who chooses to journey to God's will."

Annie was shown the admonishments and chastisements that await the world. Jesus and Mary have disclosed to her that Saint Maria Goretti Church will be a center of God's mercy and love for all. Annie's last regular apparition of the Blessed Mother occurred on October 18, 1990. She continues to see the Blessed Mother on her birthday and at times of difficulty.[6]

Steven Nelson was a steer wrestler and a calf roper when he began to hear the voice of the Blessed Mother. He claims that before his locutions, he went to church only "to keep Mom and Dad happy." As the voice spoke to Steve, his heart began to change. He moved back home, started to pray daily, and soon was attending daily Mass. "I couldn't get enough of it. I started getting involved." Steve says that both Jesus and Mary speak to him. He said of his gift, "The one thing the Blessed Mother has shown me is this: 'Steve, I need you to be you, and to show people that even though you have hard times, even though things go up and down, if you have hope and trust, you can still carry around God's joy and peace.' "

Susan Evans is dark-haired, effervescent, and filled with life. Her first locution was a male voice that startled her during a wedding reception. "Would you give up your family for me?" Susan realized immediately Who was speaking to her and she immediately responded in her heart: "Yes, Lord, because I love You more than anyone." After that experience, Susan felt compelled to pray to the Blessed Mother, even though she was somewhat afraid of her. She asked Mary to help her get near the Lord, to come back to church, to get her life in order. Within six weeks, Susan was back at church. In November 1987, the Blessed Mother told Susan that she desired a prayer group for young adults.[7] Susan subsequently approached Father Jack.

Susan was given the special symbol of charity by the Blessed Mother. Shortly thereafter, Susan felt a need to attend daily Mass. She said: "I was so drawn to the Eucharist. I cried receiving the Eucharist, because it is such a gift and because Our Lord brought me away from such a sinful life to a better life."

Jimmy Kupanoff went to Medjugorje with his family

before the spiritual phenomena began at Saint Maria Goretti parish. While he was at Medjugorje, Jimmy had a powerful realization of Jesus as Lord of all creation. In late summer 1988, the Blessed Mother spoke to Jimmy in clear interior words. He is a student at Arizona State University and works part-time. His symbol is compassion.

James Pauley, born in November 1971, is the youngest of the nine visionaries and locutionists of Scottsdale. He works full-time as the youth minister and director of the teen program in the parish. James traveled to England with Father Jack and worked with groups of young people who have given their lives in response to the messages which the Blessed Mother has given to the world at Medjugorje.

Mary Cook learned a lesson from the Blessed Mother. When Mary first began to experience locutions, her job was the center of her life. Now Mary allows only Jesus to be the center of her life. Mary first saw the Blessed Mother during the 1991 Medjugorje conference in Irvine, California. Mary says she hears both the Lord Jesus and His Blessed Mother. The following message was given to Mary for the young people's prayer group on January 17, 1992.

"My dear ones, it is I, your Mother. I am here tonight because my Son allows me to come to you, and because I love you so much! Thank you for being so devoted, so dedicated to my Son. My dear ones, tonight I ask you to make a commitment to prayer. It is crucial to my plan that you commit yourselves to prayer to my Son. Ask for my intercession and I will help you, I am always reaching my hand out to you, my little ones. Please take hold. I will lead you to my Son.

*Pray with your hearts, little ones, and you will find the
answers to my Son's will for you. Pray honestly to Him.
There is no need to hide anything. He knows everything."*

Like Steve Nelson, his younger sister Wendy grew up
on ranches in South Dakota and Nebraska. The family
moved to Scottsdale during their late teenage years. Jesus
spoke to Wendy as she worked with children at the convent of Mother Teresa's order in Phoenix: "Will you give
Me everything?" Wendy wept with joy as she committed
her life to Jesus. She saw the Blessed Mother shortly after
hearing the voice of the Lord. Wendy says that she continues to hear Jesus or His Blessed Mother. Her symbol is
strength.

Stephanie is considered a brilliant young woman. An
accountant by training and profession, she was the second
person to approach Father Jack about hearing a voice. She
had very little religious background at the time. She went
to church irregularly. Now her entire life is centered
around the will of Jesus. Stephanie receives messages and
lessons about life, ways to change her thinking so that
daily living is filled with real joy. The following message
she shares from Jesus is for all people everywhere and has
special significance for professionals:

*"Each of you women is to be an example of purity, chastity,
and innocence. I ask you, 'Can you deny your flamboyant
ways, desire to obtain this attention, and allow My
Mother's grace to enter you?' You shall shine, My dear
ones, shine with purity and grace. Clothe yourselves in
chastity, chaste garments, chaste actions, and chaste atti-*

tudes toward others, especially the men I have brought into your lives.

"Men, My sons, are you willing to give up your egotistic actions and attitudes? Will you accept these women as symbols of My Mother's purity, and treat them as you would My own dear Mother? Would you seek to possess her? Would you lust after her, the one full of grace? My dear sons, you would not. I tell you, no matter how poor in spirit one was, My Mother's grace dazzled their heart and left them with peace.

"I wish to sanctify each of these women, shearing away from them the hardness of the world. Can you accept them for the gems they shall become, and guard them carefully with your virtues? Your virtues—I tell you, they shall multiply. Man was created along with woman to be his helpmate. Do you think this statement is of the physical? It is a statement of the spiritual. Through these women, much grace shall flow, and it shall flow often upon you. Can you love them for this and not for the physical?

"My dear sons, do you think I ask much of you? I, if you say yes, shall sanctify your hearts. There are many ways to accomplish this, but what I offer to you now is the love of a pure and chaste relation between man and woman. Be one another's spiritual helpmate. Do not, I caution you, attach your own meaning to My divine words. . . ."[8]

Bishop Thomas O'Brien of Phoenix in his official capacity addressed the phenomena occurring in Saint Maria Goretti parish with wisdom that brings an explanation and a framework for all the private revelations that are reported around the world, especially those that are not officially sanctioned by the Church. In 1989, Bishop O'Brien appointed a commission to study the events in Scottsdale; in 1990, he released this statement regarding its findings:

> The commission concluded that the messages (locutions) "are explainable within the range of ordinary human experience" and they continued by stating "obviously we cannot know for certain whether or not the locutions or visions are miraculous in the true sense of the word. . . ." The commission also said, "Father Spaulding has demonstrated himself to be a good priest and he should be commended for his devotion to Our Lady."

> After much prayerful discernment, I have accepted the conclusions drawn by the commission and I have personally communicated this to Fr. Spaulding. . . . There may not be . . . any unequivocal claim of miraculous intervention. This is due to the absence of any external evidence that the messages are from Our Lord Jesus Christ or the Blessed Virgin Mary.

> Rooted in the faith of Catholics, the role of Mary is a part of the mystery of faith. This role belongs to public revelation and to the deposit of faith handed over to the apostles and presented by their successors in the official ministry of the Church. . . . However, even authentic devotions do not add anything new to our faith, but only recall what we have always believed. They remind us of our failure to practice our faith as we should, they call us to repentance and to a deeper and fuller faith in

Jesus Christ. In all time the Blessed Virgin Mary calls us to her Son who is Lord of all the ages.[9]

Phoenix, Arizona

Estella Ruiz is a happy woman filled with love. She is the mother of seven children and the grandmother of many more. Sunday afternoons have always been special at the Ruiz home. Reyes, Estella's husband, has had one requirement for his grown-up children: Those in the area must come home for Sunday dinner, and pray the Rosary together as a family.

The Ruiz home in south Phoenix is a busy place on most Saturday evenings. People from all around the world have congregated in the backyard around a shrine to the Blessed Mother that Reyes and his sons built years ago. The Ruiz family bustles about finding chairs, getting drinks of water for the sick, welcoming old friends and neighbors.

Inside, the little children jostle to get turns snuggling on their grandmother's lap. Others scurry about looking for rosary beads as they realize: "It's time for Our Lady to come!" Reyes kneels beside Estella, who is seated in a chair. "My knees are bad and the Blessed Mother knows that I need to protect them so that I can walk. She doesn't mind if I sit when she appears," Estella remarks to those who seem surprised that she does not kneel.

A loudspeaker broadcasts the voice of Reyes as he leads his family and the crowds in the recitation of the Rosary. When the apparition of the Blessed Virgin Mary occurs, a sweet silence spills over the living room where Estella gazes at what only she can see. The rest of the people see an image of Our Lady of Guadalupe that Reyes painted many years ago. He has placed photos of his children, grandchildren, and sons- and daughters-in-law in the Immaculate Heart portion of the painting.

Just as suddenly as it began, the apparition is over, and the Rosary continues. Afterward, Estella tells everyone what message the Blessed Mother has given. There are usually also a few private messages for some of the persons present.

Estella and Reyes were speaking at a healing Mass in a church in Santa Barbara, California, when first we met. Later, Estella shared the story of her first encounter with the Mother of God and the mission she has accepted in response to her apparitions. Estella laughingly admits that she did not have great devotion to the Blessed Virgin Mary before her apparitions. The following dialogue from that interview explains some of Estella's thinking.

An Interview with Estella Ruiz

Q. Why do you think the Blessed Mother began to appear to you, Estella?

A. *(Much laughter)* Because she has a good sense of humor. At the time of my first apparition, it was Reyes who was devoted to the Blessed Mother. After our children were raised, I decided to do a few things for myself. Though I had only a high school education, the women's movement made me start to think that maybe there was a chance for me to do something with my life. I began to think about a career. I got a job as a teacher's aide.

That was the beginning for me. I was able to obtain education through some of the available programs and I gradually became a leader in our school district. The more my career flourished, the farther away from the Lord I drifted. It was just that I was so busy at work, studying, and at home that I did not have much time to pray. Reyes, in the meantime, was praying for both of us. *(More laughter)* He went to daily Mass, prayed the Rosary every day.

Q. Were you happy, Estella?

A. I was having a wonderful time. I was working and studying to earn my master's degree in education. I was planning on getting my doctorate. I had a great job that I loved, and frankly, I did not believe that God or the Blessed Mother were interested or sensitive to women's rights.

Q. The Blessed Mother asked the visionary Lucia of Fatima to learn to read. That request was quite radical for the times and the culture in which Lucia lived.

A. I certainly know that now! Since I have been seeing the Blessed Mother and visiting with her during these years, I have come to know her better: her love, her wisdom, her power, her kindness, her compassion. Through these apparitions that I have had, my family, every one of us, has been blessed. We have all changed. We have all come closer to recognizing the truth.

Q. Do you know why the Blessed Mother is appearing, Estella?

A. Yes. She says the Eternal Father takes consecrations very seriously. The United States was consecrated to the Immaculate Heart of Mary by its first bishop, John Carroll, before we even had a constitution. The Blessed Mother appears to me as Our Lady of the Americas with messages for the United States.

Q. Do you remember the first apparition you had, Estella?

A. Of course! I can never forget the circumstances and the shock and the joy. Reyes went to Medjugorje. I thought he was rather a strange person to be running off to an Iron Curtain country searching for visions. I even mocked him.

Q. You mocked him for going to Medjugorje?

A. Not just for Medjugorje. He was always praying. He always had the rosary beads in his hands. I thought he lacked good, old-fashioned American ambition. I called him Holy Roly. Sometimes his prayer life was actually a source of embarrassment to me. Our son was elected a state legislator in Arizona, so I realized that there wasn't much I could do about Reyes's religiousness, and we were all managing in spite of his bizarre behavior.

Q. Don't you think God was hearing Reyes's prayers and helping everyone in your family?

A. I was a very skeptical person. I really did not believe in divine intervention in human affairs. I had seen much suffering and poverty in my life, in my work, and I thought hard work and human accomplishments were the only way to better ourselves. Our family had a lot of problems. Several of our children had problems.

Q. Is that why Reyes went to Medjugorje?

A. I don't think so. He is just in love with our Blessed Mother. In fact, I often thought he loved her more than the Lord. That really bothered me. The Blessed Mother is amazing. She never takes anything for herself. But I didn't know that then.

Q. How did your apparitions begin?

A. When Reyes was in Medjugorje, I dressed, as usual,

and was hurrying out the door of my house to drive to work. As I passed Reyes's painting of Our Lady of Guadalupe, I heard a quiet, clear, feminine voice, gentle yet so strong, say, "Good morning, my daughter." I was actually quite startled. I began to think that my imagination was playing tricks on me. I hurried off to work. But several days later, while Reyes was still in Medjugorje, the same thing happened again. This time I felt more open to the voice and I actually responded: "Good morning, dear Blessed Mother." It seemed so natural. Then I laughed at my foolishness. I said to myself: "I am getting as crazy as Reyes!" *(Laughter)*

Q. Did you think you imagined the voice?

A. I was not interested in analyzing the experience at all. I totally put it out of my mind.

Q. What happened next?"

A. When Reyes returned from Medjugorje, he was a different man. He had a peace, a gentleness, a strong love that I had never seen in anyone else before. I knew that something very special had been given to him there. Now I know that I was the one who had changed. I was now able to see what had probably been there in Reyes all along, but I didn't recognize his virtues. I was too much into the events of my career, my work to notice.

Q. Did your apparitions begin soon after Reyes's return from Medjugorje?

A. No. Our family continued to gather on Sunday afternoons to pray the Rosary and to have Sunday dinner as we always do. About three months after Reyes's pilgrimage to Medjugorje, we were all together on Sunday, praying the Rosary. It was December 3, 1988.

Suddenly, the Blessed Mother stepped out of the painting of Our Lady of Guadalupe. I recognized her voice right away as she said, "Hello, my daughter." I gasped in shock, in embarrassment and amazement. I said, "Blessed Mother, why would you appear to me? I don't even like you. It is Reyes who is your faithful child!" I can never forget her look of love. She smiled at me with so much love that I have no words to describe. I gave her my life, my family, my career—everything. She is filled with so much love! It is impossible to describe. Once you have seen her, there is really nothing that compares, even in a small way. To see the Blessed Mother is to see a part of Heaven! It makes everything here seem almost inconsequential except to love everyone and everything in God and for God.

Q. What did the Blessed Mother ask of you?

A. She told me she is Our Lady of the Americas. She asked me to be her messenger. She promised that she herself would help my family, that she would prepare us to better serve her Son Jesus.

Q. How did the Blessed Mother help your family?

A. She asked us to read the Bible every day. She asked us all to get involved in Bible study. She says we need to know the words of her Son. The apparitions happened almost daily in the beginning. If I was busy, she would call to me. Then I would kneel down and she would appear to me. After a while, the Blessed Mother asked me to get paper and pen so that she could dictate messages to me for others.

Q. What does the Blessed Mother ask of you?

A. She gives important messages for our times to prepare

our people in the United States for what lies ahead. The United States now has much spiritual sickness. The Eternal Father has sent the Blessed Mother as Our Lady of the Americas to our people in these difficult and dangerous times to help us and lead us back to her Divine Son. The United States is very dear to the Heart of God.[10]

Steubenville, Ohio

Tony Fernwalt never thought of himself as spiritual or holy. In fact, few have experienced the hardship that Tony knows well. He is no stranger to the prison system, to violence as a fact of life, or to raw poverty. On March 10, 1992, Tony was doing some cleanup work at Saint Jude's Orthodox Church. As he climbed the steps out of the basement where he had been working, he said:

> I could hear the voice of some young lady that sounded like she was singing, or crying. Then I smelled these roses. I mean the place just reeked of roses. It was so strong I couldn't believe it. . . . Then I peeked through the open door of the church and I saw this lady dressed all in red standing with her hands open in front of the altar. She was saying over and over:
>
> *"My Son's Heart is broken."*
>
> I thought, oh boy, her kid's been in an accident or something. Maybe he's in the service, or

sick, or getting a divorce. Anyway, it was none of my business. I shut the door to the basement. I figured to go to the back of the church and not bother her. As I walked past her she said again:

"My Son's Heart is broken."

She looked like she was from India or someplace like that. Long dress, draping veil, funny clothes. Everything was red. When I got to the back of the church, I sat down to rest on an old folding chair. She was right there! It scared me! First thing she says:

"As you know, my Son is Jesus."

That bothered me and I said: Yeah, and I suppose you're the Virgin Mary. I figured she was nuts and belonged in the state hospital, Fallsview or Massillon or someplace like that. I looked at her pretty close.

Then I started noticing the beauty of her. She looked too young to have a son in the service. I looked at her real close now. She looked too tall for her body. Something's wrong here, I said to myself. I started going down from her head down her whole body till I got to her feet. They were standing on a mist that was resting on the floor. Her feet were maybe a foot off the floor on the mist! She looked me right in the eye and said: *"Yes."*

Something in me told me that this was serious—it gripped me—choked me—I couldn't breathe. I'm sitting in the chair—I felt like I was dying. I grabbed my neck. She said:

"Do not be afraid."

I was scared—but some kind of peace came to me when she spoke:

"Do not be afraid."

She said:

"You have sinned against God, you have sinned against my Son and you have sinned against God's children."

I knew that I had whipped my kids, and my wife. Then she started to tell me about other things I did—she said I wanted to be cruel. I figured anybody can look up the court records. It's all there. Then she said:

"You need to pray. Pray that people come back to church. Pray that people come back to my Son. Pray for forgiveness. Ask my Son for forgiveness."

Then I started to see my sins unfold in front of me. Only now I wasn't thinking how I felt. I could feel how the others felt when I was hurting them. I felt their pain. I even felt their fear. If I hit somebody, I felt the hurt. I could feel their mental and physical pain when I hurt them. She kept asking me to ask Jesus for forgiveness for each thing I did that I was seeing. She told me about things I did that nobody ever, ever knew. I thought, I'm dying. I can't stand this. I didn't see anything good I had ever done in my life. Only the bad stuff. And there was plenty of bad stuff. I was kind of mad.

I said, If you are who you say you are, I want to know about the world, things that they say are going to happen. We talked about wars, riots, violence in the cities. She said that God does not cause these. We do. She told me about lots of things that are going to happen on the earth. I said to her, I've been bad all my life. Why would you care about me? I would have sold your Son for thirty pieces of silver too, maybe less. She looked at me—I could see her love for me. She said:

"No, you are only a child. People will come and teach you love. They will help you to love and understand. I will take you from a Saul to a Paul. I will leave signs to prove that I was here and believers will come and see and believe."

She promised that the scent of roses would be a sign. Things would turn gold. The sick would be healed and weak faith would become strong. She said:

"My Son wants all people to return to Him. Pray that sinners will be converted. Pray that their hearts turn back to my Son. My Son wants all souls. He does not want to lose even one soul."

On March 26, 1995, Jesus appeared to Tony in Our Lady of the North American Martyrs Church in Steubenville, Ohio. Tony reports that when Jesus appears, the tabernacle radiates and His form comes from within the tabernacle. He stands on a cloud of bright light. He wears a robe of glowing white. His hair and eyes are brown. Rays of light emanate from the open tabernacle. His messages to Tony include the absolute necessity of sacramental confession:

"People go to confession and do not confess their deepest sins. Unconfessed sins are not forgiven. One day they will be revealed to everyone. Only sins that are fully confessed are totally washed away. They no longer exist. There are those who received the Holy Eucharist without making a truthful confession or having real sorrow for their sins. This is an even deeper sin."

Jesus asked for perpetual adoration everywhere. Jesus said that when we receive the Holy Eucharist, a part of Him becomes a part of us. And a part of us becomes a part of Him. Jesus said to Tony:

"I am truly My Father's Tabernacle. I am truly your Tabernacle. I am also present, physically, in every Tabernacle throughout the world.

> *"Listen to the teachings of Pope John Paul II. Read Scripture. Return to church. Pray for the Pope, bishops, priests and religious.*
>
> *"Love your spouse and children. Imitate the Holy Family of Nazareth.*
>
> *"Evil grows fast. It is the responsibility of every citizen, not just the government, to help the poor.*
>
> *"Love one another. Respect one another. Do not judge one another."*[11]

Conyers, Georgia

Nancy Fowler is a registered nurse. A middle-aged housewife and mother of two young sons, she made a pilgrimage to Medjugorje in 1988. Later she reported that she had visions of the Blessed Virgin Mary on the thirteenth of the month for a few years in the early 1990s. Newspaper reporters who covered the event noted that the apparitions occurred in a farmhouse next door to Nancy's home in Conyers. Thousands of people assembled to pray the Rosary as loudspeakers carried messages during the monthly noon-hour apparitions.

Nancy also disclosed apparitions and messages from the Lord Jesus. She says that when she asked Jesus why she was chosen for such a privilege, "Jesus told me He chose me because He desired to select a soul greatly in need of His mercy."

The Washington Post featured a front-page article on October 14, 1994, about the final apparition in Conyers, Georgia, to the nurse: "On a misty, cold and muddy hill here, more than 30,000 people gathered today in near silence to listen to every amplified syllable spoken by an ordinary-looking woman in a green raincoat. The soft, childlike voice belonged to Nancy Fowler, a 46-year-old homemaker, but Fowler said the words belonged to the Virgin Mary."[12]

There is a man-made mound called "the hill" behind Nancy's home. It contains a cross; rocks of different sizes; and medals, crosses, and other memorabilia left there by the people who come to pray. There is a well nearby that Nancy says has special healing qualities.

On a cold Georgia night in January 1992, several who were gathered on "the hill" noticed that the half-moon in the starless sky seemed to split (the way one sees a cell divide under a microscope). The "second half-moon" flipped over so that now everyone observed a full moon surrounded by pulsating rays of golden light in such a way that it resembled the Holy Eucharist in a golden monstrance. Many clouds moved briskly about the full moon. Suddenly a cloud formation that resembled Our Lady of Medjugorje, with her left hand pointing to the full moon, was quite clear in the sky. At the same time other clouds formed a vertical chain, or ladder of angels, beside the cloud formation that resembled the famous image of Our Lady of Medjugorje. Counting the ladder of angels, beginning with the smallest one on the bottom rung to the huge one at the top, there were nine angels. "One for each of the nine choirs!" someone in the group observed.

At that moment, everyone present realized that each had been to Medjugorje. They decided that the scene in the sky they were witnessing identified the real title for

Our Lady of Medjugorje, "Our Lady of the Eucharist," for she continually leads all people to her Son Jesus. Her hands first presented Jesus to the Magi and shepherds who found Jesus by means of signs in the sky. Two thousand years later, on that cold night in Conyers, Georgia, the signs in the sky said much about Jesus in the Eucharist.

Before dawn the next morning, all the people in the group went to Holy Spirit Monastery in Conyers. They attended Mass with the Cistercian monks and received Jesus in the Eucharist. The chapel of the monastery was filled with pilgrims that morning. There were not enough seats to accommodate the crowds. No one, however, seemed to mind standing for the Mass.

Stories circulate of physical, spiritual, or psychological healings by those who traveled to Conyers in search of God. Signs such as the miracle of the sun, and the chains of rosaries, medals, and other religious objects mysteriously turning golden in color, are also reported.

By 10 A.M. on January 13, 1992, throngs of people were filling the grounds of Nancy's home and the neighbor's home where the announced apparition would occur at noon. News reporters were wandering through the crowds asking questions like, "Why are you here?" The sick said they were looking for miraculous cures. Other answers were as varied as the outfits the people wore on that dreary, cold day.

Only invited guests and some of the sick were permitted into the large room where the alleged apparition was to take place. All the others hovered around the porch of the farmhouse near the loudspeakers.

At 11:45, Nancy entered the large room filled with

praying people. She sat in a chair in the front left-hand corner and peered at a statue of the Blessed Mother holding the Infant Jesus. It was located high on a shelf in front of her. Someone sat beside her with pen and paper to record her words. Various preselected persons stepped in front of the standing mircophone to lead the crowds outside in the recitation of the Rosary. Suddenly a male voice said, "Quiet. The Mother of God is here." A little after the noon hour, Nancy read her message over the loudspeaker and described what she saw.

Outside, some said they saw luminary signs like the spinning of the sun, the strange formation of clouds, and sudden, unexpected lights as they prayed the Rosary. Others began to gather their belongings and return to their cars. Some walked next door to Nancy's house to procure water from the well. People began to inquire among themselves, "What did you see? What did you hear?"

Each carried the message they were told was given for them from the Mother of God. One man commented, "At least we made the effort to come here. God knows our hearts." The monthly apparitions were reported by Nancy Fowler to have ended in October 1994.[13]

Chicago, Illinois

In 1987, eighty-three-year-old retired railroad worker Joseph Reinholtz made a pilgrimage to Medjugorje. While there, Vicka Ivankovic, one of the six visionaries, prayed over him because he had partial blindness that made it difficult for him to see. As Vicka prayed, Joseph made a vow to dedicate the rest of his life to prayer for the terminally ill.

When Joseph returned to his home in a Chicago suburb, he often knelt in front of a small crucifix, purchased in Medjugorje, and a statue of the Blessed Mother. One day as he prayed, he recovered his sight. The first object that he observed was the statue of the Blessed Mother weeping. The statue continued to weep for three days and three nights.

In the spring of 1989, Joseph returned to Medjugorje to thank God for restoring his sight. Vicka noticed him one day in a crowd and she approached him to speak privately to him. The conversation lasted nearly four hours. Joseph spoke the only language he knows, English. Vicka spoke in Croatian, yet each understood the other perfectly. Padre Pio, the stigmatist Franciscan priest, once said from his monastery in San Giovanni Rotondo: "Differences of language and barriers between souls disappear when we speak the only language that really matters, that of the spirit."[14]

Vicka shared with Joseph that he had been chosen for a mission in his home diocese. She advised him to look for a special crucifix that is fifteen feet tall and stands between two trees, one of which is triple-branched. When Joseph returned to his home he began the search for the crucifix. He finally located the fifteen-foot cross in the military section of the Queen of Heaven Cemetery in Chicago, near his home. Joseph prayed daily in front of the cross for about a year. He reports that then something unusual happened.

In August 1990, Joseph, the man who had been

cured of partial blindness, saw the Blessed Mother standing near the crucifix. Joseph said the Lady from Heaven spoke to him, giving him messages for the world. Joseph says that the Blessed Mother asks all people on earth to sacrifice more and to pray sincerely with their hearts.

People flocked to the cemetery to pray. Many desired to see the Beautiful Lady from Heaven, too. They were not disappointed. Reports of healings, conversions, the mysterious scent of roses, the "miracle of the sun," and rosaries changing colors drew pilgrims from everywhere to the fifteen-foot cross in the cemetery. The triple-branched tree next to the cross was named the "Trinity tree."

Officials of the Archdiocese of Chicago investigated and stated that nothing supernatural was going on at the cross. The cross, however, has been moved to a parking lot in the cemetery to accommodate the large crowds that gather there.

On January 9, 1993, Joseph reported that the Blessed Mother, accompanied by many angels, gave a message for the world, excerpted as follows:

"Praise Jesus my children! I am the announcement of the 'New Era.' In the deep darkness of your times, if you live with me you can already glimpse the first glow of the 'new times' that await you. Look to the Light and live in peace of heart and hope. If you remain always in my Immaculate Heart, my beloved ones, even as of these moments you can begin the 'New Era' of holiness, of grace, of light, of purity, of love, and of peace. I am your Mother, the Queen of Peace."[15]

Santa Maria, California

In May 1990, I was working in Los Angeles on a project. The inaugural issue of *Mary's People*, with an insert containing the fourth *Queen of Peace Newsletter* from the Pittsburgh Center for Peace, was being prepared by the staff of Twin Circle Publishing, and I was there to participate in its preparation. Some trusted, dear friends, Bob and Clare Schaefer, offered to take me to nearby Santa Maria, where it was said that a housewife was receiving messages from the Blessed Mother, who desired that a huge cross be erected on a hill overlooking the town.[16] We drove to the hill.

To our amazement, perhaps as many as twenty thousand people, mostly of Spanish descent, were assembled on the hill. They were dressed in their Sunday finery. The men, for the most part, wore suits with white shirts and neckties. The women were beautifully attired as if they were guests at a wedding. But it was the children who were exquisite. Some of the little girls wore white dresses, white shoes, and white veils. The little boys were wearing suits, white shirts, and neckties, like the men.

People were praying the Rosary. They were singing hymns. The sun was hot and there was no room to sit down, but no one seemed to mind standing on the hillside. There was a spirit of joy and expectation in the air. Suddenly people began to exclaim: "Look—the sun!" We looked at the high noon sun, and it was spinning and pulsating. Great rays of light, of every possible color, streaked from the center of the sun across the sky like lightning. Some people near us were weeping. Some were frantically trying to film the phenomenon. Others simply gazed in silent wonder.

A little girl, perhaps six or seven, who was standing near my small group, suddenly fell to her knees and stretched her arms towards the sun, crying: *"Madre de Dios!"* [Mother of God] *Madre de Dios!"* Two little boys, perhaps two and three years old, also fell to their knees. Great tears of joy tumbled to the ground from their cheeks as they too cried out: *"Madre de Dios!"* Their little arms reached up to a figure only they saw.

People with Polaroid cameras who had photographed the spinning sun began to make loud exclamations: "Look! The Blessed Virgin!" I walked over to a woman whose Polaroid was in the process of producing such a photo and asked her if I might have it. She seemed confused, but she agreed. I held the photo in a normal way in front of eyewitnesses until it was fully developed, about three minutes. There in the photo was a white image of the traditional Blessed Virgin figure.

The Blessed Virgin had said at Medjugorje that we can always find her when we visit the Blessed Sacrament, for she is ever in union with her Divine Son. Is the spinning sun phenomenon, which people all over the world now claim to see, a symbol of Jesus, who is truly present in the Eucharist?

We were so deeply touched by the experiences around us that at first we hardly noticed a bird that appeared to fly out of the sun. It swooped before us and seemed to pause near the kneeling children for a moment. Then the bird ascended high in the sky in front of us and, surrounded and encased in a pure white light, flew back into the sun. It was then that we realized it was Pentecost Sunday. We all experienced a truly unforgettable Eucharistic celebration that special day on the hill in Santa Maria.

CHAPTER THIRTEEN

Victorious Queen

He will wipe every tear from their eyes, and there shall be no more death or mourning, wailing or pain, [for] the old order has passed away.

REVELATION 21:4

China: Our Lady of the New Advent

Over the centuries, the people of China have undergone much suffering and political upheaval. Millions perished in war and famine. Missionaries brought Christianity to China, but realized little success except where the glories of the Blessed Virgin Mother of God were extolled.[1] Many Chinese cannot comprehend how the Infant Jesus Christ can be honored as God unless His Mother is venerated as sacred.[2] Devotion to the Blessed Virgin Mary has flourished in the sparse settlements where Christianity has taken root in China. Most people in China, whatever their personal religious beliefs, do know about the Blessed Virgin Mary.[3]

Because of the ideas of Confucius and the deep veneration of ancestors which are the patrimony of the Chinese people, it is logical that the Blessed Mother of Him who is the salvation of the world should be a profound object of love and devotion in China. And she is.

The Vincentian Fathers had established a mission in Dong Lu, the poorest region in the area near Peiping. It was known as the place of beggars. In 1900, during the violent Boxer Rebellion, 10,000 warriors attacked the hamlet of Dong Lu. The 700 Christian residents had no chance of survival in the face of such armed fury. They clung together in profound, fervent prayer.

Suddenly, the ferocious soldiers began to fire their weapons into the sky as they shouted obscenities and vengeance. Then, just as suddenly, the entire force of 10,000 men turned and fled the village with a speed that only those consumed with mortal fear can muster. Legend says that the villagers beheld a Beautiful Woman surrounded with celestial light in the sky above. The bullets of the warriors did no harm to her presence, her beauty, or her peace. Suddenly, however, a mighty horseman galloped from the horizon with a power that shocked the warriors. The mighty figure on the horse was enveloped in a light so dazzling that the 10,000 warriors wasted no time in fleeing the village, never to return. The local people had no doubt that the Blessed Virgin Mother whose Son is God had come to protect them. Her trusted warrior captain, Saint Michael the Archangel, routed the enemy.

A church was built on the site and a painting of the Blessed Mother, attired in the robes of an empress, with the Christ Child on her knees, was placed on the high altar. This image has become the Chinese tradition of the reality and presence of the Blessed Virgin Mother and her Divine Son, Jesus Christ.[4]

Though the church was destroyed in 1951, the painting remains. Perhaps a day will come when it will be housed in a beautiful shrine that welcomes people from all over the world who revere the blessings of family life in God.

In early summer, June 2, 1995, the front page of *The Washington Post* carried a feature article about two apparitions of the Blessed Mother that occurred at the pilgrimage site at Dong Lu in front of 10,000 people in late May 1995. Thousands of Chinese Catholics had gathered at Dong Lu to celebrate a Mass attended by priests and bishops of the underground Roman Catholic Church. On two separate occasions, the vast crowds turned and stared directly into the hot afternoon sun for a glimpse of the Blessed Virgin Mary. "The crowd broke into applause on one of the occasions," the paper reported.[5]

Those 10,000 who saw the apparitions were defying the Communist government by gathering publicly for an unauthorized Mass at this pilgrimage site.[6] They sang in Gregorian chant that drifted over the surrounding rice fields. Great columns of incense rose. The faces of the people shone with love and gratitude as they recited the Rosary. The apparitions of the Blessed Mother are perceived as their sign of God's continued presence in the affairs of humans.

The Blessed Virgin Mary is being seen throughout China. Rural people in remote districts who do not know her as the Mother of Jesus Christ recognize her as the Virgin Mother of God. They report her Infant as God in human form.[7] People of all faiths, or in some cases no faith at all, are seeing the miracle of the sun; rosary beads are turning gold; and the sick are being healed as prayer increases, prayer groups meet, and Mass attendance escalates. Major pilgrimages are taking place, not only at Dong Lu, but also on a hillside outside Shanghai.[8]

There are far more Christians in China now than when the Communists took power in 1949, with a party line designed to exterminate the faith. The estimates are anywhere from six to twelve million Catholics in China faithful to Rome. Some published estimates indicate that as many as one-third of the government-appointed bishops of the Chinese Patriotic Association are secretly loyal to Rome.[9] Negotiations are ongoing between the Chinese government and the Vatican. The total number of Christians in China is not precisely known.

A group of pilgrims brought the statue of Our Lady of Fatima to Peking in October 1994. Among the hundreds of devout were Gianna Talone Sullivan and her husband, Dr. Michael Sullivan, of Emmitsburg, Maryland. Gianna reported that the Blessed Virgin Mary appeared to her in the Church of the Immaculate Conception, seat of the bishop of Peking of the Chinese Catholic Church associated with the Chinese Patriotic Association.

Gianna Sullivan says that the Blessed Mother was attired in a long white robe and wore a sheer white veil. She stood on a cloud and was enveloped in extraordinary lavender lights that were so intense that Gianna could barely see. She said: "The first apparition took place on Friday, October 28, 1994, at 2 P.M. The Mother of God also appeared to me the next day in the same church. These two apparitions are foundational. They mark a new era in the Church of Jesus Christ in China." Gianna spoke of her apparitions:

The Blessed Mother looked different than I am used to seeing her. Her features were the same, but she was surrounded with so much light—shades of lavender. Oh—and the angels! There were hundreds of angels around her! Hundreds of chubby angel faces! They were emitting so much light themselves—lavender shades. The angels seemed to envelop the Blessed Mother! But the Blessed Mother's hands! The light from her hands was tremendous! She wore a gold crown. I received this message from the Blessed Mother in the Church of the Immaculate Conception in Peking:[10]

"I am Our Lady of All Grace. I am Our Lady of Joy. I am Mother of All People. My Immaculate Heart will reign, but not in the way you now think. The purpose of my coming here is to obtain unity in the churches.

"It is God's joy for me to appear here. There are many in China who are dear to my Immaculate Heart. They have great love for God. They are not forgotten. They too are my children.

"I greatly desire unity in the churches of China now. Work tirelessly for God's glory! May the peace of Jesus fill your hearts and minds and souls forever."

The rays that were pulsating from the hands of the Blessed Mother were so dazzling that even the sun was dull by comparison. The hundreds of angels who surrounded her were filled with energy and love. Their presence with the Mother of God in the Church of the Immaculate Conception in Peking is a great sign of the reign of peace and joy and love. The call is now. The reign of God is at hand.

The message becomes clear. Mary is the Mother of God and the Mother of all His people. The Blessed Mother of Jesus Christ is appearing all over the world to reconcile all people and all nations. As the Indian chief in Venezuela who threw his spear at his apparition of the Blessed Mother learned many centuries ago, and the atheist guerrillas in Bosnia who shot at the apparitions of the Blessed Mother discovered recently, no human can thwart the plan of God for long.

The Mother of Jesus Christ appears now all over the world by the special providence of God. She is sent to this generation with her pure Mother's heart of love and compassion to reclaim the children of God for whom her Son died.

Russia: Our Lady of Kazan

Russia has been known as the Garden of Mary since it was Christianized over one thousand years ago. During the 800s two Greek monks, Saints Cyril and Methodius, brought Christianity to the lands of Russia. They translated the liturgy into what is now referred to as Old Church Slavonic. About 988 A.D., Grand Prince Vladimir I married a Byzantine princess and consequently became a Christian. Under his reign, most of his people also became Christians. Shrines, monasteries, churches, and basilicas, some of which date back to those early times, dot the landscape of the former Russian Empire with tributes to the Blessed Virgin Mary. A true Russian has deep veneration for the Mother of God at the root of his soul.

The sacred and revered icon of Our Lady of Kazan, which depicts the Mother of God holding her Divine yet fully human Infant near her left cheek, is considered one of the most precious spiritual treasures of the Russian people and has been a vital cultural expression of their collective soul during the last thousand years.

The icon's origins are rooted in the early founding days of the church of the apostles. The icon's journey to Russia began in Constantinople. From there, it was brought across the Black Sea and up the Volga River to a monastery in the city of Kazan, which lies deep in the interior of the former Mongolian Empire.

The sacred Presence of God that believers experienced as they prayed before the icon led them to deep levels of interior illumination that vastly enriched their understanding of God's heavenly Kingdom. By approximately 1101, the icon was revered throughout the Russian lands wherever the Christian faith flourished. Russian pilgrims traveled vast distances on foot to pray before the holy Presence they experienced in the icon of Our Lady of Kazan. Folk dances, songs, and festivals commemorated its power and beauty. Yet the icon's fame was just beginning.

In 1209, the city of Kazan was overrun and conquered. Angry mobs destroyed the city and the monastery with it. The icon was lost in the rubble, but its memory lingered in the songs and festivals of the faithful.

Three hundred seventy years later, July 8, 1579, a small, nine-year-old girl named Matrona was suddenly startled by an immense flash of light. She fell to her knees in amazement at the beauty, holiness, and eternal kindness of the Mother of God, who stood on a cloud and was clothed in the brilliance of God's unconditional love for His people of the earth. The Beautiful Lady from Heaven asked the child to rescue the ancient and holy icon of Our Lady of Kazan from the burnt-out ruins of the old monastery near Matrona's home.

"The icon of Our Lady of Kazan lives!" the people shouted as they heard the news of Matrona's apparition. "What have we done to deserve such a gift!" some of the wiser ones dared ask. With great joy and expectation, they quickly assembled in the ruins.

Matrona quietly repeated the instructions she had heard from the Beautiful Lady from Heaven. The people began to sing the folk songs that assured them of God's love and providence as they dug in the ruins. In the blink of an eye, they found the miraculous icon.

"It's true! It's true!" they shouted one to another. Suddenly there was total silence. People had fallen to their knees in astonishment and awe as they experienced the sacred Presence in the icon. The Patroness and Protectress of the Russian People was once again among the flock of Mary's Divine Son.

Word spread like the light of dawn after a dark night. Thousands upon thousands, once again singing the ancient songs of their spiritual heritage, gathered at the site of the apparition of the Mother of God. Festivals and celebrations filled the people's hearts with love, gratitude, and joy. Even the high-ranking clergy and aristocracy wept with amazement. Intellectuals agreed with the peasants that although of an ancient age, the image seemed clear, beautiful, unforgettable. People spoke of a divine light that radiated forth from the sacred icon of Kazan.

Almost immediately, miracles and healing occurred in the lives of those who gazed with reverence upon the holy and, by now, miraculous icon of Our Lady of Kazan. As the centuries rolled along, the icon of Our Lady of Kazan, housed in a convent especially constructed for it by the czar, became known throughout the Russian Empire as the Liberatrix and Protectress of Holy Mother Russia.

Peter the Great carried the Holy and Miraculous Icon of Our Lady of Kazan for his banner as he marched into battle against the enemies of Russia. When he transferred the capital from Moscow to St. Petersburg, he carried the Holy and Miraculous Icon of Our Lady of Kazan with great homage across the vast stretch of Russian soil that separated the two cities, amid the prayerful songs of the Russian people who lined his path. At St. Petersburg, Peter the Great enshrined the sacred icon within his city and the transfer of the capital was complete.

Later, when Napoleon was making inroads into Russian territory in his attempt to conquer Russia, the people gathered in prayer vigils before the sacred and revered icon to implore the intercession of the Mother of God on behalf of Holy Mother Russia. They sang the ancient songs that commemorate the icon. They prayed the prayers of their ancestors. When Napoleon was finally defeated, the people of Holy Mother Russia attributed the victory to the intercession of the Mother of God through their veneration of the Holy and Miraculous Icon of Our Lady of Kazan.

During the reign of Alexander II, a magnificent basilica, modeled after St. Peter's in Rome, was constructed in

Moscow at what would later be called Red Square. The faithful thronged in pilgrimage to the beautiful basilica created to house the sacred icon. Families spoke about the Presence that each succeeding generation of Russians treasured in the icon of Our Lady of Kazan. Until the Revolution of 1917, miracles and healings proliferated at the Shrine of Our Lady of Kazan in Moscow and were attributed to the presence of the holy icon.

The Bolsheviks recognized the danger to their plans that the icon of Our Lady of Kazan symbolized as the "soul of the Russian people." After all, their goal was to convince the world that there is no such thing as an eternal soul in a human being. Therefore, in an act of violent terrorism, the revolutionaries destroyed the Basilica of Our Lady of Kazan on October 13, 1917. The revolutionaries intended to prove, by this senseless act of destruction, that God does not exist. Officials mocked the faith and ridiculed the spiritual heritage of the Russian people as they boasted of their violence.

What the Bolsheviks, and most of the Russian people, did not know was that as the Basilica of Our Lady of Kazan fell, the Mother of God was appearing in another location in Europe where she spoke about the Russian people and their fate. The place where the Patroness and Protectress of all Russia spoke to her children in Russia, and in all the world, on October 13, 1917, was Fatima, Portugal. She said:

> *"If humanity does not turn back to God, Russia will spread errors and terrors worldwide. In the end my Immaculate Heart will triumph. Russia will be converted. A period of peace will be given to the world."*

God never forgets His children. The sacred and revered icon of Our Lady of Kazan was mysteriously removed from Russia at the time of the Bolshevik Revolution. Later in the century, it was discovered in a castle in England.[11]

People throughout the world who heard the messages of Our Lady of Fatima began to pray, even as early as 1917, for the conversion of Russia, as the Blessed Mother requested. Billions of individual prayers and sacrifices have ascended as incense before the throne of God from all over the earth on behalf of the people of Russia since that time.

Many citizens in Holy Mother Russia have fallen even deeper into poverty, oppression, ignorance, and suffering during the absence from Russian soil of the Holy and Miraculous Icon of Our Lady of Kazan. There is a shortage of food: fresh vegetables and fruit are particularly scarce and quite costly in the cities. The black market thrives. Russian mothers do the same work as men and have little time to spend with their families. Children are placed in state-run day-care centers.

The collapse of the Iron Curtain followed the unprecedented apparitions of the Mother of God at Medjugorje, where the Patroness and Protectress of all Russia identified herself as the Queen of Peace. Seventy-five years after its destruction, the great Basilica of Our Lady of Kazan is being reconstructed at Red Square, largely through the generosity of children of the Mother of God throughout the world.

The Patriarch of Moscow and of all Russia, His Holiness Aleksey II, received a delegation of foreign Christian pilgrims, including Catholics, Protestants, and Orthodox worshipers from the United States, Europe, Asia, Africa, and Australia, in Moscow Cathedral at Red Square on October 13, 1992. He announced:

> We know of the message of Fatima. During the dark years, that message was our hope. We know that the original Icon of Our Lady of Kazan is housed in a beautiful, Byzantine-style Shrine constructed especially for its exile at Fatima. We look forward to its return to Russia. Perhaps then, we the people of Russia shall know peace and abundance once again. Those who have kept the faith should not be proud. We are all sinners. Now, together, we have a great task to accomplish.[12]

Slovakia: The Immaculate Purity

A shrine that is now attracting people from all five continents was once a woodcutter's shack until a most amazing series of apparitions occurred in it and turned the tiny hamlet of Litmanova, Slovakia, into a place of worldwide pilgrimage. In 1990, two young girls ventured out into the forest behind their homes in the mountainous hamlet of Litmanova, situated in Slovakia near the border of Poland. The weather was beautiful that summer Sunday afternoon and the children went deeper and deeper into the cool forest. After a while they became tired and went into a woodcutter's shack to rest. Thirteen-year-old Ivetka Korcakova and Katka Ceselkova began to play jacks.

Suddenly the wind began to howl. It bombarded the

old woodcutter's shack and made it shake to its very foundation. The children were frightened. Ivetka exclaimed: "Let's pray!" The children fell to their knees and began to recite the Our Father. No sooner had they begun their prayer than a brilliant light filled the room. In the dazzling brightness, the two girls beheld a most extraordinary woman, beautiful beyond their capacity to describe. Only Ivetka could hear her speak, though Katka also saw her. The children later said they knew they were in the sacred presence of God as they beheld His glorious, ever-holy Mother, surrounded with many brilliant angels, though they did not see Jesus.

As the apparition ended and the light faded, the children became filled with fear. They exited the woodcutter's shack and fled through the forest as fast as they could run. Ivetka said that she wondered whether the Beautiful Lady was behind her but she dared not turn around to look.

Finally, as the children reached the edge of the forest, they paused and looked intently at their surroundings. There was no Beautiful Lady, there were no angels, only one another. Yet, for the first time, the children were aware that they were standing on holy ground. During those timeless seconds when they beheld the blessed woman of the Apocalypse, the grace of the Mother of Jesus Christ had touched them and forever changed them, though they had no language to articulate the experience. They knew they now saw the world and their relationship to it in a new light. Each made a promise to tell no one about their experience.

During the next several weeks, the parents of the children noticed a difference in their behavior. There was no priest for their Byzantine Catholic church except on Sundays, when a traveling missionary would come by to say Mass. The small church was usually locked, but the girls were seen sitting on the steps by passersby who noticed that their hands were folded and they had a faraway look in their eyes.

At home, the girls began to spend time withdrawn from family and friends in quiet meditation. Finally, Ivetka's father prevailed upon her to share what she was thinking about that had so changed her behavior. When he heard of the Beautiful Lady in the forest he summoned his wife and they gathered Katka and returned to the woodcutter's shack.

No sooner did they enter the door than a brilliant light sent the small group to their knees. Immediately Katka and Ivetka saw the Beautiful Lady in the dazzling light. Only Ivetka heard her say:

"Dear children, I am the Immaculate Purity. God has sent me to your world, to your times with messages as never before in history. Please pray, my children."

The date was August 5, 1990. The children and the adults prayed fervently in response to the Beautiful Lady's request.

Word spread quickly throughout the region. Pilgrims began to make the arduous journey up the steep mountain to the woodcutter's shack. On the first Sunday of every month the Blessed Mother presented a message through Ivetka to the world from Litmanova.

The beautiful Immaculate Purity medal has been

struck at the request of the Blessed Mother, and people of all corners of the globe seek to obtain it. It is especially efficacious for those who knowingly or unknowingly need divine protection in the area of purity.

A person in London wore the Immaculate Purity medal for several hours and, during that time, he received a most extraordinary healing and enlightenment. He was amazed to be set free from a problem he carried from birth that was related to his sexual identity. He said that before wearing the medal, intense suffering was a great part of every moment of his every day. He wore the Immaculate Purity medal for only three hours yet was amazingly freed from all his pain, illness, and distortion. He publicly stated that he was healed in body and soul by wearing the medal. He said that his newfound freedom gave him the first joy he had ever known in his life.[13]

On July 3, 1993, pilgrims from Litmanova heard the following message delivered by Ivetka on behalf of the Blessed Mother.

Under her title, the Immaculate Purity, the Blessed Mother of Jesus calls out to her faithful children everywhere:

"Please help me with your prayers and fasting. How desperately my errant children need your help. Please pray, pray, pray. Please help me."[14]

CHAPTER FOURTEEN

Mother of Divine Mercy

Then I saw a new heaven and a new earth. The former
heaven and the former earth had passed away, and the sea
was no more. I also saw the holy city, a new Jerusalem, coming down out of heaven from God, prepared as a bride
adorned for her husband. I heard a loud voice from the
throne saying, "Behold, God's dwelling is with the human
race. He will dwell with them and they will be his people
and God himself will always be with them."

REVELATION 21:1–3

Love's Promise: Veronica's Story

Veronica was two months old when her mother died. In
1954, Veronica's Spanish-speaking grandmother moved
into the family house to care for the three motherless children, especially the new baby. Seven years later, Veronica's
father remarried—his bride a beautiful young woman.
Veronica felt betrayed and unwanted. She ran away from
home and was captured by the police in a distant state. Her
father flew by plane to retrieve his troubled youngest child.

The teenage years were difficult for Veronica. She continued to experience deep feelings of abandonment and
found solace in alcohol, marijuana, and other mood-altering

drugs. She was able to complete only one year of college because her addictions had become so pervasive in her life.

Veronica never thought of God, of church, of the commandments, of any responsibilities except, as she says, "the next high. I never looked at my actions as being sinful . . . and, of course, when you don't go to sacramental confession, you become even less aware of what sin is . . . thereby making sin habitual, much like taking drugs."

When she was twenty-four years old, Veronica married. Her husband was irresponsible and unemployed, and, at thirty-four, he depended on marijuana for his pleasure. Veronica was certain she could change him. It was a shock when Veronica learned on her wedding night that her husband had no intention of having only one wife. In fact, he informed her that he had every intention of having more than one wife—at the same time! Veronica felt hopeless as she realized that her husband would always bring other women into their home.

Veronica was four months pregnant when she finally mustered the strength to leave her husband for the first time. She said she found the courage, not for herself, but for her baby. Her husband, however, persuaded her to return to him. When her daughter was born, Veronica realized that her marital situation was never going to improve. Her husband was drunk when he came to the hospital to pick up his new baby daughter and Veronica. When they walked into a house filled with empty beer bottles and filth, something in Veronica snapped. "I knew then that I could not live in this situation," she said.

Veronica filed for divorce. She then sank into deep depression and considered suicide. Her stepmother said to her: "Take a long look in the mirror at yourself. God does not make junk. Try giving yourself back to God, give Him all your mistakes, all your problems, all your hopes for a good life. He is perfectly capable of making your life great. Why don't you ask?"

Veronica hung up the phone and picked up her little daughter. She desperately wanted a better life for her child. Then Veronica fell on her knees and prayed the only way she knew. She spoke words of desperation rooted in disappointment, abandonment, even anger. She dared to ask God for a miracle. Veronica says: "I told Him how I was feeling and how lost I was. I told Him that if He were the God everyone thought He was, now would be a pretty good time to perform one of His miracles. I prayed in this manner as if it was the end of my life—which I thought it really was. From the moment I finished praying, I felt as if a huge load was lifted from my shoulders. I knew I had to try living again."

Veronica stumbled from circumstance to event without much direction in her life. She remarried. Her second husband was also addicted to marijuana, but he did not drink alcoholic beverages.

In 1988, one of Veronica's aunts went to Medjugorje. She returned on fire with the messages of the Blessed Mother. Veronica says: "I just patted her on the back, saying, 'How nice for you!' I thought the Rosary was only prayed at funerals and when you were old." But something began to awaken in Veronica after her aunt came back from Medjugorje.

She read all she could find about the apparitions of the Blessed Mother to the six children in Medjugorje. She was intrigued about the Blessed Mother's urgent request for people to return immediately to sacramental confession. "No way! Not after all I had done. . . . Since I had sinned so much, God was not going to have me back." Then Veronica found a short story about Mary Magdalene. The kindness of Jesus to Mary Magdalene changed her understanding of God's love and forgiveness.

Veronica began to think about the mercy of God. She even bought a Bible. Then she realized that she had broken all the commandments. When Veronica found Psalm 51 in the Bible, she read it several times. Then she closed her Bible, got down on her knees, and said, "Jesus, I'll make You a deal. If You forgive me, I'll promise I will spend the rest of my life bringing souls back to you." Veronica was very much afraid to go to sacramental confession. So she decided to travel to Medjugorje and go to confession there.

The trip to Medjugorje took place in October 1989. It was an event in Veronica's life that she says she will carry with her into eternity. Groups around the world listen to Veronica's testimony as she travels now to share her experiences there. Veronica did go to sacramental confession at Medjugorje.

When she returned to her home in Denver, Colorado, she had a deep interior urge to start a prayer group. Veronica went to a local priest and asked his permission to use his church. When Veronica accepted the key in her hand, she believed that it was her sign from God of His complete forgiveness for her entire past life. He had handed her the key to His house through the priest!

It would never be the same again for Veronica. She began to pray with real confidence in God's unconditional love for her. She tried to live the messages of the Blessed Mother that she learned from all the apparitions around the world. She began to treasure her Bible. Now the words were filled with meaning and methods to deal with the realities of day-to-day living.

Veronica had tried on many occasions to rid herself of her addiction to marijuana. As her life in Christ grew, she decided to stop using drugs of any kind, for Jesus. She says, "Once I stopped trying to quit for myself, I was able to stop. It happened instantly and without complications. I'll never forget the first Christmas I was able to kneel in front of the Infant Jesus and give Him the gift of a totally clean body and soul. I realized I was returning the gift He had given me."

In October 1990, Veronica returned to Medjugorje. Afterwards, she had a glorious dream. She saw the Lord Jesus Christ. He looked directly into her heart. He gazed deeply into her eyes and spoke consoling words of immense love. Later she began to receive messages from Jesus about once a month. The Blessed Virgin Mary began to speak to Veronica. She taught her how to pray the Our Father, the Apostles' Creed, and the Glory Be to the Father prayers. Veronica began to experience interior visions of the Blessed Mother at work and at home. The visions were always at times of difficulty. They were a source of great encouragement.[1]

Veronica has frequently described an experience she had during the celebration of Mass.

All of a sudden my attention was drawn from the presence of the Blessed Mother beside me, because of the commotion I noticed coming from behind the altar. It was then that I saw hundreds of angels crowding around the altar, preparing for the Consecration.

It seemed that all the angels were trying to get into the best position to see their Jesus. The priest was standing in a solid beam of light which appeared to go straight up. As he was lifting up the consecrated Host, the Blessed Mother said: "Behold my Son!" An angel came from behind and in one swift moment, took the Host straight up the beam of light. It was at that instant that I truly believed for the first time that Jesus is present in the Eucharist. I knew deep in my soul that the consecrated Host is not just a symbol of Jesus. It is Jesus! The angels remained until after I received Holy Communion. Then I was no longer able to see the angels. I was left with real faith now. I knew for the first time in my life that Jesus is alive. He is with us. He is in the Eucharist in a powerful way. What a gift!

Veronica says that God is now the center of her life. She goes to daily Mass and to sacramental confession weekly. She says that conversion is a daily process. It happens moment by moment. Veronica has founded a retreat center for those who wish to increase their prayer life or to overcome any kind of addiction.

Veronica Garcia turned to the Blessed Mother for help when her life was in shambles. She learned, as everyone who turns to Mary does, that the Mother of God gives all her children to Jesus.[2] Jesus gives life and abundance.

The Marian Movement of Priests: Father Stefano Gobbi

Father Stefano Gobbi was born in 1930. He holds a doctorate in sacred theology from the Pontifical University of the Lateran in Rome. Father Gobbi founded the Marian Movement of Priests in 1972, when he began to receive messages from the Blessed Virgin Mary. It has become the fastest-growing movement in the Catholic Church, numbering cardinals, bishops, priests, sisters, and laypeople among its vast worldwide membership.

The movement's U.S. national headquarters is located in St. Francis, Maine, and the Reverend Albert G. Roux is the national director. The messages that Father Gobbi receives from the Blessed Mother are compiled in booklet form and distributed in the various languages of the world. In the United States alone, there are more than 2,500 cenacles of priests, religious brothers and sisters, youths, laypeople, and couples, and even family cenacles. Such groups gather on a regular basis. They read the messages of the Blessed Mother, pray the Rosary, and recite the Act of Consecration to the Immaculate Heart of Mary for protection in these times.

Father Gobbi says the Blessed Mother requests the cenacles of prayer as a means of combating the darkness of evil in the world.

On September 29, 1988, the Blessed Mother imparted the following message to Father Gobbi for all her children:

"Entrust yourselves to the protection of your Guardian Angels, and especially of the Archangels, Saints Gabriel, Raphael, and Michael, whose feast you celebrate today.

Thus you will be clothed in the virtue of fortitude, so needed today. You will be healed of the deep wounds which you have been dealt and especially you will always be protected by Saint Michael in the terrible battle which, during these last times, is being waged between heaven and earth.

"And in the end you will be able to form part of the victorious army, guided by me, your heavenly Mother, the Woman clothed in the Sun, for the soon-to-come triumph of her Immaculate Heart in the world."[3]

An Interview with Father Gobbi*

Q. Father Gobbi, why is the Blessed Mother giving messages to you?

A. She is drawing all her children to unity with the Holy Father by love, by prayer, and by patient suffering. These messages are a gift of God's love.

Q. Do you know why there are so many apparitions, locutions, and experiences of the presence of the Blessed Mother in these times?

A. There is a deep bond that unites Mary's little children. Why? Because we all love Jesus' Mother so much. Jesus rewards love. The apparitions, locutions, messages spread His love throughout the world.

Q. Does the Blessed Mother speak to you about the Triumph of her Immaculate Heart?

A. Yes. The dominion of the Saints has come into the world. The reign of Satan is about to end. You are all called to be apostles of Mary in these last times.

*Translation by Father Roux.

Q. How does one become an apostle of Mary in these last times?

A. Consecrate yourselves to her Immaculate Heart. She sends me throughout the world to gather all her little children and help them to entrust themselves to her Immaculate Heart.

Q. Father, many people do not know what consecration to the Immaculate Heart of Mary means. Will you please explain the significance of the consecration?

A. The Blessed Mother asks me to tell you: "Just as Noah, in the name of the Lord, made his family enter into the ark, in these times, those who would be protected, defended, and saved from the trials that have come upon the earth shall enter the Ark of the Immaculate Heart."

Q. What does the Blessed Mother ask of those who desire to enter the Ark of her Immaculate Heart?

A. She desires everyone to realize that God lives in us. We are children of God. She wants us to live as His children. God is the joy of our lives. We were created to experience His joy, to be His joy. We have been created for God. We have been created for Paradise. Life on earth is simply a time of preparation for the fullness of life in God.

Q. Are there problems on earth that the Blessed Mother asks her children to solve?

A. The Blessed Mother says that we must not live to possess the earth, or money, or entertainment, or any of the things we will leave behind when we no longer have the use of our bodies. We are to live for God. We are to use our time and our strength for the glory of God. We are to love and help one another in any way we are able, always for the love of God.

Q. What message does the Blessed Mother want us to have today?

A. Love glorifying God as Mary did by doing His will. How great the Blessed Virgin is. All she ever did was obey God's will! That is what she asks of us. Only that. God wills to possess your soul. But He will not take your soul. You must give it to Him by obeying His will. If your soul is possessed by God, it becomes a garden of light, and Mary enters into the garden and makes her virtues flourish there. Faith, hope, charity, prudence, justice, fortitude, temperance, humility, prayer. Your soul becomes a garden perfumed by all these virtues. The Blessed Virgin carries you in her arms before the Eucharistic Jesus. You become Eucharistic souls. You experience the need to receive Him, to adore Him, to be one with Him. Then you spread the life of Christ, you become Apostles of the New Advent, you become instruments of the Triumph of the Immaculate Heart in the world.

Q. Father Gobbi, do you know when the Triumph of the Immaculate Heart will occur?

A. Before the year 2000.[4]

Apparitions, visions, and locutions of the Blessed Mother are an infusion of divine grace to facilitate the conversion and reconciliation of all people. God is patient. How long must humanity wait for peace, joy, and love?

The history of authentic apparitions, visions, and locutions of the Mother of God, since the time of the Prophet Elijah, is a love story. The effect of these divine favors is divine light in the world as people labor to become open to God's omnipresence and all-pervading love.

Heartfelt prayer, fasting, and discipline of the sensual appetites sweep away the fantasy of all forms of illusion and selfishness and elevate our human will to the pursuit of the supernatural. In that enlightened state, generosity, love, and service to humanity flower. Mother Teresa of Calcutta is a renowned twentieth-century example. Her mission to the dying in India began with a divine invitation, to which she responded wholeheartedly with great love. Her ministry is sourced in her obedience to God's will for her. Everyone has a role to play in the unfolding of God's great plan for His children. We must, however, choose to respond. Our choices are stepping-stones to Paradise or anchors lodged in hell.

Apparitions of the Mother of God present a divinely beautiful woman filled with peace and unconditional love for each child of God. Her apparitions bring fortitude and endurance to God's people and inspire obedience to His will. The Blessed Mother's entrance into global consciousness in these times presents the radical journey of God's children from darkness to light.

Faith untested is no faith at all. Christ reminds His disciples after His Resurrection:

"Blessed are they who do not see but who believe."

The ways of God are gracious and gentle. God's Presence, His providence, His eternal, unconditional love for each child of His is the path of truth and the source of human peace, joy, and love. That path is obscured without the light of God's power. The maternal solicitude of the Blessed Mother and the virtue she inspires is a gift of God's love.

When an enlightened person believes in God's Word or revelation there remains much that he must accept without full understanding. In these times, the Blessed Mother calls all people on earth to strictly fast two days per week. Is she bringing divine enlightenment about the need for humans to eat more grains, fruits, and vegetables—to abstain from those foods that science even now begins to discover are injurious to health? It takes discipline, virtue, and grace to bend the mind under the yoke of faith. Only a humble person can bow his reason before truths beyond his power to comprehend.

The Eternal Now: Matthew Kelly's Story

On the 7th of April, 1993, as I knelt beside my bed saying my evening prayers, I found myself at what seemed to be a crossroads in my life. I had many unanswered questions in my mind and I desperately yearned for the gift of discernment, believing that it was in doing God's will that I would find my happiness.

Unresolved, I finished my prayer in a hurry and climbed into bed. As always, I said the Hail Mary three times: one that Our Lady might take care of me during the night, one for my family and friends, and one for society. Then I reached for my Walkman thinking I might find some comfort in the words of a song.

As I reached for my Walkman, I felt a strong internal presence and a feeling that urged me not to pick up my Walkman. I ignored that and reached for it all the same and as I put the head-phones on, I had a similar feeling only it was twice as powerful. I ignored it.

Finally, I turned the Walkman on and after two or three minutes of music I had that same feeling again, but this time it was unmistakable. I knew that this was something I had never experienced before. And so I got out of bed, knelt down and I put myself in the presence of God. During that day and throughout this experience I felt God was asking something of me, yet I couldn't pinpoint it. I felt God wanted to speak to me. So kneeling there in my bedroom I said, "I am listening." All in an instant, I heard what I now know to be the voice of God the Father speak to me.

Matthew was nineteen years old when he heard the voice of God the Father for the first time. Since that extraordinary night, Matthew receives dictation from the Eternal Father. He has spoken about his messages around the world and he has published two books containing his messages for the world from the Eternal Father. Matthew now also hears the voice of the Blessed Mother and the Lord Jesus. He says the voice of Jesus is the same voice as the Eternal Father though they are two separate persons.

Matthew's experiences are unique. God the Father has disclosed some crucial information to Matthew about these times and the role that Mary plays. The following are messages received by Matthew Kelly:[5]

"During these end times, Mary plays the greatest part in preserving the faith and building a cohort to continue to live on in My love by prayer, the Mass, the Rosary, the Eucharist, Confession and sacrifice. You ask Me what it is I ask of you. This is what I ask: Entrust yourself to your Mother Mary's guidance and do these things constantly.

"Mary is fruit. She is sweet and beautiful. She is full of love and compassion. Speak to her, for she hears you and will answer your call.

"You are living in a time often spoken about by false prophets, for this is a time of change in the world. The evil one is running wild, but . . . you will be able to see it {evil} as light as day. This time should not alarm you or disturb you. . . .

"But faith, My children. I am your Father. I will look after you. A time is coming when you will live united to Me. That is what you live for. Live for My love.

"The only way to prepare for these end times is by personal sanctification. You must all aim to be saints. This is My will for each and every one of you.

"You must pray, sacrifice, go to confession and communion, say the Rosary, read good spiritual material to develop your understanding of the basic doctrines of the Church, do charitable works, and love all souls as though they were Me, the Lord your God.

"This is the only preparation for the times that await at the doorstep of the world. I am the Lord your God. I come to you out of My infinite mercy in these words, but before long I will come to you out of My infinite justice. . . . Now is the time to respond My children.

> *"Seek My will in each moment and live not for pleasure in this life but in hope of Heaven.*
>
> *"My children, spread these messages. These messages are for each and every one of My children throughout the world. You are presently in the end times. These years are the most important since Jesus walked on the earth. His second coming is at hand. Be ready. Follow My Son Jesus Christ. He will lead you to Me, your Father."*

The Blessed Mother sends this message to each and every person on earth:

> *"I am your Mother. I hold you close to my heart always. I care for you and watch over you. You do not see me but know that I am there, never letting you out of my sight."*

Those who belong to the Blessed Mother are her gift to Jesus. Jesus cares for His Mother's children with delight.

Divine Favors:
Mary, Spiritual Mother of the Human Race

The Eternal One brought His heart into the world through His Virgin Mother. The unseen God that nothing in the universe can contain rested in Mary's arms clothed in her flesh, which He had made out of the clay of the earth. Such humility blinds the proud. The Blessed Mother's Divine Son is the light all people crave (John 1:4–5).

God's love extinguishes anger, hate, resentment, anxiety, nervousness, illness, fear, failure, greed, avarice, jeal-

ousy, envy, sickness, and death. Light begets light. God's people are His delight. Never did He intend for them to live in poverty, ignorance, filth, and despair. Love begets love. Sin begets sin. Those who sow in sin reap in sin. Those who sow in love reap in love. God makes all things well. His will is done. Those who rest in His will reap His bounty. Those who rest in their own will build castles in the sands of illusion.

The famous Marian apparitions embody themes reminiscent of the Gospel of Jesus Christ, of the great patriarchs and prophets. Recorded in the art, architecture, music, and literature of the world, they represent threads in the mystery of the Blessed Mother. She remains ever the hidden masterpiece of the Divine Mind. Her apparitions are a glimpse into the unfathomable depths of God's love and mercy.

Humans stand on holy ground. Each person God creates is a glorious living basilica of inestimable beauty who is the pleasure of our Creator. He desires to dwell within His living basilicas. He waits to be invited, for He is love. He longs for each of us to love Him by loving one another as we bask in His love and providence. Love begets love. Those who love live on in the Triumph of the Immaculate Heart. There will be no others, for the spirit of evil is driven from the earth in the light of the Spirit of Truth. And so ends the world of darkness.

The Blessed Mother calls for the last time to the people of God to enter the Kingdom of love; to persevere, for her Son the Messiah comes soon. Those who recognize Him, and who will follow Him to the Promised Land, are being prepared now in the holocaust of Satan's last stand. Satan's days of reign are drawing to an end.

The Blessed Virgin Mary is being revealed all over the world as the spiritual Mother of the human race. Her apparitions, visions, locutions have produced a networked spiritual family that emerges like precious flowers in the early dawn of springtime. Her flowers are brothers and sisters in the Sacred Heart of Mary's Divine Son Jesus. Her flowers are old and young, tall and short, black and white, Asian and African, Caucasian and Native American, Middle Eastern, Eskimo, and tribal. Her flowers are Christian, Jew, Muslim, Hindu, Buddhist, even former unbelievers who have found their real Mother and now live in the Spirit of Truth.

A front-page article in *The Washington Post* on October 14, 1994, noted that "visions of Mary have proliferated throughout the United States and the world since the 1980s. It is one of the most intense concentrations of such occurrences since they [apparitions] were first noted. . . ."

A great outpouring of the Holy Spirit of truth has burst upon the earth through the apparitions of the Blessed Virgin Mary. God's little children pine for His love. She who is the Mother of love brings love to all those who respond to her call. Those who love live forever.

The Blessed Virgin Mary, always faithful to God's will no matter what the cost, teaches her children to be faithful to God's will. In these times, those who respond to her call allow new flowers of God's love to blossom in all four corners of the globe. The old world passes away in the blinking of an eye. God's Kingdom comes when we least expect it.

But of that day or hour, no one knows, neither the angels in heaven, nor the Son, but only the Father.

Be watchful! Be alert! You do not know when the
time will come. . . . Watch, therefore; you do not
know when the lord of the house is coming,
whether in the evening, or at midnight, or at
cockcrow, or in the morning. May he not come
suddenly and find you sleeping. What I say to you,
I say to all: "Watch!"

MARK 13:32–33, 35–37

Those who have ears to hear and eyes to see recognize
the signs of the times. They live on the Island of Beauty
where winds of myrrh blow over the hills and scent the
earth with God's sweet mercy.

God shall walk among His people. The Divine Grower
has planted seeds of His own flowers throughout the
world. Their seed is His love. His Garden is His delight.
He shall walk the earth amid the profusion of His flowers.
The Triumph of the Immaculate Heart sees the earth restored to the heart of God our Creator and Father.

The voice of God is sweet. The melodies of His graciousness fill the deepest longings of each human heart.
The Blessed Mother, mystery of God's unfathomable love
for all His people of the earth, emerges on the dawn of the
twenty-first century bringing countless mornings of hope.

EPILOGUE

A Special Message for You from the Blessed Mother

Dear children,

You are responsible for the messages. The source of grace is here, but you, dear children, are the vehicles transmitting the gifts. Therefore, dear children, I am calling you to work responsibly. Everyone will be responsible according to his own measure. Dear children, I am calling you to give the gift to others with love and not keep it for yourselves. Thank you for having responded to my call.

GIVEN AT MEDJUGORJE
ON MAY 8, 1986

ENDNOTES

AUTHOR'S NOTE

1. Saint John of the Cross, *The Ascent of Mount Carmel*, Book II of *Selected Writings*, trans. Kieran Kavanaugh and Otilio Rodriguez. Washington, D.C.; ICS Publications, 1979. pp. 179–180.

2. Ibid., pp. 163–165.

CHAPTER ONE

1. Captain Scott O'Grady, interview by Jane Pauley, *Dateline NBC*, National Broadcasting Co., Inc., June 13, 1995.

2. Consecration to Jesus, the Incarnate Wisdom, through the Blessed Virgin Mary, as recorded in Saint Louis de Montfort, *True Devotion to Mary* (1941, reprint, Rockford, Ill.: Tan Books, 1985), pp. 196–199.

3. Janice T. Connell, *Angel Power* (New York: Ballantine Books, 1995), p. 182, citing Pope Gregory I, *Forty Gospel Homilies: Gregory the Great* (Kalamazoo, Mich.: Cistercian Publications, 1990), p. 285.

4. Ibid., pp. 141–175.

5. Ibid., pp. 26, 27.

6. Saint Louis de Montfort, *True Devotion to Mary*, p. 18.

7. Ibid., p. 33.

8. Ibid, p. 28.

9. *Newsweek*, August 1, 1994, cover story.

10. Saint Louis de Montfort, *True Devotion to Mary*, p. 30.

11. *The Washington Post*, June 5, 1995.

12. *The Washington Post*, March 9, 1992.

13. *U.S. News & World Report*, March 29, 1992.

14. *The Washington Post*, March 9, 1992.

15. A photo journal by James L. Carney, The Seton Miracles, presents color photos of some of the phenomena surrounding Father Jim Bruse and is available from the Marian Foundation: P. O. Box 2589, Dale City, Virginia, 22193-2589.

16. Richard Preston, *The Hot Zone* (New York: Random House, 1994).

17. Ibid., pp. 16, 17.

18. Ibid., p. 260.

19. *The New York Times*, June 13, p. A4.

20. *Catechism of the Catholic Church*, Article 67 (Liguori, Mo.: Liguori Publications, 1994), p. 23.

21. Ibid.

22. Vatican II, *Lumen Gentium*, Chapter 12.

23. Reverend William Watson, S.J., address delivered at Georgetown University, May 4, 1995.

24. Peter M. J. Stravinskas, ed., *Our Sunday Visitor's Catholic Encyclopedia* (Huntington, Ind.: Our Sunday Visitor Publishing, 1991), p. 90.

25. René Laurentin and Henry Joyeux, *Scientific and Medical Studies on the Apparitions at Medjugorje* (Dublin: Veritas Publications, 1987).

26. Pope John Paul II, *Crossing the Threshold of Hope* (New York: Alfred A. Knopf, 1994), p. 213.

27. Ibid., p. 214.

28. John Hampsch, interview by author, Los Angeles, Calif. *See also* John Hampsch, *Preparation for the End Times* (Chicago, Ill.: Claretian Missionaries Publications), 1992.

29. Hampsch, interview.

30. Ibid.

CHAPTER TWO

1. National Conference of Catholic Bishops, *Behold Your Mother, A Pastoral Letter on the Blessed Virgin Mary*

(Washington, D.C.: United States Catholic Conference, November 21, 1973), p. 27.

2. Pope Pius IX, *Ineffabilis Deus*, Apostolic Letter, December 8, 1854.

3. In 431 A.D. the Council of Ephesus declared that Mary is truly the Mother of God because she is the Mother of Jesus, who is the Second Person of the Holy Trinity made man. Council of Ephesus, 431 A.D., as cited in Henricus Denzinger, *Enchiridion Symbolorum, Definitionum et Declarationum de Rebus Fidei et Morum*, ed. Herder (Barcelona: 1946), n. 113, and quoted in Mark Miravalle, *Mary: Coredemptrix, Mediatrix, Advocate* (Santa Barbara, Calif.: Queenship Publishing, 1993), p. xiii.

4. Lateran Council, 649 A.D., as cited in Denzinger, *Enchiridion Symbolorum*, n. 256, and quoted in Miravalle, Ibid.

5. Pope Pius IX, *Ineffabilis Deus*.

6. Jude Langsam, ed., *Welcome to Carmel* (Washington, D.C., Teresian Charism Press, 1982), p. 27.

7. Pope John Paul II, *Redemptor Hominis*, Encyclical Letter 1979, n. 1.

8. Pope Pius IX, *Ineffabilis Deus*.

9. Adapted from William J. Walsh, ed., *The Apparitions and Shrines of Heaven's Bright Queen*, 4 vols. (New York: T.J. Carey, 1904), vol. 1, pp. 165–172.

10. Ibid., pp. 219–221.

11. Ibid., pp. 329–339.

12. Ibid., vol. 2, pp. 77–87.

CHAPTER THREE

1. Ignatius of Loyola, *A Pilgrim's Journey: The Autobiography of Ignatius of Loyola* (Collegeville, Minn.: Liturgical Press, 1991), pp. 16, 126.

2. The author wishes to acknowledge the graciousness of Betty and Ricardo Marino, who provided photo reproductions of

the facial image of the *tilma* of Juan Diego as well as the official messages of the apparitions to Juan Diego. Words ascribed to Our Lady of Guadalupe are adapted from information available from the Shrine of Our Lady of Guadalupe in Mexico City.

3. Ibid.

4. Ibid.

5. Ibid.

6. Ibid.

7. Saint Teresa of Ávila, *The Way of Perfection*, trans. and ed. E. Allison Peers (Garden City, N.Y.: Doubleday Image Books, 1964), pp. 139–140.

8. Saint Teresa of Ávila, *Collected Works of Saint Teresa of Avila*, trans. K. Kavanaugh and O. Rodriguez, 3 vols. (Washington, D.C.: ICS Publications, 1978), vol. 1, pp. 193–194.

9. Saint Teresa of Ávila, *The Way of Perfection*, as quoted in Benedict J. Groeschel, *A Still, Small Voice* (San Francisco: Ignatius Press, 1993), p. 114.

10. Saint Teresa of Ávila, *Collected Works*, vol. 3, p. 140.

11. Ibid.

12. Adapted from Saint Margaret Mary, *The Autobiography of Saint Margaret Mary*, trans. V. Kerns (Rockville, Ill: Tan Books, 1952), p. 106.

13. Saint Margaret Mary, as quoted in William J. Walsh, ed., *The Apparitions and Shrines of Heaven's Bright Queen*, 4 vols. (New York: T. J. Carey, 1904), vol. 3, pp. 210–211.

14. Saint Margaret Mary, *Autobiography* (Tan Books), p. 113.

15. Ibid., pp. 67–68 (slightly adapted to simplify the language).

16. Adapted from Saint Margaret Mary, *Autobiography*, as quoted in Walsh, ed., *Apparitions and Shrines*, vol. 3, pp. 218–219.

17. Ibid., pp. 219–220.

CHAPTER FOUR

1. Adapted from the writings of Alphonse de Ratisbonne as quoted in William J. Walsh, ed., *The Apparitions and Shrines of Heaven's Bright Queen*, 4 vols. (New York: T. J. Carey, 1904), vol. 3, pp. 295–301.
2. Ibid.
3. Ibid.
4. Ibid.
5. Sandra L. Zimdars-Swartz, *Encountering Mary from La Salette to Medjugorje* (Princeton: Princeton University Press, 1991), pp. 27–28.
6. Ibid., pp. 165–189.
7. Ibid., pp. 36–39.
8. Ibid., p. 166.
9. Ibid., pp. 177–178.
10. Ibid., p. 178.
11. Ibid., p. 198.
12. Ibid., p. 183.
13. Excerpted from the original translation, "La Salette, the Apparitions of the Blessed Virgin Mary on the Mountain in 1846," as quoted in Ted and Maureen Flynn, *The Thunder of Justice* (Sterling, Va.: Max-Kolbe Communications, 1993), pp. 112–117.
14. *See* Zimdars-Swartz, *Encountering Mary*, pp. 165–189.
15. *See* Janice T. Connell, *The Triumph of the Immaculate Heart* (Santa Barbara, Calif.: Queenship Publishing, 1993), pp. 41–46.
16. J. B. Estrade, *My Witness, Bernadette* (Springfield, Ill.: Templegate, 1946), pp. 25–26.
17. Ibid., p. 97.
18. Connell, *Triumph of the Immaculate Heart*, p. 46.
19. The National Shrine of the Immaculate Conception in

Washington, D.C., is a tribute to the prophetic pastoral care of the first bishop of the United States, John Carroll, S.J., who in 1792 solemnly declared the young nation to be under the patronage of the Blessed Virgin Mary. Daily, docents guide visitors from around the world through the basilica speaking of apparitions on all the continents that are memorialized with individual shrines. The spiritual heritage centered in devotion to the Blessed Virgin Mary and brought to the United States by people from the four corners of the earth is embodied in this edifice. In 1994, Hollywood humanitarian Bob Hope and his wife Delores donated a special shrine here to Our Lady of Hope of Pontmain, in memory of Mr. Hope's mother. Some of the facts about Our Lady of Hope have been adapted from information available at the National Shrine of the Immaculate Conception. *See also* Catherine M. Odell, *Those Who Saw Her: The Apparitions of Mary* (Huntington, Ind.: Our Sunday Visitor Publishing, 1986), pp. 93–102.

CHAPTER FIVE
1. Lucia of Fatima, as quoted by Joseph A. Pelletier in *The Sun Danced at Fatima* (Garden City, N.Y.: Doubleday Image Books, 1983), chapter 1, n. 1.
2. Ibid., p. 17.
3. Ibid.
4. Ibid., p. 18.
5. Lucia of Fatima, *Fatima in Lucia's Own Words* (Fatima, Portugal: Postulation Centre, 1976), pp. 60–63.
6. Janice T. Connell, *The Triumph of the Immaculate Heart* (Santa Barbara, Calif.: Queenship Publishing, 1993), p. 56.
7. Lucia of Fatima, *Fatima in Lucia's Own Words*, p. 107.
8. Ibid.
9. John Haffert, interview by author.

10. Lucia of Fatima, *Fatima in Lucia's Own Words*, p. 104.
11. Ibid.
12. Christopher Rengers, O.F.M.Cap., *The Youngest Prophet* (New York: Alba House, 1986), pp. 32–33, quoting Lucia of Fatima, *Fatima in Lucia's Own Words*, p. 107.
13. Monsignor Peter Mimnagh, Diocese of San Diego, Calif.
14. Haffert, interview.
15. Rengers, *Youngest Prophet*, p. 37.
16. Lucia of Fatima, *Fatima in Lucia's Own Words*, pp. 111–112.
17. Rengers, *Youngest Prophet*, p. 42.
18. *Lucia of Fatima, Her Own Words to the Nuclear Age: The Memoirs of Sr. Lucia*, comm. by John Haffert (Asbury Park, N.J.: 101 Foundation, 1993), p. 256.
19. Ibid.
20. Rengers, *Youngest Prophet*, p. 42.
21. Ibid.
22. Ibid., pp. 54–55.
23. Ibid., p. 57.
24. Ibid., pp. 58–59.
25. Ibid., p. 62.
26. Lucia of Fatima, *Fatima in Lucia's Own Words*, p. 145.
27. Pelletier, *Sun Danced at Fatima*, p. 137.
28. Ibid.
29. John Haffert, *To Prevent This* (Asbury Park, N.J.: 101 Foundation, 1993), p. 77.
30. Pelletier, *Sun Danced at Fatima*, language slightly adapted, p. 156; *see also* Lucia of Fatima, *Fatima in Lucia's Own Words*, pp. 189, 195, 196.
31. Teiji Yasuda, *Akita: The Tears and Message of Mary*, English version by John Haffert (Asbury Park, N.J.: 101 Foundation, 1989), p. 149.
32. Ibid., pp. 77, 78.

CHAPTER SIX

1. Joseph Pelletier, *Our Lady Comes to Garabandal; Including Conchita's Diary, 1971* (reissue, Worcester, Mass.: Assumption Publications, 1985), pp. 40, 41.

2. René Laurentin, interview by author, Notre Dame University, May 1989.

   See also Marian Apparitions of the Twentieth Century: A Message of Urgency (Lima, Pa.: Marian Communications, 1991), video documentary. This video is an excellent resource for documentary film footage of the ecstasies of the children of Garabandal.

   See also Robert François, *O Children Listen To Me* (Lindenhurst, N.Y.: Workers of Our Lady of Mount Carmel, 1980). The ordinary of the diocese in which the village of Garabandal is located, Bishop Doroteo Fernandez, was the apostolic administrator of the diocese of Santander. His three-member commission visited Garabandal three times during a four-year period, beginning shortly after the alleged apparitions began. The finding was that all the events of Garabandal had a natural explanation and were based on "child's play." Bishop Fernandez and his successor, Bishop Eugenio Beitia, issued official notice advising the faithful of "caution" concerning the alleged events at Garabandal. They further advised that nothing supernatural had occurred there. However, they did emphasize that "we have found no grounds for Ecclesiastical Condemnation either in doctrine or in the spiritual recommendations that have been divulged in the events and addressed to the Christian faithful." In 1986 Bishop Del Val Gallo appointed a new commission and announced to the Vatican that he was reopening the investigation of the events of Garabandal. Visiting priests are now permitted to bring the faithful; they say Mass and administer the sacraments there. The many people who have spent time, assets, and years of service to spread the messages of Garabandal include Stanley J. and Marjorie Karminski; Dolores Tierney, S.F.O.; and Maria Carmela Saraco, Workers of Our Lady of Mount Carmel.

3. Supplied by Stanley J. Karminski.

4. *Marian Apparitions of the Twentieth Century*, video documentary.

5. Ibid.

6. Sandra L. Zimdars-Swartz, *Encountering Mary from La Salette to Medjugorje* (Princeton: Princeton University Press, 1991), p. 130.

7. Ibid., p. 132.

8. Personal research by Stanley J. Karminski.

9. *Marian Apparitions of the Twentieth Century*, video documentary.

10. Ibid. This video contains photojournalism of the apparitions in Zeitoun.

11. The author gratefully acknowledges the hospitality of the sisters at the Convent of the Servants of the Eucharist at Akita, Japan, where these spiritual phenomena occurred and from whom much of the information herein has been gathered. Sister Agnes graciously consented to be interviewed by the author and her recollections are incorporated into the text. Also interviewed were June Keatley, Bishop John Shojiro Ito, Mutsuo [Francis] Fukushima, and John Haffert. For additional information *see* Teiji Yasuda, O.S.U., *The Meaning of Akita*, trans. J. Haffert (Asbury Park, N.J.: 101 Foundation, 1989), *and* Mutsuo [Francis] Fukushima, *Akita: Mother of God as CoRedemptrix: Modern Miracles of the Eucharist* (Santa Barbara, Calif., Queenship Publishing, 1994). For more information, write to the author.

12. Sister Agnes Katsuko Sasagawa, and Sister Teresa Toshiko Kashiwagi, Mother Superior of the convent, interviews by author, summer of 1991.

13. The replica statue of Our Lady of All Nations of Amsterdam exhibited lacrimotions and bleeding 101 times in the chapel of the convent at Akita. It is carved from wood and was imported to Japan from Holland.

14. Sisters at the Convent at Akita, interview by author.

15. Sister Agnes, interview by author.

16. The dialogue recounted in the experiences of Sister Agnes is based upon the testimony of Sister Agnes to author, the eyewitness experiences of Mutsuo [Francis] Fukushima, and the narratives contained in Teiji Yasuda, *Akita: The Tears and Message of Mary*, English version by John Haffert (Asbury Park, N.J.: 101 Foundation, 1989), especially pp. 4, 110, 188, and 189, and used with the permission of the 101 Foundation. The author wishes to acknowledge and thank John Haffert for his foundational research and analysis of the apparitions of Akita, and for his gracious interviews with the author.

17. Sister Agnes's diary is contained in Yasuda, *Tears and Messages of Mary*.

CHAPTER SEVEN

1. The author traveled to Venezuela in 1991 and gratefully acknowledges the hospitality of Lian and Norberto Azqueta, Isabelle Tanremo, and Mercedes Stone. Spanish translations for speeches were arranged through the graciousness of John Donovan of the United States Pentagon Prayer Group. Simultaneous translations for extemporaneous talks in Venezuela were provided by Isabelle Tanremo.

The interviews with Maria Esperanza Biancini and her family were conducted during and after the First Archdiocesan Annual Marian Conference, sponsored by Archbishop John Murphy, of Spokane, Wash., on October 21–23, 1994. The author is most grateful for the many kindnesses of the committee, especially Hank De Goede and Dean Carmichael. The author wishes to note the kindness and sacrifices of all those who have made the events in Venezuela available for people everywhere.

2. *Land of Grace, Betania, Venezuela*, video documentary (Lima, Pa.: Marian Communications, 1993), is an excellent resource of video footage of the background, ecstasies of the people, Eucharistic miracle, and surrounding circumstances. *See also* Michael H. Brown, *The Bridge to Heaven* (Lima, Pa.: Marian Communications, 1993) *and* Sister Margaret Catherine Sims, *Apparitions in Betania, Venezuela* (Framingham, Mass.: Medjugorje Messengers, 1992).

3. *Land of Grace*, video documentary.

4. Ibid.

5. Ibid.

6. *See Land of Grace*, video documentary, for footage of the Host. Please contact the office of the Roman Catholic Bishop of Caracas, Venezuela, for any on-going, official, ecclesiastical position regarding the Host.

7. Maria Esperanza Biancini and her family, interview by author, October 1994.

8. Ibid.

9. Ibid.

10. The author wishes to acknowledge the graciousness of Rita Sarges, Vienna, Va., for information concerning the apparitions in Nicaragua, including the official messages

and statements from the office of Monsignor Pablo Antonio Vega, Prelate Bishop of Juigalpa, and from the Nicaraguan Community in Exile, headquartered in Alexandria, Va.

11. *See* René Laurentin, *An Appeal From Mary in Argentina* (Milford, Ohio: Riehle Foundation, 1990), which contains the history and messages of the apparitions. Additional information is available from the Riehle Foundation, Milford, Ohio. The author wishes to acknowledge the formidable contributions in the area of private revelation of Bill Reck of the Riehle Foundation and his late wife, Frances.

12. The author thanks Professor René Laurentin for his patient contributions concerning all the apparitions of the twentieth century, and especially in Argentina.

CHAPTER EIGHT

1. Father Michael Scanlan, T.O.R., interview by author.

2. *See* Raoul Auclair, *The Lady of All Nations*, translated by Earl Massecar (Lac Etchemin, Quebec: L'Armée de Marie, 1978).

3. Mark Miravalle, President, Vox Populi Mariae Mediatrici.

4. *See* Sandra L. Zimdars-Swartz, *Encountering Mary from La Salette to Medjugorje* (Princeton: Princeton University Press, 1991), pp. 256–259. *See also* Auclair, *The Lady of All Nations*.

5. This statement and those that follow are abstracted from the compiled messages of Our Lady of All Nations.

6. René Laurentin, interview by author. The author wishes to thank Stanley J. Karminski for providing the translated messages and history of the apparitions in Amsterdam. For

additional information concerning the position of the Church regarding events in Amsterdam, contact Professor Mark Miravalle, Franciscan University of Steubenville, Steubenville, Ohio.

7. *See* Janice T. Connell, *Queen of the Cosmos* (Orleans, Mass.: Paraclete Press, 1990), pp. 61–69, *and* Janice T. Connell, *Visions of the Children* (New York: St. Martin's Press, 1992), pp. 99–120.

8. *See* June Keithley, *Lipa* (Manila: Anvil Publishing, 1992), which chronicles the events surrounding the apparitions of Lipa. Mrs. Keithley has also produced a video documentary series entitled *The Woman Clothed with the Sun.* She has filmed documentaries on location at the world's famous Marian shrines where apparitions of the Blessed Mother have occurred; the documentaries have been aired throughout Asia.

9. Teresita Castillo, interview by the author, Lipa, Philippines, July 1991. The author wishes to acknowledge the graciousness of all those who extended their hospitality, especially the Azores family; the sisters at the Carmelite Convent at Lipa; Father James B. Reuter, S.J.; June Keithley; Cristina Ponce-Enrile; Alice Reyes; Mercy Thason; Lydia Sison; Minetta Ayala; government officials; and members of the clergy, the Center for Peace in Asia, and all the prayer groups.

CHAPTER NINE

1. Villagers in Medjugorje, interviews by author.
2. Ivanka Ivankovic and Mirjana Dragicevic, interviews by author.
3. Mirjana, interview by author.
4. Jacov Çolo, interview by author.
5. Mirjana, interview by author.

6. The six visionaries of Medjugorje, interviews by author.

7. Marija Pavlovic, interview by author.

8. René Laurentin; Father Robert Faricy, S.J.; and villagers in Medjugorje; interviews by author.

9. Dr. Slavko Barbaric, O.F.M., and Father Jozo Zovko, O.F.M., interviews by author.

10. Vicka Ivankovic, interview by author.

11. Father Faricy, in conversation with author.

12. *See* Albert Shamon, *The Power of the Rosary* (Milford, Ohio: Riehle Foundation, 1989).

13. Janice T. Connell, *Visions of the Children* (New York: St. Martin's Press, 1992), pp. 174–175.

14. Mirjana, interview with author, as cited in Janice T. Connell, *Queen of the Cosmos* (Orleans, Mass.: Paraclete Press, 1990), p. 19.

15. Ibid., p. 18.

16. The monthly messages of Our Lady from Medjugorje are available by telephoning local Marian or Medjugorje Centers throughout the world. Those who desire to receive the messages by fax or mail may contact:

   The MIR GROUP, 400 Poydras Street, Suite 2650, New Orleans, LA 70130. Fax: 504-595-6923.

   Marian Movement of Priests, National Headquarters, P.O. Box 8, St. Francis, ME 04774-0008.

   Mary's People, Twin Circle Publishing Company, 15760 Ventura Blvd., Suite 1201, Encino, CA 91436.

   Pittsburgh Center for Peace, 6111 Steubenville Pike, McKees Rocks, PA 15136.

17. *See* Connell, *Visions of the Children*, pp. 75–87, *and* Connell, *Queen of the Cosmos*, pp. 35–48.

18. Connell, *Visions of the Children*, pp. 77–79.

19. René Laurentin and René Lejeune, *Messages and Teachings of*

Mary at Medjugorje (Milford, Ohio: Riehle Foundation, 1988), p. 207.

CHAPTER TEN

1. The information on the Rwanda apparitions is based upon primary documents and eyewitness accounts supplied to the author. René Laurentin traveled to Kibeho and personally witnessed certain apparitions in 1988. He spoke with diocesan experts assigned to the Rwanda apparitions and studied the messages. He has written about the theological implications of the apparitions in Africa in many publications. His synthesized report is contained in *The Apparitions of the Blessed Virgin Mary Today* (Dublin: Veritas Publications, 1990), pp. 68–70.

   The author also wishes to acknowledge the timely video done by Drew Mariane of the final apparition of Alphonsine and contained in *Marian Apparitions of the Twentieth Century: A Message of Urgency* (Lima, Pa.: Marian Communications, 1991), video documentary. Some of the data herein were supplied by Gabriel Maindron in his 1992 letter, "Message of Mary from the Heart of Africa," p. 61. The author also wishes to thank Mabel and Charles Ipok of London for providing some of the facts and documentation regarding the apparitions in Kibeho.

2. Maindron, "Message of Mary."

3. Ibid.

4. René Laurentin, interview by author.

5. Maindron, "Message of Mary."

6. Ibid.

7. *Kibeho, Africa; Apparitions of the Blessed Virgin* (Lima, Pa.: Marian Communications, 1989), video documentary; available from Marian Video Productions, P.O. Box 8,

Lima, PA 19037. Personal testimony of the bishop is included.

8. Ibid.

9. The Publican, *The Miracle of Damascus* (Glendale, Calif.: Messengers of Unity, 1989), p. 2.

10. Ibid.

11. Ibid., p. 4.

12. Ibid., p. 6.

13. Ibid., p. 7.

14. Ibid., pp. 7–8.

15. Ibid., p. 10.

16. Ibid., p. 11.

17. Ibid., back cover.

18. Ibid., p. xix.

19. Ibid., p. vi.

20. Video available from Messengers of Unity, 249 N. Brand Blvd., Suite 584, Glendale, CA 91203. Phone: 1-800-88-UNITY.

CHAPTER ELEVEN

1. See *Mary's Touch*, Special Issue, spring 1995; available from Mary's Touch by Mail, P.O. Box 1668, Gresham, OR 97039.

2. *See*, for example, *The Queen of the Holy Rosary in Naju, Korea: Mary Draws Us to the Eucharist*, video; available from Mary's Touch by Mail.

3. The author wishes to thank all those who supplied information about the gifts of Julia Kim, and/or arranged meetings, especially Father Martin Lucia; Father Ernie Santos; Father William Watson, S.J.; June Keithley; Eleanor Wetzel; Maureen and Ted Flynn; Tom Petrisko; Marie Mueller; Stanley Karminski.

4. Marie Mueller, ed., *Mary's Newsroom*, P.O. Box 101308, Pittsburgh, PA 15237.

5. Michael O'Carroll, C.S.Sp., *Theotokos: A Theological Encyclopedia of the Blessed Virgin Mary* (Collegeville, Minn.: Liturgical Press, 1982), p. 342, defines *Theotokos:* "The ancient Eastern title for Mary, Mother of God, prominent especially in liturgical prayer in the Orient down to our time. It was formally sanctioned at the Council of Ephesus."

6. Most Reverend Stephen Sulyk, Metropolitan of Ukrainian Catholics, as quoted in the foreword to: John Bird, *Queen of Ukraine* (Asbury Park, N.J.: 101 Foundation, 1992).

7. Bird, *Queen of Ukraine*, pp. 39–40.

8. Ibid., p. 40.

9. Ibid.

10. Ibid.

11. Josyp Terelya, Ukrainian visionary, interview by author.

12. Bird, *Queen of Ukraine*, p. 41.

13. Ibid.

14. Ibid., p. 42.

15. Josyp Terelya, interview.

16. Janice T. Connell, *Visions of the Children* (New York: St. Martin's Press, 1992), pp. xvii, xviii.

17. Bird, *Queen of Ukraine*, p. 44.

18. Ibid., p. 46.

19. Ibid., p. 48.

20. Ibid., p. 50.

21. Ibid., p. 51.

22. Terelya, interview.

23. Bird, *Queen of Ukraine*, p. 52.

24. Ibid., p. 53.

25. Ibid.

26. Father Michael Scanlan, T.O.R. (who was present for the apparition on the mountain), interview by author.

27. For information about the apparitions and messages of Patricia Talbot, contact Sister Isabel Bettwy, Merciful

Mother Association, P.O. Box 4505, Steubenville, OH
43952.

CHAPTER TWELVE
1. The U.S. apparitions reported in this chapter are not
   officially sanctioned by the Church. The experiences
   recounted may in some cases, as mentioned in the text, be
   under investigation by Church authorities, or may have
   statements by the presiding bishops. For more
   information, please write to the author.
2. Father Jack Spaulding, interview by author.
3. Sister Lucy Rooney, S.N.D. deN., Father Robert Faricy, S.J.,
   and Father René Laurentin, interviews by author.
4. *I Am Your Jesus of Mercy*, in three volumes, is available from
   the Riehle Foundation, P.O. Box 7, Milford, OH 45150.
   Volume 4 of *I Am Your Jesus of Mercy* is available from
   Queenship Publishing, P.O. Box 42028, Santa Barbara,
   CA 93140-2028. Fax: 805-569-3274.
5. *I Am Your Jesus of Mercy* (Milford, Ohio: Riehle Foundation,
   1989), p. 9.
6. *See* Robert Faricy, S.J. and Lucy Rooney, S.N.D. deN.
   Return to God: The Scottsdale Message (Santa Barbara, Calif.:
   Queenship Publishing, 1993). *See also* René Laurentin, *Our
   Lady and Our Lord in Scottsdale* (Milford, Ohio: Faith
   Publishing, 1992), pp. 40–45.
7. The Blessed Mother first began to request prayer groups
   for everyone in the world, especially the youth, to survive
   the evil of the times. The Blessed Mother gave specific
   rules for members of prayer groups. *See* Janice T. Connell,
   Visions of the Children (New York: St. Martin's Press,
   1992), pp. 174–175. Also quoted in René Laurentin and
   René Lejeune, *Messages and Teachings of Mary at Medjugorje*
   (Milford, Ohio: Riehle Foundation, 1988), pp. 202–203.

8. Faricy and Rooney, *Return to God*, pp. 18–19.

9. Bishop Thomas O'Brien, as quoted in "Bishop Issues Statement on Scottsdale Locutions," *The Catholic Sun* 6, no. 2 (January 18, 1990), p. 14.

10. Estella Ruiz, interview by author. For additional information, write to the author.

11. Information supplied through the graciousness of Elizabeth Connell Minno, Marie Mueller, Ellen McGrath, and Mark Miravalle, S.T.D. For additional information, write to: Christ in the Hills, 4198 Post Road, Jewett, OH 43986; Mary's Newsroom, P.O. Box 101308, Pittsburgh, PA 15237, fax: 412-367-1997; The Woman's Voice, P.O. Box 454, Kent, OH 44240, fax: 216-673-6141.

12. *The Washington Post*, October 14, 1994.

13. Ibid.

14. James Carrigan, confidant of Padre Pio, interview with author.

15. Information supplied through the graciousness of Marie Mueller, Mary's Newsroom.

16. For information, contact the Riehle Foundation, P.O. Box 7, Milford, OH 45150.

CHAPTER THIRTEEN

1. Zsolt Aradi, *Shrines to Our Lady around the World* (New York: Farrar, Straus & Young, 1954), p. 135.

2. Ibid.

3. Ibid.

4. Ibid., p. 140.

5. *The Washington Post*, June 2, 1995.

6. Ibid.

7. Ibid.

8. Ibid.

9. Ibid.

10. Gianna Talone Sullivan, interview by author.

11. John Haffert of the Blue Army of Our Lady of Fatima and the 101 Foundation, interview by author.

12. His Holiness Aleksey II, quoted in Janice T. Connell, *The Triumph of the Immaculate Heart* (Santa Barbara, Calif.: Queenship Publishing, 1993), pp. 76–77.

13. Public testimony at London Town Hall, January 1993.

14. The author wishes to acknowledge the graciousness of Sue Ellis in providing information about the Litmanova apparitions. For additional information about the apparitions in Litmanova, or to obtain the Immaculate Purity Medal, contact Sue Ellis, Spring Marian Center, Surrey, England, or contact the author.

CHAPTER FOURTEEN

1. *See* Janice T. Connell, *Visions of the Children* (New York: St. Martin's Press, 1992), pp. 163–169, for information on how those who so desire may "see" with the heart.

2. Veronica's story adapted from her interviews with author, her public testimonies, and an article by Tony Hickey in *Medjugorje Herald*, May 1995, available from P.O. Box Ten, Galway, Ireland. Those who wish to contact Veronica may do so at the retreat center she has founded, where all are welcome. Write to: Veronica Garcia, c/o American Christian Mission, Rural Route 2, Box 258, Velpen, IN 47590.

3. Father Don Stefano Gobbi's messages are available from Marian Movement of Priests, National Headquarters, P.O. Box 8, St. Francis, ME 04774-0008.

4. Father Don Stefano Gobbi, interview by author, Washington, D.C., 1990.

5. Matthew Kelly's messages are available from the author.

SELECTED BIBLIOGRAPHY

Alacoque, Saint Margaret Mary. *The Autobiography of Saint Margaret Mary*. Translated by V. Kerns. Westminster, Md.: Newman Press, 1961.

Aradi, Zsolt. *Shrines to Our Lady around the World*. New York: Farrar, Straus & Young, 1954.

Auclair, Raoul. *The Lady of All Nations*. Translated by Earl Massecai. Lac Etchmin, Quebec: L'Armée de Marie, 1978.

Augustine, Saint. *The Confessions*. Garden City, N.Y.: Doubleday Image Books, 1960.

Barbaric, Slavko, O.F.M. *Fasting*. Steubenville, Ohio: Franciscan University Press, 1988.

———. *Pray with the Heart*. Steubenville, Ohio: Franciscan University Press, 1988.

Bennett, William J. *The Book of Virtues*. New York: Simon & Schuster, 1993.

Bird, John. *Queen of Ukraine*. Asbury Park, N.J.: 101 Foundation, 1992.

Blackbourn, David. *Marpingen: Apparitions of the Virgin Mary in Nineteenth-Century Germany*. New York: Alfred A. Knopf, 1994.

Bojorge, Horatio. *The Image of Mary According to the Evangelists*. New York: Alba House, 1978.

Brigid, Saint. *The Magnificent Prayers of Saint Brigid of Sweden*. Rockford, Ill.: Tan Books, 1983.

Brigitta of Sweden, Saint. *Brigitta: Life and Selected Revelations*. Mahwah, N.J.: Paulist Press, 1990.

Brown, Michael H. *The Bridge to Heaven.* Lima, Pa.: Marian Communications, 1993.

Bryant, Christopher. *The Heart in Pilgrimage.* New York: Seabury Press, 1980.

Burghardt, Walter J., S.J. *Sir, We Would Like to See Jesus.* Ramsey, N.J.: Paulist Press, 1982.

Burrows, Ruth. *Fire upon the Earth.* Denville, N.J.: Dimension Books, 1981.

Carberry, John J., Cardinal. *Mary Queen and Mother: Marian Pastoral Reflections.* Boston: Daughters of Saint Paul, 1979.

Carroll, Michael P. *The Cult of the Virgin Mary: Psychological Origins.* Princeton: Princeton University Press, 1986.

Carter, Edward, S.J. *The Spirituality of Fatima and Medjugorje.* Milford, Ohio: Faith Publishing, 1994.

Cataneo, Pascal. *Padre Pio Gleanings.* Sherbrooke, Quebec: Editions Paulines, 1991.

Catechism of the Catholic Church. Liguori, Mo.: Liguori Publications, 1994.

Catherine of Genoa, Saint. *Purgation and Purgatory: The Spiritual Dialogue.* Ramsey, N.J.: Paulist Press, 1979.

Catherine of Siena, Saint. *The Dialogue.* Ramsey, N.J.: Paulist Press, 1980.

Caussade, Jean-Pierre de. *The Joy of Full Surrender.* Orleans, Mass.: Paraclete Press, 1986.

Ciszek, Walter J., S.J. *With God in Russia.* Garden City, N.Y.: Doubleday Image Books, 1966.

Cloud of Unknowing, The. Edited by William Johnson. Garden City, N.Y.: Doubleday Image Books, 1973.

Connell, Janice T. *Angel Power.* New York: Ballantine Books, 1995.

———. *Queen of the Cosmos.* Orleans, Mass.: Paraclete Press, 1990.

———. *The Triumph of the Immaculate Heart.* Santa Barbara, Calif.: Queenship Publishing, 1993.

————. *Visions of the Children.* New York: St. Martin's Press, 1992.

Daniélou, Jean, S.J. *The Angels and Their Mission according to the Fathers of the Church.* Westminster, Md.: Christian Classics, 1988.

Delaney, John J. *A Woman Clothed with the Sun.* Garden City, N.Y.: Doubleday Image Books, 1961.

Dossey, Larry, M.D. *Healing Words.* San Francisco: Harper San Francisco, 1993.

Dubay, Thomas, S.M. *Fire Within.* San Francisco: Ignatius Press, 1989.

Dupre, Louis and James A. Wiseman, eds. *Light from Light: An Anthology of Christian Mysticism.* Mahwah, N.J.: Paulist Press, 1988.

Eadie, Betty J. *Embraced by the Light.* Calif.: Gold Leaf Press, 1992.

Emmerich, Anne Catherine. *The Life of the Blessed Virgin Mary.* Rockford, Ill.: Tan Books, 1954.

Escriva, Blessed Josemaria. *The Way.* Manila: Sinag-Tala Publishers, 1982.

Estrade, J.B. *My Witness, Bernadette.* Springfield, Ill.: Templegate, 1946.

Faricy, Robert, S.J. *The Lord's Dealing: The Primacy of the Feminine in Christian Spirituality.* Mahwah, N.J.: Paulist Press, 1988.

————. *Praying for Inner Healing.* Ramsey, N.J.: Paulist Press, 1979.

Faricy, Robert, S.J., and Lucy Rooney. *The Contemplative Way of Prayer.* Ann Arbor, Mich.: Servant Books, 1986.

————. *Return to God: The Scottsdale Message.* Santa Barbara, Calif.: Queenship Publishing, 1993.

Flynn, Ted, and Maureen Flynn. *The Thunder of Justice.* Sterling, Va.: Max-Kolbe Communications, 1993.

Fowler, Nancy. *To Bear Witness That I Am the Living Son of*

God. Newington, Va.: Our Loving Mother's Children, 1992.

Francis of Assisi, Saint. *The Best from All His Works.* Christian Classics Collection, Nashville: Thomas Nelson, 1989.

Francis of Assisi, Saint, and Saint Clare. *Francis and Clare: The Complete Works.* Translated by R. J. Armstrong and I. C. Brady. Ramsey, N.J: Paulist Press, 1982.

Francis of Sales, Saint. *The Sermons of Saint Francis de Sales on Our Lady.* Edited by Lewis S. Fiorelli. Rockford, Ill.: Tan Books, 1985.

François, Robert. *O Children Listen to Me.* Lindenhurst, N.Y.: Workers of Our Lady of Mount Carmel, 1980.

Fukushima, Mutsuo [Francis]. *Akita: Spiritual Oasis of Japan.* Santa Barbara, Calif.: Queenship Publishing, 1994.

Gertrude of Helfta. *The Herald of Divine Love.* Mahwah, N.J.: Paulist Press, 1993.

Gillett, H.M. *Shrines of Our Lady in England and Wales.* London: Samuel Walker, 1957.

Glenn, Paul J. *A Tour of the Summa.* Rockford, Ill.: Tan Books, 1978.

Gobbi, Don Stefano. *To the Priests, Our Lady's Beloved Sons.* 11th ed. Toronto: Marian Movement of Priests, 1990.

Griffiths, Bede. *Sacred Wisdom of the World.* London: HarperCollins, 1994.

Groeschel, Benedict, C.F.R. *A Still Small Voice.* San Francisco: Ignatius Press, 1992.

Haffert, John. *To Prevent This.* Asbury Park, N.J.: 101 Foundation, 1993.

Heine, Max. *Equipping Men for Spiritual Battle.* Ann Arbor, Mich.: Servant Books, 1993.

Hempsch, John. *Preparation for the End Times.* Chicago: Ill. Claretian Missionaries Publications, 1992.

Hickey, James Cardinal. *Mary at the Foot of the Cross.* San Francisco: Ignatius Press, 1988.

Huber, Georges. *My Angel Will Go before You.* Westminster, Md.: Christian Classics, 1988.

Ignatius of Loyola, Saint. *A Pilgrim's Journey: The Autobiography of Ignatius of Loyola.* Collegeville, Minn.: Liturgical Press, 1991.

————. *The Spiritual Exercises.* Translated by Anthony Mohola. New York: Doubleday Image Books, 1989.

Jelly, Frederick M. *Madonna: Mary in the Catholic Tradition.* New Huntington, Ind.: Our Sunday Visitor Publishing, 1986.

John of the Cross, Saint. *Selected Writings.* Translated by Kieran Kavanaugh and Otilio Rodriguez. Washington, D.C.: ICS Publications, 1979.

John Paul II, Pope. *Crossing the Threshold of Hope.* New York: Alfred A. Knopf, 1994.

————. *Mary: God's Yes to Man* (*Mother of the Redeemer,* Encyclical Letter). San Francisco: Ignatius Press, 1988.

————. *Redemptor Hominis,* Encyclical Letter. 1979.

————. *The Splendor of Truth,* Encyclical Letter. Boston: Saint Paul Books & Media, 1993.

Johnson, Francis. *Fatima: The Great Sign.* Rockford, Ill.: Tan Books, 1980.

Julian of Norwich. *Showings.* Introduction by Edmund Cooledge, O.S.A., and James Walsh, S.J. Ramsey, N.J.: Paulist Press, 1978.

Keithley, June. *Lipa.* Manila: Anvil Publishing, 1992.

Kelly, Matthew. *Words from God.* Batemans Bay, N.S.W., Australia: Words from God, 1993.

Kowalska, Blessed M. Faustina. *Divine Mercy in My Soul: The Diary.* Stockbridge, Mass.: Marian Press, 1990.

Langsam, Jude, ed. *Welcome to Carmel.* Washington, D.C.: Teresian Charism Press, 1982.

Laurentin, René. *The Apparitions at Medjugorje Prolonged.* Translated by J. Lohre Stiens. Milford, Ohio: Riehle Foundation, 1987.

————. *The Apparitions of the Blessed Virgin Mary Today.* Dublin: Veritas Publications, 1990.

————. *An Appeal from Mary in Argentina.* Milford, Ohio: Riehle Foundation, 1990.

————. *Bernadette at Lourdes.* Minneapolis: Winston Press, 1979.

————. *The Church and Apparitions—Their Status and Function; Criteria and Reception.* Milford, Ohio: Riehle Foundation, 1989.

————. *Our Lord and Our Lady in Scottsdale.* Milford, Ohio: Faith Publishing, 1992.

————. *A Year of Grace with Mary.* Dublin: Veritas Publications, 1987.

Laurentin, René, and H. Joyeux. *Scientific and Medical Studies on the Apparitions at Medjugorje.* Translated by L. Griffin. Dublin: Veritas Publications, 1987.

Laurentin, René, and René Lejeune. *Messages and Teachings of Mary at Medjugorje.* Milford, Ohio: Riehle Foundation, 1988.

Lewis, C.S. *The Screwtape Letters.* New York: Macmillan, 1943.

Liguori, Saint Alphonso Maria de'. *The Glories of Mary.* Rockford, Ill.: Tan Books, 1977.

Lucia of Fatima. *Fatima in Lucia's Own Words.* Edited by L. Kondor. Fatima, Portugal: Postulation Centre, 1976.

————. *Her Own Words to the Nuclear Age: The Memoirs of Sr. Lucia.* Comments by John Haffert. Asbury Park, N.J.: 101 Foundation, 1993.

Lymann, Sanford M. *The Seven Deadly Sins: Society and Evil.* New York: St. Martin's Press, 1978.

Maloney, George A., S.J. *Called to Intimacy.: Living in the Indwelling Presence.* New York: Alba House, 1983.

Margaret Mary, Saint. *The Autobiography.* Rockford, Ill.: Tan
    Publishers, 1952.

Mary of Agreda, Venerable. *Mystical City of God.* 4 vols.
    Washington, N.J.: Ave Maria Institute, 1971.

McKenzie, John L., S.J. *Dictionary of the Bible.* Milwaukee:
    Bruce Publishing, 1965.

McSorley, Richard, S.J. *New Testament Basis for Peace Making.*
    Scottsdale, Pa.: Herald Press, 1985.

Michel, Frère de la Sainte Trinité. *The Whole Truth About
    Fatima.* Buffalo, N.Y.: Immaculate Heart Publications,
    1989.

Miravalle, Mark, S.T.D. *Introduction to Mary.* Santa Barbara,
    Calif.: Queenship Publishing, 1993.

————. *Mary: Coredemptrix, Mediatrix, Advocate.* Santa Barbara,
    Calif.: Queenship Publishing, 1993.

————. *The Message of Medjugorje.* Lanham, Md.: University
    Press of America, 1986.

————. *The Apostolate of Holy Motherhood.* Milford, Ohio:
    Riehle Foundation, 1991.

Mohr, Sister Marie Helene, S.C. *Saint Philomina, Powerful with
    God.* Rockford, Ill.: Tan Books, 1988.

Montfort, Louis-Marie Grignion de, Saint. *God Alone: The
    Collected Writings of St. Louis de Montfort.* Washington,
    N.J.: Blue Army, 1989.

————. *The Secret of the Rosary.* Washington, N.J.: Blue Army,
    1951.

————. *True Devotion to Mary.* Edited by Fathers of the
    Company of Mary. Translated by F. W. Faber. 1941.
    Reprint, Rockford, Ill.: Tan Books, 1985.

Moore, Thomas. *Care of the Soul.* New York: HarperCollins,
    1992.

Morse, Melvin, M.D. *Transformed by the Light.* New York:
    Ballantine/Ivy Books, 1992.

Most, William G. *Our Father's Plan.* Manassas, Va.: Trinity Communications, 1988.

Mowatt, Archpriest John J. *The Holy and Miraculous Icon of Our Lady of Kazan.* Fatima, Portugal: Domus Pacis, 1974.

Muto, Susan A. *Pathways of Spiritual Living.* Garden City, N.Y.: Doubleday Image Books, 1984.

National Conference of Catholic Bishops. *Behold Your Mother: A Pastoral Letter on the Blessed Virgin Mary.* Washington, D.C.: United States Catholic Conference, Nov. 21, 1973.

Neumann, Erich. *The Great Mother.* Translated by Ralph Manheim. Princeton: Princeton University Press, 1955.

Newman, John Henry. *Mary the Second Eve.* Rockford, Ill.: Tan Books, 1982.

Nikodimos, Saint, and Saint Makarios of Corinth. *The Philokalia.* 4 vols. London: Faber & Faber, 1984.

Northcote, J. *Celebrated Sanctuaries of the Madonna.* London: Longmans Green, 1968.

O'Carroll, Michael, C.C.Sp. *Medjugorje Facts, Documents, Theology.* Dublin: Veritas, 1986.

————. *Theotokos: A Theological Encyclopedia of the Blessed Virgin Mary.* Wilmington, Del.: Liturgical Press, 1982.

O'Connor, Edward D., C.S.C. *The Catholic Vision.* Huntington, Ind.: Our Sunday Visitor Publishing, 1992.

Odell, Catherine M. *Those Who Saw Her: The Apparitions of Mary.* Huntington, Ind.: Our Sunday Visitor Publishing, 1986.

Origen. *An Exhortation to Martyrdom, Prayer, First Principles: Book IV.* Ramsey, N.J.: Paulist Press, 1979.

Pelletier, Joseph. *Our Lady Comes to Garabandal; Including Conchita's Diary.* Worcester, Mass.: Assumption Publications, 1971, reissued 1985.

————. *The Queen of Peace Visits Medjugorje.* Worcester, Mass.: Assumption Publications, 1985.

————. *The Sun Danced at Fatima.* Garden City, N.Y.: Doubleday Image Books, 1951.

Petrisko, Thomas W. *Call of the Ages.* Santa Barbara, Calif.: Queenship Publishing Company, 1995.

Pius IX, Pope. *Ineffabilis Deus*, Apostolic Letter. 1854.

Pius XII, Pope. *Munificentissimus Deus*, Apostolic Constitution. 1950.

————. *Signa Magna*, Encyclical Letter. 1948.

Preston, Richard. *The Hot Zone.* New York: Random House, 1994.

Prince, Derek. *Blessing or Curse: You Can Choose.* Tarrytown, N.Y.: Chosen Books, 1990.

Publican, The. *The Miracle of Damascus.* Glendale, Calif.: Messengers of Unity, 1989.

Reck, William A. *Thoughts on Apparitions.* Milford, Ohio: Riehle Foundation, 1993.

Rengers, Christopher. *The Youngest Prophet.* New York: Alba House, 1986.

Rouvelle, Alexander de. *Imitation of Mary in Four Books.* New York: Catholic Book Publishing, 1985.

Sanford, Agnes. *The Healing Gifts of the Spirit.* Philadelphia: Harper & Row, 1966.

Sanford, John A. *The Kingdom Within.* San Francisco: Harper & Row, 1987.

Scanlan, Michael, T.O.R. *Appointment with God.* Steubenville, Ohio: Franciscan University Press, 1987.

————, and Randall J. Cirner. *Deliverance from Evil Spirits.* Ann Arbor, Mich.: Servant Books, 1980.

Schouppe, F.X., S.J. *The Dogma of Hell.* Rockford, Ill.: Tan Books, 1989.

Scupoli, Dom Lorenzo. *The Spiritual Combat and a Treatise on Peace of Soul.* Rockford, Ill.: Tan Books, 1990.

Shamon, Albert. *The Power of the Rosary.* Milford, Ohio: Riehle Foundation, 1989.

Silvestrini, Achille. *The Life of the Madonna in Art.* Boston: Daughters of Saint Paul, 1985.

Sims, Sister Margaret Catherine. *Apparitions in Betania, Venezuela.* Framingham, Mass.: Medjugorje Messingers, 1992.

Singer, Jim Z. *Use My Gifts: The Messages of Our Lord.* Toronto: Ave Maria Center of Peace, 1993.

Stravinskas, Peter M.T., ed. *Our Sunday Visitor's Catholic Encyclopedia.* Huntington, Ind.: Our Sunday Visitor Publishing, 1991.

Sullivan, Gianna Talone. *I AM Your Jesus of Mercy.* 3 vols. Milford, Ohio: Riehle Foundation, 1989.

————. *I AM Your Jesus of Mercy.* Vol. 4. Santa Barbara, Calif.: Queenship Publishing, 1993.

Terelya, Josyp, with Michael Brown. *Josyp Terelya, Witness.* Milford, Ohio: Faith Publishing, 1991.

Teresa of Ávila, Saint. *Collected Works.* 3 vols. Translated by K. Kavanaugh and O. Rodriguez. Washington, D.C.: ICS Publications, 1985.

————. *The Interior Castle.* Translated by K. Kavanaugh. New York: Paulist Press, 1979.

————. *The Way of Perfection.* Translated and edited by Allison Peers. Garden City, N.Y.: Doubleday Image Books, 1964.

Thérèse of Lisieux, Saint. *The Autobiography: The Story of a Soul.* Garden City, N.Y.: Doubleday Image Books, 1957.

Thomas Aquinas. *Summa Theologiae: A Concise Translation.* Westminster, Md.: Christian Classics, 1989.

————. *Summa Theologica.* 5 vols. Westminster, Md.: Christian Classics, 1981.

Two Friends of Medjugorje. *Words from Heaven.* Birmingham, Ala.: St. James Publishing, 1990.

Van Kaam, Adrian, C.S.Sp. *The Mystery of Transforming Love.* Denville, N.J.: Dimension Books, 1981.

————. *The Roots of Christian Joy.* Denville, N.J.: Dimension Books, 1985.

Vincent, R. *Please Come Back to Me and My Son.* Westmeath: Ireland's Eye Publications, 1992.

Walsh, Michael, ed. *Butler's Lives of the Saints.* Foreword by Cardinal Basil Hume. San Francisco: Harper & Row, 1984.

Walsh, William J., ed. *The Apparitions and Shrines of Heaven's Bright Queen.* 4 vols. New York: T. J. Carey, 1904.

Weible, Wayne. *Medjugorje, the Message.* Orleans, Mass.: Paraclete Press, 1989.

Weil, Simone. *Waiting for God.* New York: Harper & Row, 1951.

Werfel, Franz. *The Song of Bernadette.* Translated by Ludwig Lewisohn. New York: Saint Martin's Press, 1970.

Yasuda, Teiji. *Akita: The Tears and Message of Mary.* English version by John Haffert. Asbury Park, N.J.: 101 Foundation, 1989.

Zimdars-Swartz, Sandra L. *Encountering Mary from La Salette to Medjugorje.* Princeton: Princeton University Press, 1991.

Zovko, Jozo, O.F.M. *A Man Named Father Jozo.* Milford, Ohio: Riehle Foundation, 1989.

If you are interested in writing to the author for more information, or to receive a newsletter, please include return postage and address all correspondence to:

Jan Connell
Two Gateway Center
Suite 620
Pittsburgh, PA 15222

Many people all over the world are experiencing spiritual gifts in these times. If you have experiences or stories about the Blessed Mother, the angels, the saints, or perhaps the Lord that you would like to share, please direct all correspondence to the above address.

PERMISSIONS ACKNOWLEDGMENTS

Grateful acknowledgment is made to the following for permission to reprint previously published material:

Mary's Newsroom: Mary's Messenger. Reprinted in Marie Mueller, editor, *Mary's Newsroom* (March–April 1995). Reprinted with the permission of the publishers.

The Most Rev. Thomas J. O'Brien: Excerpts from Bishop Thomas O'Brien's statement on Saint Maria Goretti parish. Excerpted with the permission of the Most Rev. Thomas J. O'Brien.

Reproduction Without Commentary: Excerpts from *La Salette: The Apparitions of the Blessed Virgin Mary on the Mountain in 1846*, Reproduction Without Commentary, 12, Avenue of Grand f 'or, 49600 Beaupreau, France. Reprinted with the permission of the publishers.

TAN Books and Publishers: Excerpts from *The Autobiography* by Saint Margaret Mary. Copyright © 1952 by TAN Books and Publishers, Rockford, IL. Reprinted with the permission of the publishers.

Doubleday: Excerpts from *The Way of Perfection* by Teresa of Ávila, translated by Allison Peers. Copyright © 1964 by Allison Peers. Reprinted with the permission of Doubleday, a division of Bantam Doubleday Dell Publishing Group, Inc.

United States Catholic Conference: Scripture selections are taken from the *New American Bible*. Copyright © 1991, 1986, 1970 by the Confraternity of Christian Doctrine, Washington, D.C., and are used with permission. All rights reserved.

Princeton University Press: Excerpts from *Encountering Mary: From La Salette to Medjugorje* by Sandra L. Zimdars-Swartz. Copyright © 1991 by Princeton University Press. Reprinted with the permission of the publishers.

PICTURE CREDITS

frontispiece: *The Coronation of the Virgin*, detail, by Botticelli, Alinari/Art Resource, New York

p. xxii: Culver Pictures

p. 86: *La Madonna del Granduca* by Raphael, Alinari/Art Resource, New York

p. 196: *The Virgin Immaculate* by Padre Sarullo, Alinari/Art Resource, New York

p. 280: *The Coronation of the Virgin* by Fra Angelico, Girandon/Art Resource, New York

p. 350: *The Sistine Madonna* by Raphael, Alinari/Art Resource, New York

Ted Connell

ABOUT THE AUTHOR

JANICE T. CONNELL is a practicing attorney with a master's degree in public and international administration and is a graduate of the Georgetown University School of Foreign Service. She is married and has four children and two grandchildren. She is the author of *Visions of the Children: The Apparitions of the Blessed Mother at Medjugorje, Queen of the Cosmos, The Triumph of the Immaculate Heart,* and *Angel Power.*

Janice Connell presents business seminars, professional workshops, and lectures throughout the world on social, economic, and environmental issues that impact the well-being of everyone on the planet. For information, write to the author at:

Two Gateway Center
Suite 620
Pittsburgh, PA 15222